THE ARCHITECTURE OF
MICHELANGELO

JAMES S. ACKERMAN

PROFESSOR OF FINE ARTS

HARVARD UNIVERSITY

TEXT AND PLATES

1966

A. ZWEMMER LTD

LONDON

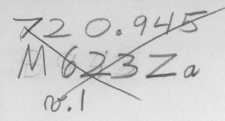
TO MY PARENTS

This book has received the Alice Davis Hitchcock
Book Award of the Society of Architectural
Historians and the Charles Rufus Morey
Award of the College Art Association of America

© 1961

FIRST PUBLISHED 1961

REVISED EDITION 1966

A. ZWEMMER LTD, 76–80 CHARING CROSS ROAD, LONDON WC2

MADE AND PRINTED IN GREAT BRITAIN

BLOCKS ETCHED BY W. F. SEDGWICK LTD, LONDON SE1

TEXT AND ILLUSTRATIONS

PRINTED BY PERCY LUND, HUMPHRIES AND CO. LTD, BRADFORD

TEXT REPRINTED PHOTOGRAPHICALLY

BY THE YSEL PRESS

DEVENTER, HOLLAND

BOUND BY KEY AND WHITING, LONDON N1

Contents

List of Plates

Unless otherwise indicated all works are by Michelangelo

1a. Francesco di Giorgio. Ideal church plan. Florence, Bibl. Naz., Cod. Magliabecchiano, fol. 42v

1b. C. Cesariano. Plate from Vitruvius, *De Architectura*, ed. Como, 1521, Bk. III, fol. xlix

1c. Albrecht Dürer. Study of human proportion. Bremen, Kunsthalle (after Lippmann)

1d. Profile studies. Haarlem, Teyler Museum, No. 20v

CASTEL SANT' ANGELO

2a. Chapel of Leo X. Exterior (1514)

2b. Giovanni Battista da Sangallo. Drawing after Michelangelo's Chapel exterior

FLORENCE, FAÇADE OF SAN LORENZO (1515–1520)

3a. Giuliano da Sangallo or assistants. Façade project. Uffizi, *Arch.* 277

3b. Anonymous copy of Michelangelo's first project. Casa Buonarroti, No. 45

3c. Façade project. Casa Buonarroti, No. 91

3d. Façade project. Casa Buonarroti, No. 44

4a. Façade project. Casa Buonarroti, No. 47

4b. Aristotile da Sangallo. Copy of a project by Michelangelo. Munich, Staatl. graphische Sammlung, No. 33258

4c. Antonio da Sangallo the younger. Copy of a project by Michelangelo. Uffizi, *Arch.* 790r

5a. Façade project. Casa Buonarroti, No. 43

5b. Wooden model. Casa Buonarroti

6a. Notes on blocks quarried for the façade. Archivio Buonarroti, Vol. I, 144–145, fols 260v, 261r

6b. Notes on blocks quarried for the façade. Archivio Buonarroti, Vol. I, 134–135, fols 250v, 251r

6c. Florence, Medici Palace. Ground-floor window (*ca.* 1517)

6d. Sketch-plan for the "Altopascio" house. Casa Buonarroti, No. 117

List of Text Illustrations

Photographic Sources

Alinari, Florence: 2a, 3a, 3b, 5a, 6c, 9, 13b, 14a (coll. Mannelli), 17, 21, 25b, 27a, 50, 66b, 67, 68, 73a, 77b, 78a

Anderson, Rome: 18a, 40, 45, 46a, 64, 73c

Berlin, Kunstbibliothek: 48b, 49a, b

Boston Public Library: 43a, 72a, b

British Museum, London: 11a, b, 12a, c, 25a, 30b, 83a

Brogi, Florence: 8, 26a, b, 58a, 65b

Brunswick, Germany, Herzog Anton-Ulrich Museum: 31a, 42b

Ciacchi, Florence: 42a, 47b, 48a

Columbia University, New York; Avery Library: 35a, 36b, 37, 51c, 59b, 71b, 80b

Florence, Soprintendenza alle Gallerie: 3c, d, 4a, 5b, 6a, b, d, 7a, b, 8, 10, 14c, 16, 18b, 19a, b, 20b, 22, 23, 27b, 28a, 57a, 65c, 69a, 72c, 77a, 79a

W. Gernsheim, Florence: 2b

Haarlem, Teyler Museum: 1d, 20a, 54, 79b

Harvard University, Cambridge: 1a, b, 13a, 75, 80a, c, 81b, 82a

Louvre, Paris: 31b

Dr E. Luporini: 70b

Rollie McKenna: 15

Leonard von Matt: 29, 33, 44, 63, 83b

Metropolitan Museum, New York: 41, 43b, 53b, 59a, 60, 61

Mr Sigmund Morgenroth: 51a

Munich, Staatliche graphische Sammlung: 4b

New York University Institute of Fine Arts: 69b

Oxford, Ashmolean Museum: 14b, 34b, 46b, 55b

Rome, Gabinetto Fotografico nazionale: 38b (courtesy W. Lotz)

Rome, Fototeca di Architettura e Topografica: 57b

Dr C. de Tolnay: 12b, 71a, 73b

Vatican, Musei e Gallerie pontificie: 52b, 58b, 65a, 76a, b

John Vincent: 35b, 38a, 39, 74

Warburg Institute, London: 38c (courtesy H. Bober)

Windsor Castle Library: 78b (by gracious permission of H.M. the Queen)
Dr Rudolf Wittkower: 24 (photo made for Tolnay)
The author: 47a, 51b, 66a, 62b

The following Plates were made from publications indicated in the captions (see List of Plates): 1c, 4c, 25c, 28b, 30a, 32, 34a, 36a, 52a, 53a, 55a, 56a, b, 62a, 70a, 81a, 82b

List of Abbreviations

Aufzeichnungen	Wolf Maurenbrecher, *Die Aufzeichnungen des Michel-angelo Buonarroti im Britischen Museum*, Leipzig, 1938.
B. (followed by catalogue no.)*	Paolo Barocchi, *Michelangelo e la sua scuola I, II, I. disegni di Casa Buonarroti degli Uffizi* (Accademia Toscana di scienze e lettere, Studi, VIII) Florence, 1962.
Briefe	Karl Frey, ed., *Sammlung ausgewählter Briefe an Michelagniolo Buonarroti*, Berlin, 1899.
Condivi	*Vita di Michelagnolo Buonarroti raccolta per Ascanio Condivi de la Ripa Transone*, Rome, 1553. Ed. P. D'Ancona, Milan, 1928.
Corr.	Gaetano Milanesi, ed., *Les correspondants de Michel-Ange, I, Sebastiano del Piombo*, Paris, 1890.
Dicht.	Karl Frey, ed., *Die Dichtungen des Michelagniolo Buonarroti*, Berlin, 1897.
D. (followed by catalogue no.)*	Luitpold Dussler, *Die Zeichnungen des Michelangelo; kritischer Katalog*, Berlin, 1959.
F. (followed by catalogue no.)	Karl Frey, *Die Handzeichnungen Michelagniolos Buonarroti*, 3 vols, Berlin, 1909–1911. The same designation is used for F. Knapp, *Nachtrag zu den von K. Frey herausgegebenen drei Bänden*, Berlin, 1925.
Gaye	Giovanni Gaye, *Carteggio inedito d'artisti dei secoli XIV–XVI*, 3 vols, Florence, 1839–1840.
Lettere	Gaetano Milanesi, ed., *Le lettere di Michelangelo Buonarroti pubblicate coi ricordi ed i contratti artistici*, Florence, 1875.
Nachlass	Karl Frey, *Der literarische Nachlass Giorgio Vasaris*, I, Munich, 1923; II, Munich, 1930.
Pastor, *Geschichte*	L. von Pastor, *Geschichte der Päpste seit dem Ausgang des Mittelalters*, Freiburg i. B., 1885 ff.
Vasari	*Le vite de' più excellenti pittori, scultori, e architettori, scritte da Giorgio Vasari pittore aretino*, Florence, 1568. Ed. Gaetano Milanesi, 9 vols., Florence, 1906.
Venturi, *Storia*	Adolfo Venturi, *Storia dell'arte italiana*, 11 vols., Milan, 1901–1948.

*In citations of drawings from the Casa Buonarroti the letter "A" (=Architectural) at the close of the number has been omitted.

Preface

IT is one of the delights of art historical studies that our predecessors have not exhausted – or even adequately surveyed – subjects as stimulating as Michelangelo's architecture. A foundation was laid in this field by H. von Geymüller's monograph of 1904 which, however, dealt principally with the Florentine projects, and was already outdated following the systematic publication of drawings and documents by Karl Frey and Henry Thode before and during the first World War. Dagobert Frey's book on the later buildings (1920) initiated a fifteen-year period of basic research including many studies by Charles de Tolnay (notably the Prussian *Jahrbuch* articles of 1930–1932) and Rudolf Wittkower's exemplary work on the Laurentian library (1934). The first and only comprehensive survey is Armando Schiavo's *La vita e le opere architettoniche di Michelangelo* (1953), which contains some useful original scholarship but otherwise is vitiated by the author's ignorance of essential writings published outside Italy. It would be impossible even today to solve many of the historical problems raised by Michelangelo's architecture if Charles de Tolnay and Johannes Wilde had not further developed the meticulous science of a Karl Frey and enriched it with rare sensitivity in analysis and criticism. They are leaving to their successors an impression that no useful tools of Michelangelo's scholarship remain untouched.

It seems unjust that this book, which owes so much to Tolnay's publications, should appear before his own on the same subject, long planned as the sixth and final volume of his Michelangelo monograph; but I trust that the following pages, by their occasional divergence from Tolnay's conclusions as well as by their tokens of the riches to be expected from his writings, may further whet the reader's appetite for the anticipated work.

When I first discussed my project with the Editors of this series in 1956, I proposed to write a critical summary based on knowledge of Michelangelo's architecture as it had been established by others. But I soon found that a thorough re-study of the original sources for each building was needed to answer even basic questions of chronology and authorship. The change of emphasis and of scope threatened to appeal to specialists alone, and this neither the Editors nor I intended; so my solution was to write, in a sense, both books: a general text for the non-specialist, composed of essays on Michelangelo's major designs in the context of comparable Renaissance structures, and a Catalogue for colleagues and students, where the history of each structure and the genesis of its design is reconstructed by the analysis of documents, letters, drawings, views and other sources.

In the text, as in the Catalogue, I have treated each building separately in order to avoid clouding my conclusions by preconceived images of Michelangelo's style and its "evolution". For similar reasons I have not referred to one of the most successful artifacts of twentieth-century art history – the concept of Mannerism. Though there is disagreement on the chronological and geographical limits of the Mannerist style in architecture, nearly every definition includes – or begins with – the Laurentian library and occasionally other designs of Michelangelo. I believe that while the concept of Mannerism has facilitated criticism in the past, gradually it has come to obstruct our perception by urging us to find in the work of art what our definition of it states we must find. The same may be said of the Baroque, a category into which Michelangelo was placed by critics of the period before the invention of Mannerism. While we do find in Michelangelo's buildings characteristics which conform to our definitions of the Baroque, it is surely more illuminating to say that they aroused architects of the seventeenth century to emulation rather than that Michelangelo "anticipated" Baroque architecture or that his design was "proto-Baroque", as if he had miraculously benefited from a glimpse into the future. In short, my approach has been guided by the conviction that generalizations on style should emerge from, rather than guide the examination of works of art themselves.

To simplify reference to the Bibliography and Plates, the Catalogue is being published in a separate volume. Because the Catalogue traces the evolution of each design by means of graphic sources, and because it discusses minor as well as major projects, the reader will find illustrations among the Plates to which no reference is made in the text volume. To reduce production costs, we have restricted the size of many of the documentary illustrations; all but a few are handsomely reproduced elsewhere. The scholarly apparatus has been condensed wherever possible; Catalogue references are shortened to include only the surname of the author and the date of his work, and I hope to have lessened the reader's discomfort by following the same unconventional pattern in the Bibliography. Footnotes appear in the text only where it was necessary to supplement the references in the Catalogue. I have also economized on the citation of studies that have been superseded by recent research which incorporates their findings (e.g., the classification of drawings by Thode [1908–1913] and Berenson [1938], now supplanted – at least for architectural studies – by Dussler, *Die Zeichnungen des Michelangelo*, of 1959; the K. Frey catalogue [1909–1911] remains valuable because every entry is reproduced in facsimile). While adopting British orthography, I have retained one Americanism: what I refer to as the second and third stories of a structure are known abroad as the first and second stories respectively.

With warm gratitude I acknowledge the assistance I have had from many students, colleagues and friends: Carroll Brentano and Elizabeth Breckenridge who helped me with research; Frank Krueger, Gustavo de Roza, and Timothy Kitao, whose draughtsmanship brought life to my reconstructions, and the Research Fund of the University of California, which helped to provide this aid as well as a large part of the photographic material. Lapses in my chronology of St Peter's were keenly detected by Susan Mc. Killop.

Walter Gernsheim, Eugenio Luporini, Walter and Elizabeth Paatz, Herbert Siebenhüner and Charles de Tolnay have generously allowed me to reproduce illustrations made by or for them and have otherwise helped with their advice. I have been graciously assisted in locating and procuring photographs by Luciano Berti, Ulrich Middeldorf, Michelangelo Muraro, James van Derpool, Carl Weinhardt, jun., and particularly by Ernest Nash of the *Fototeca di architettura e topografia* in Rome. Four plates by John Vincent reproduced here are among the fruits of a campaign of architectural photography which he kindly undertook with me in the Summer of 1956; others I owe to the generosity of Rollie McKenna, Sigmund Morgenroth, and Leonard von Matt.

I am particularly grateful to Elizabeth MacDougall for sharing with me her discoveries on the later buildings, especially the Porta Pia, to Wolfgang Lotz for more ideas than I can account for, much less acknowledge, and to John Coolidge for his brilliant intuitions concerning the early works.

When the bulk of my manuscript was completed, it had the rare good fortune of being read by three scholars supremely qualified to judge it: Charles de Tolnay, Johannes Wilde and Rudolf Wittkower; their comments have led to substantial improvements, as have those of my wife, whose wise criticisms of style have saved the reader incalculable anguish.

June, 1960.   Berkeley, California.

PREFACE TO THE REVISED EDITION

The need for a second edition of these volumes has given me the opportunity to correct a few of my errors, and to take some account of the publications on Michelangelo's architecture that have appeared since 1961, including the thoughtful reviews of the first edition. Because the original printing of the Catalogue volume was sold out earlier than the text, it was emended and issued in 1963; changes in the text volume take account of subsequent contributions through 1965. In a forthcoming Italian edition, the catalogue will be corrected further for the period 1963-1965. Two substantive changes in my conclusions involve Michelangelo's part in the design of the Medici Chapel, which was clarified with the generous help of Johannes Wilde and by the discovery of an important document by Corti and Parronchi, and the history of the podium of the Marcus Aurelius statue on the Capitoline Hill, the subject of a study by Künzle. Important contributions also have been made in the beautifully illustrated volume *Michelangelo Architetto*, edited by Portoghesi and Zevi.

February, 1966   Cambridge, Mass.

Introduction

IN the early years of the sixteenth century the extraordinary power, wealth, and imagination of the Pope, Julius II della Rovere (1503–1513) made Rome the artistic centre of Italy and of Europe and attracted there the most distinguished artists of his age. Chiefly for political reasons, the rise of Rome coincided with the decline of great centres of fifteenth-century Italian culture: Florence, Milan, and Urbino. The new "capital" had no eminent painters, sculptors, or architects of its own, so it had to import them; and they hardly could afford to stay at home. This sudden change in the balance of Italian culture had a revolutionary effect on the arts; while the fifteenth-century courts and city-states had produced "schools" of distinct regional characteristics, the new Rome tended to encourage not so much a Roman as an Italian art. No creative Renaissance artist could fail to be inspired and profoundly affected by the experience of encountering simultaneously the works of ancient architects and sculptors – not only in the ever-present ruins but in dozens of newly founded museums and collections – and those of his greatest contemporaries. Like Paris at the beginning of the present century, Rome provided the uniquely favourable conditions for the evolution of new modes of perception and expression.

I described the results as revolutionary. Since Heinrich Wölfflin's great work on this period,[1] the traditional concept of the High Renaissance as the ultimate maturing of the aims of the fifteenth century has been displaced by an awareness that many of the goals of early sixteenth-century artists were formed in vigorous opposition to those of their teachers. What Wölfflin saw in the painting and sculpture was characteristic of architecture, too.

But there is an important difference in the architectural "revolution": it was brought about by one man, Donato Bramante (1444–1514). This reckless but warranted generalization was concocted by a contemporary

1. Heinrich Wölfflin, *Die klassische Kunst*, Munich, 1899.

theorist, twenty-three years after Bramante's death; Sebastian Serlio called him "a man of such gifts in architecture that, with the aid and authority given him by the Pope, one may say that he revived true architecture, which had been buried from the ancients down to that time".[2] Bramante, like Raphael, was born in Urbino; he was trained as a painter and ultimately found a position at the court of Milan under Lodovico Sforza. Already in his first architectural work of the late 1470's his interest in spatial volume, three-dimensional massing, and perspective illusions distinguishes him from his contemporaries, though the effect of his innovations was minimized by a conservative and decorative treatment of the wall surfaces. When Milan fell to the French at the end of the century, Bramante moved on to Rome, where the impact of his first introduction to the grandiose complexes of ancient architecture rapidly matured his style. The ruins served to confirm the validity of his earlier goals; they offered a vocabulary far better suited to his monumental aims than the fussy terra-cotta ornament of Lombardy, and they provided countless models in which his ideal of volumetric space and sculptural mass were impressively realized.

Architecture is a costly form of expression, and the encounter of a uniquely creative imagination with a great tradition could not have been of much consequence without the support of an equally distinguished patron. That Julius II sought to emulate the political grandeur of the Caesars just as Bramante learned to restore the physical grandeur of ancient Rome continually delights historians, because the occasion may be ascribed with equal conviction to political, social, or economic determinants, to the chance convergence of great individuals, or to a crisis of style in the arts.

As soon as Bramante had completed small commissions in his early years in Rome (e.g., the cloister of Santa Maria della Pace, 1500; the *Tempietto* of San Pietro in Montorio, 1502), the Pope saw in his work the echo of his own taste for monumentality and lost interest in Giuliano da

2. *Il terzo libro di Sebastiano Serlio bolognese*, Venice, 1540 (quoted from the edition of Venice, 1584, fol. 64v).

Sangallo, the brilliant but more conservative Florentine architect whom he had consistently patronized when a Cardinal. A year after his election to the pontificate, Julius commissioned Bramante to design a new façade for the Vatican Palace and the huge Cortile del Belvedere; in the following year, 1505, he requested plans for the new St Peter's, to replace the decaying fourth-century Basilica. Another commission of unknown date initiated projects for a "Palace of Justice" that would have rivalled the Vatican if it had been finished.

The new papal buildings confirm the decisive break with early Renaissance architecture already announced in the *Tempietto*. This building, though one of the smallest in Rome, is the key to High Renaissance architecture because it preserves traditional ideals while establishing the forms of a new age. It is traditional in being a perfect central plan, a composition of two abstract geometrical forms: the cylinder and the hemisphere. But fifteenth-century geometry had never (except in the drawings of Leonardo, which surely influenced Bramante) dealt so successfully with solids: buildings before Bramante, even those with some sense of plasticity, seem to be composed of planes, circles and rectangles rather than of cylinders and cubes, and to be articulated by lines rather than by forms. In the *Tempietto* the third dimension is fully realized; its geometric solids are made more convincing by deep niches that reveal the mass and density of the wall. Members are designed to mould light and shade so as to convey an impression of body. We sense that where the earlier architect drew buildings, Bramante modelled them. Because the *Tempietto* recites the vocabulary of ancient architecture more scrupulously than its predecessors, it is often misinterpreted as an imitation of a Roman temple. But just the feature that so profoundly influenced the future – the high drum and hemispherical dome – is without precedent in antiquity, a triumph of the imagination.

In the projects for St Peter's (Pl. 51a, Fig. 11a) the new style attains maturity. Here for the first time Bramante manages to coordinate his volumetric control of space and his modelling of mass. The key to this achievement is a new concept of the relationship between void and solid.

Space ceases to be a mere absence of mass and becomes a dynamic force that pushes against the solids from all directions, squeezing them into forms never dreamed of by geometricians. The wall, now completely malleable, is an expression of an equilibrium between the equally dynamic demands of space and structural necessity. Nothing remains of the fifteenth-century concept of the wall as a plane, because the goal of the architect is no longer to produce an abstract harmony but rather a sequence of purely visual (as opposed to intellectual) experiences of spatial volumes. It is this accent on the eye rather than on the mind that gives precedence to voids over planes.

Bramante's handling of the wall as a malleable body was inspired by Roman architecture, in particular by the great Baths, but this concept of form could not be revived without the technique that made it possible. The structural basis of the Baths was brick-faced concrete, the most plastic material available to builders. For the Roman architect brick was simply the material that gave rigidity to the concrete, and protected its surface. In the Middle Ages the art of making a strong concrete was virtually forgotten, and bricks, now used as an inexpensive substitute for stone blocks, lost the flexibility afforded by a concrete core. Bramante must have rediscovered the lost art of the Romans. The irrational shapes of the plan of St Peter's (Fig. 11a) – giant slices of toast half eaten by a voracious space – are inconceivable without the cohesiveness of concrete construction, as are the great naves of the Basilica, which could not have been vaulted by early Renaissance structural methods.[3] Bramante willed to Michelangelo and his contemporaries an indispensable technical tool for the development of enriched forms.

In the evolution of the design of St Peter's, Bramante left for Michelangelo the realization of an important potential in the malleability of concrete-brick construction; for in spite of his flowing forms, the major spatial volumes of his plan are still isolated from one another. The chapels in the angles of the main cross and, more obviously, the four

3. On Bramante's revival of Roman vaulting technique, see O. Förster, *Bramante*, Munich, 1956, pp. 277 f.

corner towers, are added to the core rather than fused into it, as may be seen more clearly in elevations (Pl. 51a).

The dynamic characterization of space and mass which was the essence of Bramante's revolution is equally evident in his secular buildings, even when he was concerned primarily with façades. In the fifteenth century it was the nature of a façade to be planar, but Bramante virtually hid the surface by sculptural projections (half-columns, balconies, window pediments, heavy rustications) and spatial recessions (ground floor arcades, and loggias on the upper story, as in the court of the Belvedere and the façade of the Vatican). These innovations are not motivated by mere distaste for the flat forms of the early Renaissance façade but by a positive awareness of the range of expression available in a varied use of light. His projections capture the sun in brilliant high-lights and cast deep shadows; his half-columns softly model the light; his loggias create dark fields that silhouette their columnar supports. In the façades, as in the interior of St Peter's, the purely sensual delights of vision inspire the design. The philosophical impulse of fifteenth-century architecture had become sensual.

Bramante's style rapidly changed the course of Renaissance architecture. This was due not only to its novelty, but to the unprecedented situation created by the great size of his papal projects: for the first time in the Renaissance it became necessary to organize a modern type of architectural firm with a master in charge of a large number of younger architects who were in one sense junior partners, in another sense pupils. Almost every eminent architect of the first half of the sixteenth century, Michelangelo excepted, worked under Bramante in the Vatican "office": Baldassare Peruzzi, Raphael, Antonio da Sangallo, Giulio Romano, and perhaps Jacopo Sansovino. Of these only Peruzzi actually practised architecture before Bramante's death (e.g. the Villa Farnesina in Rome, 1509); the others learned their profession at the Vatican and later developed Bramante's innovations into individual styles that dominated the second quarter of the century. The effect was felt all over Italy: Peruzzi built in Siena, Raphael in Florence, Sansovino in Venice, Giulio in Mantua, and

Sangallo throughout the Papal States. The death of Julius II in 1513 and of Bramante in 1514 simultaneously removed the co-authors of High Renaissance architecture, leaving the monumental Basilica and palaces in such an inchoate state that the next generation found it hard to determine precisely what the original intentions had been. Paradoxically, this was a favourable misfortune, because it liberated the imagination of the younger architects just as they reached maturity. Raphael, Peruzzi and Sangallo, inheriting the leadership of St Peter's and the Vatican, were free to compose variations on the theme of their master, and were actually encouraged to do so by successive popes who wanted distinctive evidence of their own patronage.

The fact that Michelangelo's career as an architect began in 1516 is directly related to this historical scene. Michelangelo's animosity toward the powerful Bramante kept him out of architecture during Bramante's lifetime. But the election of a Medici, Leo X (1513–1521), as the successor to Julius II, provided opportunities in Florence. Leo, although he chose Bramante's chief disciple, Raphael, to continue the Vatican projects, needed an architect to complete the construction of San Lorenzo, the major Medici monument in Florence. Michelangelo was the obvious choice for this job because he was not only the leading Florentine artist but also a sculptor-painter, ideally equipped to carry out the half-figurative, half-architectural programme envisaged by the Medici family. Besides, the commission served the dual purpose of removing Michelangelo from Rome and of frustrating the completion of the Tomb of Julius II, which would have competed with Medici splendour.

Although Michelangelo's achievements in Florence proved that he was as eminent in architecture as in the other arts, he was excluded from any important Roman commissions so long as any member of Bramante's circle was alive. When Antonio da Sangallo died in 1546, the only member of the circle who survived was Giulio Romano (Raphael d. 1520, Peruzzi d. 1536), and it is significant that the Fabbrica of St Peter's called Giulio from Mantua to forestall Michelangelo's appointment as chief architect. But his death, immediately following Sangallo's, finally left the field open to Michelangelo, now 71 years old.

Yet Michelangelo's personal conflict with Bramante cannot by itself explain why the intrigues that it engendered were so successful in excluding him from architectural commissions in Rome. That the popes of this period – Leo X; another Medici, Clement VII (1523–1534); and Paul III, Farnese (1534–1549) – recognized Michelangelo's pre-eminence is proven by the fact that they tried to monopolize his services as a painter and sculptor. The Medici were even willing to retain him as an architect in Florence after he had fought against them for the independence of the city. The long delay in recognition at Rome must be attributed to the unorthodoxy of his style. It lacked what Vitruvius called *decorum:* a respect for classical traditions. And in the first half of the century cultivated Roman taste was attuned to a correct antique vocabulary in a classic context. Bramante had formed this taste, and it took a generation to assimilate his innovations.

Raphael was the ideal successor to Bramante. That his concerns as a painter for massive forms and volumetric space in simple compositions of geometric solids were a counterpart of Bramante's architectural goals may be seen in such architectural frescoes as the *School of Athens* and the *Expulsion of Heliodorus*. Consequently, when he succeeded to Bramante's post he could pursue his own interests and at the same time design almost as Bramante would have done if he had lived another six years. If Raphael had been less sympathetic to his master, his architecture would certainly be better known. But in major Vatican works, at the Cortile di San Damaso and Belvedere, the two designers are indistinguishable, and uncertainty about the authorship of projects for St Peter's has always worried us. In his work outside the papal circle – Palazzo Vidoni-Caffarelli, Palazzo Branconio d'Aquila, Villa Madama in Rome, and Palazzo Pandolfini in Florence – Raphael developed Bramantesque principles and vocabulary into a more individualized expression notable for its greater sophistication, elegance of decoration, and for its success in binding into a unity masses and spaces that Bramante had tended to individualize. The propriety of Raphael's accession to Bramante's throne is further shown by the fact that the very qualities which distinguish him from his predecessor – moderation, respect for continuity, sophistication and elegance, unification of discrete elements – also distinguish his patron, Leo X, from Julius II.

A comparable poetic justice guided the careers of other Bramante followers. Peruzzi, who often worked with the linear and planar means of fifteenth-century architecture while concentrating his great ingenuity on exploring new forms and rhythms in plan and elevation (he was the first to exploit the oval plan and curved façade), was employed more in his native Siena than in Rome. That medieval town must have valued him rather for his superficial conservatism than for the extraordinary inventiveness which had too little opportunity for expression, and which now can only be appreciated properly in hundreds of drawings preserved in the Uffizi Gallery.

Giulio Romano, whose three or four small Roman palaces represent a revolt against Bramante's grandeur in the direction of repression, tight-ness, and an apparently polemic rejection of plasticity and volume, found himself more at home outside Rome, in the court of Mantua, where the tensions induced by the weakness of humanist duchies in a world of power-states could be given expression in a Mannerist architecture of neurotic fantasy (The Ducal Palace, Palazzo del Tè).

So the Rome which rejected Michelangelo was equally inhospitable to other non-classic architects. Though Peruzzi, as a Bramante follower, was frequently given a chance to aid in the design of St Peter's and the Vatican and to compete for major commissions (the great hospital of S. Giacomo degli Incurabili, San Giovanni dei Fiorentini), he never was chosen as a chief architect. The victor was always Antonio da Sangallo the Younger, who gave the classic movement its definitive form.

Sangallo's dictatorship in the style of 1520–1545 can be explained more by his propriety than by his eminence; he was probably the least gifted of Bramante's pupils. The first major Renaissance architect to be trained exclusively in the profession, he began as a carpenter at the Vatican in the early years of the century. His practice never had to be set aside for

commissions in the other arts and, being a gifted organizer and entre-
preneur, he was able not only to undertake all the important civil and
military commissions of the papacy but those of private families, among
them the Farnese, as well. Nearly a thousand surviving drawings in the
Uffizi are evidence of vast building activity throughout central Italy. He
is distinguished less for his innovations than for his capacity to apply the
experiments and aesthetic of the High Renaissance to the complete reper-
tory of Renaissance building types. The façade of Santo Spirito in Sassia
in Rome is the uninspired source of later sixteenth-century façade design;
the Banco di Santo Spirito (Rome) has a two story colossal order over
a drafted basement in a context that delighted Baroque architects and has
never been entirely abandoned; the Farnese palace (Pl. 39) is the definitive
secular structure of the Roman Renaissance, though major components
of its design were anticipated by Bramante and Raphael. It is in the plans
and models of St Peter's that the symptomatic weakness of Antonio's
architecture may be seen (Pl. 51c, Fig. 11). The project is unassailable on
the grounds of structure or of Vitruvian *decorum*, but it is confusing in its
multiplicity: infinite numbers of small members compete for attention
and negate the grandeur of scale required by the size of the building; the
dome is obese, and the ten-storied campanili are Towers of Babel.
Antonio's superior technical and archaeological knowledge proved to be
no guarantee of ability to achieve coherence or to control fully such raw
materials of architecture as space, proportion, light and scale.

Sangallo, as the first architect of the Renaissance trained in his profession, knew more than his contemporaries about the technical aspects of
construction. He was frequently called upon to right major faults in
Bramante's structures: to fortify the piers of St Peter's and the foundations of the Vatican façade, to rebuild the loggie of the Belvedere, which
collapsed in 1536, all of necessity to the detriment of the original design.
But technical competence was not a pre-eminent qualification in the
eyes of Renaissance critics: Bramante, though called *maestro ruinante* in
allusion to his engineering failures, was universally recognized as the
superior architect. Of course, this may be attributed simply to a difference

in creative ability, or genius, or whatever one may call it, but it raises an important question for Renaissance architecture, and for Michelangelo in particular: was it possible, in the age of Humanism, for an individual to be fully successful as a specialist? Sangallo, in gaining the advantage of a long apprenticeship in architectural construction, lost the benefits of a generalized body of theoretical knowledge and principles traditionally passed on in the studios of painters and sculptors. Problems of proportion, perspective (the control of space), composition, lighting, etc, as encountered in the figurative arts, were more important in the development of Renaissance architecture than structural concerns, partly because, by contrast to the Gothic period or to the nineteenth century, technology was restricted to a minor role.

In our day, when the concern for technique has threatened to overwhelm all other values in architecture, it is difficult to appreciate the Renaissance view that sculptors and painters were uniquely qualified as architects by their understanding of universal formal problems. The view was vindicated by the fact that it was the artist who made major technical advances – the technician merely interpreted traditional practices.

The Renaissance architect was forced into a preoccupation with broad principles in one way or another. First of all, he had to find a way to justify a revival of pagan grandeur in a Christian society; this involved, among other dilemmas, a rationalization of the conflicting architectural principles of antiquity and the Middle Ages. Further, as is demonstrated by Sangallo's failure to construct a theory out of devoted study of Vitruvius and Roman monuments, antiquity itself taught no clear and consistent body of principles. To give order to a chaos of inherited concepts, many Renaissance architects – Alberti, Francesco di Giorgio and others in the fifteenth century, Palladio in the sixteenth – developed and published theories of architecture of a metaphysical-mathematical cast. But formalized philosophies were not the sole solution; it is intriguing that nothing was written about architecture (or any other art) in the High Renaissance. This reveals a desire to solve the same problems in a new way; a reaction in all the arts against the abstract principles of the

fifteenth century produced a temporary shift from intellectual-philo-
sophical precepts to visual and psychological ones that could better be
expressed in form than in words. This change of emphasis is a key to
Michelangelo's achievement, and for this reason I begin the study of his
work with some observations on what we know of his architectural
ideas.

CHAPTER I

Michelangelo's "Theory" of Architecture

MICHELANGELO, one of the greatest creative geniuses in the history of architecture, frequently claimed that he was not an architect.[1] The claim is more than a sculptor's expression of modesty: it is a key to the understanding of his buildings, which are conceived as if the masses of a structure were organic forms capable of being moulded and carved, of expressing movement, of forming symphonies of light, shadow and texture, like a statue. The only surviving evidence of Michelangelo's theory of architecture is the fragment of a letter of unknown date and destination in which this identity of architecture with painting and sculpture is expressed in a manner unique in the Renaissance:

Reverend Sir (Cardinal Rodolfo Pio?): When a plan has diverse parts, all those (parts) that are of one kind of quality and quantity must be adorned in the same way, and in the same style, and likewise the portions that correspond [e.g. portions in which a feature of the plan is mirrored, as in the four equal arms of St Peter's]. But where the plan is entirely changed in form, it is not only permissible but necessary in consequence entirely to change the adornments and likewise their corresponding portions; the means are unrestricted (and may be chosen) at will [or: as the adornments require]; similarly the nose, which is in the centre of the face, has no commitment either to one or the other eye, but one hand is really obliged to be like the other and one eye like the other in relation to the sides (of the body), and to its correspondences. And surely, the architectural members derive [dipendono] from human members. Whoever has not been or is not a good master of the figure and likewise of anatomy cannot understand (anything) of it . . .[2]

For a general view of Michelangelo's theories of art, see E. Panofsky, Idea . . ., Leipzig and Berlin, 1924 (2nd ed., Berlin, 1960), pp. 64 ff.; Idem, "The History of Proportions as a Reflection of the History of Styles", Meaning in the Visual Arts, N.Y., 1955, esp. pp. 88–107; C. de Tolnay, Werk und Weltbild des Michelangelo, Zürich, 1949, pp. 87–110. Reflections of Michelangelo's theories appear in Vincenzo Danti, Il primo libro del trattato delle perfette proporzioni, Florence, 1567.

   1. Lettere, p. 431; Wilde 1953, pp. 109 f.; Condivi, ch. LIII.

   2. Lettere, p. 554; Schiavo 1949, Fig. 96 (facsimile). Interpreted by Tolnay 1949, p. 95.

It is not unusual for Renaissance theorists to relate architectural forms to those of the human body; in one way or another this association, which may be traced back to ancient Greece and is echoed in Vitruvius, appears in all theories of the age of Humanism. What is unique in Michelangelo is the conception of the simile as a relationship which might be called organic, in distinction to the abstract one proposed by other Renaissance architects and writers. It is anatomy, rather than number and geometry, that becomes the basic discipline for the architect; the parts of a building are compared, not to the ideal overall proportions of the human body but, significantly, to its functions. The reference to eyes, nose, and arms even suggests an implication of mobility; the building lives and breathes.

This scrap of a letter cannot be taken as evidence of a theory of architecture: in fact, it expresses an attitude which in the Renaissance might have been called anti-theoretical. But there is more in it than the fantasy of a sculptor, and it may be used as a key to the individuality of Michelangelo's architectural style, primarily because it defines his conscious and thoroughgoing break with the principles of early Renaissance architecture.

When fifteenth-century writers spoke of deriving architectural forms from the human body, they did not think of the body as a living organism, but as a microcosm of the universe, a form created in God's image, and created with the same perfect harmony that determines the movement of the spheres or musical consonances.[3] This harmony could not be discovered empirically, since it was an ideal unattainable in actuality, but it could be symbolized mathematically. Thus the ideal human form was expressed either in numerical or geometrical formulae: numerical proportions were established for the body that determined simple relationships between the parts and the whole (e.g., head : body$=1:7$) or the body was inscribed within a square or a circle or some combination

3. On fifteenth-century theory, see: R. Wittkower, *Architectural Principles in the Age of Humanism*, London, 1949; H. Saalman, "Early Renaissance Architectural Theory and Practice in Antonio Filarete's *Trattato . . .*", *Art Bulletin*, XLI, 1959, pp. 89 ff.

of the two, sometimes with the navel exactly in the centre. Architectural proportions and forms could then be associated with these formulae (Pl. 1a).

This entirely intellectual attempt to humanize architecture really made it peculiarly abstract, for rather than actually deriving useful mathematical symbols and proportions from a study of the body, it forced the body, like Procrustes, into figures already idealized by a long metaphysical tradition traceable to Plato and Pythagoras (Pl. 1b). The perfect mathematical figures and ratios and the way in which they were used to establish the form and proportions of buildings remained quite unaffected by this attempt to "humanize" them. But if reference to the human body was superfluous in practice, it gave fifteenth-century architects a timely philosophical justification for their method and helped to transform them from medieval craftsmen to Renaissance humanists.

If the human body was to be adapted by the fifteenth-century theorist to a system of proportions, it had to be treated as a static object to be analysed into a complex of numerically or geometrically interrelated parts. This method inevitably emphasized units: the whole became a harmony among discrete members. By contrast, Michelangelo's demand for an architecture based on anatomy was motivated by a desire to restore the indivisibility of the human form, a unity to be found in the function of the brain and of the nerve and muscle systems, rather than in external appearances.

Michelangelo was fully aware of the significance of these differences and felt compelled to attack the abstract analytical principles of his predecessors and contemporaries. Condivi noted (ch. LII):

I know well that when he read Albrecht Dürer,[4] it seemed to him a very weak thing, seeing with his (great) insight how much more beautiful and useful was his own concept of this problem [the human figure]. And to tell the truth, Albrecht deals only with the measurement and variety of bodies, concerning which no sure rule can be given, conceiving his figures upright like posts (Pl. 1c). But what is more important, he says not a word about human actions and gestures.

4. *Vier Bücher von menschlicher Proportion*, Nürnberg, 1528. Cf. E. Panofsky, *Dürer*, Princeton, 1943, pp. 260 f.

At the same time, Condivi speaks of Michelangelo's desire to write a treatise on anatomy with emphasis on human *moti* and *apparenze*. Obviously this treatise would not have made use of abstract ratio and geometry; nor would it have been the more empirical one that Leonardo might have written; for the words *moti* (suggesting "emotions" as well as "motions") and *apparenze* imply that Michelangelo would have emphasized the psychological and visual *effects* of bodily functions.

Michelangelo sensed the necessary relationship between the figurative penetration into human beings that gave his art its unique psychological force, and a literal penetration that would reveal the workings of nerves, muscles and bones. His study of anatomy, in contrast to Leonardo's, was motivated by an incalculably important shift from an objective to a subjective approach to reality.

Early Renaissance theories of proportion, when applied to buildings, produced architecture that was abstract in the sense that its primary aim was to achieve ideal mathematical harmonies out of the interrelationship of the parts of a building. Simple geometrical figures were preferred for the plan; walls and openings were thought of as rectangles that could be given a desired quality through the ratio of height to width. Given the basic concept of well-proportioned planes, the ultimate aim of architectural design was to produce a three-dimensional structure in which the planes would be harmonically interrelated. At its best, this principle of design produced a highly sophisticated and subtle architecture, but it was vulnerable to the same criticism that Michelangelo directed against the contemporary system of figural proportion. It emphasized the unit and failed to take into account the effect on the character of forms brought about by movement – in architecture, the movement of the observer through and around buildings – and by environmental conditions, particularly light. It could easily produce a paper architecture more successful on the drawing board than in three dimensions.

Toward the end of the fifteenth century, architects and painters began to be more concerned with three-dimensional effects, particularly those produced by solid forms emphasized by gradations of light and shadow.

Leonardo pioneered in the movement away from the planar concept of architecture in a series of drawings which, while still dependent for their effect on mathematical ratios, employed the forms of solid, rather than of plane geometry: cubes, cylinders, hemispheres. Leonardo's theoretical experiments must have inspired the extraordinary innovations of Bramante discussed in the Introduction. These innovations, which substituted mass and spatial volume for planar design cannot, however, be taken as evidence of a fundamental change in architectural theory. I believe that Bramante still thought in terms of proportion and ratio, as demonstrated by his tendency to emphasize the interplay of distinct parts in a building. In his project for St Peter's the exterior masses and interior spaces are semi-independent units harmoniously related to the central core (Pl. 51a).

Seen in this perspective, Michelangelo's approach to architecture appears as a radical departure from Renaissance tradition. His association of architecture to the human form was no longer a philosophical abstraction, a mathematical metaphor. By thinking of buildings as organisms, he changed the concept of architectural design from the static one produced by a system of predetermined proportions to a dynamic one in which members would be integrated by the suggestion of muscular power. In this way the action and reaction of structural forces in a building – which today we describe as tension, compression, stress, etc, – could be interpreted in humanized terms. But, if structural forces gave Michelangelo a theme, he refused to be confined to expressing the ways in which they actually operated: humanization overcame the laws of statics in his designs to the point at which a mass as weighty as the dome of St Peter's can appear to rise, or a relatively light attic-facing to oppress.

While fifteenth-century architecture required of the observer a certain degree of intellectual contemplation to appreciate its symbolic relationships, Michelangelo's was to suggest an immediate identification of our own physical functions with those of the building. This organic approach suggests the injection of the principle of empathy into Renaissance aesthetics by its search for a physical and psychological bond between observer and object.

In Michelangelo's drawings we can see how the concept was put into practice.[5] Initial studies for a building are vigorous impressions of a whole which search for a certain quality of sculptural form even before the structural system is determined (Pls. 3d, 68). Often they even deny the exigencies of statics, which enter only at a later stage to discipline fantasy. Details remain indeterminate until the overall form is fixed, but at that point they are designed with that sense of coherence with an unseen whole which we find in Michelangelo's sketches of disembodied hands or heads. Drawings of windows, doors, cornices are intended to convey to the mason a vivid experience rather than calculated measured instructions for carvings (Pls. 46b, 79b). Where his contemporaries would sketch profiles to assure the proper ratio of a channel to a torus, Michelangelo worked for the evocation of physical power (Pl. 1d); where they copied Roman capitals and entablatures among the ruins to achieve a certain orthodoxy of detail, Michelangelo's occasional copies are highly personalized reinterpretations of just those remains that mirrored his own taste for dynamic form. Rome provided other architects with a corpus of rules but gave Michelangelo a spark for explosions of fancy, a standard that he honoured more in the breach than in the observance.

This indifference to antique canons shocked Michelangelo's contemporaries, who felt that it was the unique distinction of their age to have revived Roman architecture. They interpreted a comparable indifference in fifteenth-century architects as evidence of a faltering, quasi-medieval search for the classic perfection of the early 1500's. Implicit in humanist philosophy was the concept that the goal of endeavour, whether in art, government, or science, was to equal – not to surpass – the ancients. Thus, Michelangelo's bizarre variations on classic orders, coming on the

5. On the development of architectural drawing in the Renaissance, see W. Lotz, "Das Raumbild in der italienischen Architekturzeichnung der Renaissance", *Mitt. des Kunsthist. Inst. in Florenz*, VII, 1956, pp. 193 ff.; J. Ackerman, "Architectural Practice in the Italian Renaissance", *Journ. Soc. Architectural Historians*, XIII, 1954, pp. 3 ff.

heels of the climactic achievements of Bramante and Raphael, frightened Vasari, who dared not find fault with the Master, but worried that others might emulate him.[6] When Michelangelo claimed for his design of San Giovanni dei Fiorentini in Rome that it surpassed both the Greeks and the Romans, the Renaissance concept was already obsolete; for the moment any improvement on antiquity is conceivable, the door is opened for a modern philosophy of free experiment and limitless progress.

Michelangelo's plan studies appear as organisms capable of motion: the fortification drawings obey a biological rather than a structural imperative (Pls. 26a–28a). But even in more orthodox plans (Pls. 66b–68) the masses swell and contract as if in response to the effort of support. Elevation sketches minimize the planes of the wall to accent plastic forms – columns, pilasters, entablatures, frames, etc. – which dramatize the interaction of load and support. I say "dramatize" because the sculptural members, seen as bones and muscles, create an imagined epic of conflicting forces, while it is the anonymous wall that does the mundane job of stabilizing the structure. In building, the wall is further distinguished from its expressive articulation by the choice and treatment of materials.

By contrast to contemporaries trained in fifteenth-century proportions, Michelangelo rarely indicated measurements or scale on his drawings, never worked to a module, and avoided the ruler and compass until the design was finally determined. From the start he dealt with qualities rather than quantities. In choosing ink washes and chalk rather than the pen, he evoked the quality of stone, and the most tentative preliminary sketches are likely to contain indications of light and shadow (Pls. 19b, 46b); the observer is there before the building is designed.

Michelangelo rarely made perspective sketches, because he thought of the observer as being in motion and hesitated to visualize buildings from a fixed point. To study three-dimensional effects he made clay models. The introduction of modelling into architectural practice again demonstrates the identity of sculpture and architecture in Michelangelo's

6. See the quotation from Vasari on p. 22.

mind. It is also a further sign of his revolt against early Renaissance principles, since the malleability of the material precludes any suggestion of mathematical relationships or even any independence of parts: only the whole could be studied in terra-cotta. We can infer that when Michelangelo used clay models he sought effects of mass rather than of enclosed space, as in his paintings, where the spatial environment exists only as a receptacle for the bodies. The architectural drawings show the same preference; they communicate mass by contrast to those of Bramante or Sangallo, where lines are drawn around spaces.

This approach to architecture, being sculptural, inevitably was reinforced by a special sensitivity to materials and to effects of light. Michelangelo capitalized upon the structure of his materials because of his desire to get a maximum contrast between members used to express force or tension and "neutral" wall surfaces. He invariably minimized the peculiarities of surface materials such as stucco and brick, while he carved and finished the plastic members in order to evoke – even to exaggerate – the quality and texture of the stone (Pls. 35b, 46a). No one had a comparable sensitivity to the character of the traditional Roman masonry, Travertine, the pitted striations of which became richly expressive in his design.

In speaking of modern architecture we often associate sensitivity to materials with an exposition of their technical functions, but in Michelangelo's work the latter is characteristically absent. In laying masonry, Michelangelo notably avoided any emphasis on the unit (block or brick). He disguised joints as much as possible in order to avoid conflict between the part and the whole, and to sustain the experience of the building as an organism (Pl. 64). He was the only architect of his time who did not use quoins, and he rarely employed rusticated or drafted masonry, the favoured Renaissance means of stressing the individuality of the block. If his buildings were to communicate muscular force, the cubic pieces had to be disguised.

Light, for Michelangelo, was not merely a means of illuminating forms; it was an element of form itself. The plastic members of a building

were not designed to be seen as stable and defined elements but as changing conformations of highlight and shadow. Much of Michelangelo's
unorthodoxy in the use of antique detail can be explained by his desire
to increase the versatility of light effects. If more of his interiors had been
completed according to his design, I believe we would find an astounding
variety of compositions in light, creating moods quite unknown in the
Renaissance. It is fascinating to imagine, for example, what the interior
of St Peter's might have been like if the lantern had been screened by
an interior canopy as Michelangelo planned (Pls. 57a, 61). No doubt
Michelangelo's sympathetic adjustment to the brilliance of the Mediter-
ranean sun was a factor that inhibited the exportation of his style to
hazier northern countries, where the intellectual reserve of Palladio was
much preferred.

The common practice in the sixteenth century of building from large
wooden scale models, rather than from drawings, explains the absence
of any complete plans or elevations among Michelangelo's surviving
sketches. But these sketches differ from those of other Renaissance
designers in one significant respect: with two or three exceptions none
represents even a small detail as it was ultimately built. It was Michelangelo's habit to keep his design in a constant state of flux until every
detail was ready for carving, a method entirely consistent with his
organic approach. His conception of a building literally grew, and a
change in any part involved sympathetic changes in other parts. The
final solution was not reached even in the model: the wooden model for
St Peter's was executed without an attic, and probably without a façade
or dome, in order to permit Michelangelo to alter those portions in
response to his impressions of the body of the building as it was constructed. There and at the Farnese palace, wooden mockups of cornices were
made to full scale and hoisted into position to enable the architect to
judge, and possibly to redesign, his project at the last moment; had funds
been available he doubtless would have destroyed portions already
finished in order to improve them, as he did with his later sculptures. In
all his work he seems to have carried the generative drive to a point at

which it became an obstacle to completion, an obstacle so frustrating that most of his architectural projects were not executed, and no building was completed according to his plans. So contemporary engravers had to record his projects by combining scattered records of different stages in the process of conception with touches of pure fancy. And the problem is the same for the modern historian. We shall never know for certain what Michelangelo's unexecuted projects – whether abandoned or partly completed – were to have been; in fact, the attempt to do so implies at the outset a misunderstanding of his conception of architecture. To visualize any of Michelangelo's designs, we must seek to capture not a determinate solution, but the spirit and the goals of a process.

CHAPTER II

The Façade of San Lorenzo in Florence

NOTHING troubled medieval and Renaissance architects as much as façades. Among the great cathedrals of Gothic Italy only one – Siena – has a façade that is not largely modern, and the finest churches of Florence hide behind anonymous walls of stone or the brittle veneers of nineteenth-century antiquarians. Beyond the Alps this rarely happened; the façade was the showpiece of the Gothic cathedral, dominating the town and fields with its twin towers fused into the structure, and with its great portals and rose window becoming progressively more complex in order to carry the panorama of the Old and New Testaments in sculpture and painting.

The differences are deeply rooted in custom and taste. Italian cities meant to have luxurious façades as a pious obligation, but they were not called for by either the aesthetic or the structure of the architecture. The spirit of the Early Christian church survived with its splendidly decorated inner walls and simple geometric exteriors. Since narthexes and sculptured portals were never widely adopted in Italy, and campanili were never integrated with the church structure, the façade became no more than a protective screen where the building stopped growing, having no organic relation to the structural system. It could be laid up hastily by masons in the hope that it would be clothed later in a thin coat of elegance. So it is not strange that surviving drawings for Italian Gothic façades are barely distinguishable from those painted triptychs of the period with expanses of flat surface bordered by delicate gilt frames and pinnacles.

Since Italy became the pre-eminent centre of culture at the close of the medieval period, one of the shortcomings of her Gothic churches naturally became a major problem for Renaissance architecture. The problem was intensified by a conflict of traditions: the Renaissance church, with its high nave and low side aisles, preserved the outlines of the medieval basilica, but the new taste required that it be dressed in the forms of the ancient temple with its columns (or pilasters), entablatures, and pediment. Antiquity prescribed fixed proportions for the Orders; if more than one story had to be faced with columns or pilasters, either these members had to be greatly broadened to gain height, or one Order had to be superimposed upon another. Consequently it was difficult to achieve a uniform system as a facing for the low aisles and high nave of a church. But this was not the only problem; the interior nave elevation of Renaissance churches tended to be divided, as was Brunelleschi's San Lorenzo, into three levels – columns or piers, arches, and clerestory – of which the second or arch level was by its nature substantially less high than the others. Such a division could not be employed easily on the exterior while preserving the vocabulary of the Roman temple, since the second of the three levels was too narrow to admit a proper Order of its own. If, on the other hand, the elevation were to be disguised behind a two-story façade, one of these stories was apt to become disproportionately high.

Starting with Alberti's ingenious experiments, architects of the fifteenth century tried every solution for the problem, but the very variety of results – in notable contrast to the uniformity of later Renaissance façades – testifies to their failure to reach a viable standard. This may be due partly to the unsuccessful attempt to abandon the basilical form in favour of central plan churches, where façade design, though equally challenging, was at least not complicated by reminiscences of medieval forms.

This is one explanation of the absence of a façade on San Lorenzo, a church which Medici patronage had in other respects made one of the most splendid in Florence (Pl. 15, Fig. 3). When the first Medici Pope, Leo X (1513–1521), decided to finish the church, Florentine architects swarmed to the Vatican to get the commission, because the sum assigned to construction, in addition to the prestige of the patron, assured it of being the most important basilical façade of the generation. Michelangelo, normally modest about his work, said that he could make it "the mirror of architecture and sculpture of all Italy". There was a competition for the design in 1515, Vasari says, involving Antonio da Sangallo (Elder), Andrea and Jacopo Sansovino, Raphael and others, in addition to Michelangelo.

We would know much more about Renaissance architecture if the competing projects had survived, but unfortunately we have only a few drawings by Giuliano da Sangallo, a candidate whom Vasari overlooked. These are the last records of the aged Quattrocento architect, and while they show his ability to rise to the demands of the new Roman style, they also betray his insecurity in the face of the old problems. He offers two solutions: one is a three-story elevation (Uffizi, *Arch*. 276, 281) with an extremely tall lower Order, set forward as a porch, a rather squashed upper one, and between them a mezzanine with stunted unclassical pilasters; the other (Uffizi, *Arch*. 280) is more successful, proposing two stories of equal height and also of equal width, a solution which, except for a low pediment that covers only the central bays, disguises the difference in elevation between the side aisles and the nave. The latter design includes a pair of five-story campanili loosely related to the façade, which would have clashed with the scale of the church. These are important because Michelangelo seems to have studied them for his project, together with another drawing by Giuliano (Pl. 3a; Uffizi, *Arch*. 277) which, though made at an earlier date for another church, probably was shown to the Pope at the time of the competition. Like the first solution, it has a mezzanine, but of the same width as the lower Order, since the latter does not project forward from the plane of the façade. Here the disproportionate heights of the lower and upper Orders are minimized by raising the ground floor pilasters on high socles.

Apparently Michelangelo was initially engaged to direct the façade sculpture, while others were invited to compete for the architectural commission. Ultimately his inability to collaborate with anybody brought him both jobs, but whether this attests to the success of his designs or of his intrigues is uncertain. In any event, he was appointed, though lacking previous architectural experience, because the Pope envisaged the façade as a great framework for statues and reliefs. Nobody had had such an idea in Quattrocento Tuscany; it was too pictorial to appeal to humanists and rather suggests late medieval practice (Giovanni Pisano at Siena) or the North Italian Renaissance (Certosa of Pavia). Perhaps boredom with fifteenth-century purism explains the change of taste already evident in Giuliano da Sangallo's drawing originally done for Julius II (Pl. 3a). The pictorial style gained impetus from a rapidly growing interest in theatre design, from the new vogue for painted palace façades, and from temporary festival architecture such as the façade erected on the Cathedral of Florence for the entry of Leo X in 1515. The Cathedral decoration may have suggested to Leo a scheme for San Lorenzo that would make the most of Michelangelo's genius.

In the first of three stages in the development of the design (Pl. 3b), the sculpture is really more important than the building, which becomes a skeleton for relief panels and statue niches; probably one of the reasons for abandoning this project was that some of the sculptures would have been monstrously big while others were dispersed without much cohesion, if we can trust at all the weak copies that are preserved. We may compare the architectural solution at this stage to one of Sangallo's drawings (Pl. 3a) which it echoes in some obvious ways: the lower Order raised high on socles and the upper Order in the guise of a somewhat stunted temple front; alternation of recessed entrance bays and projecting bays with paired pilasters or half columns; the outermost bays crowned by curved pediments; the profusion of sculpture; etc. Yet Michelangelo grappled more seriously with the façade problem; his project succeeds in being at the same time two and three stories high by the dissimilar design of the central and outer bays, and avoids the disruption of Giuliano's mezzanine; it unifies the nave portion of the façade by giving the four central columns a single entablature – a device retained in all subsequent studies. Though the solution is far from perfect, Michelangelo from the beginning of his architectural career exhibited an ability to fuse discrete members into a convincing whole. The far more experienced Giuliano was unable to keep the parts of his façade from scattering; he was too interested in the individual pilasters and courses.

In all remaining schemes, Michelangelo chose a three-story system in which the second story was a kind of mezzanine or attic extending the whole width of the façade; a little sketch that may have been the first of his surviving drawings (Pl. 3c) gives the mezzanine undue prominence by muting vertical accents. This departure from the unity of the original solution (Pl. 3b) was encouraged by the side elevations of Brunelleschi's church, which had an emphatic three-story elevation accented by three cornices all around; the height of the mezzanine level was dictated by the height of the nave arches. Pl. 3b was abandoned because of the divisions of its outer bays, which did not correspond to those of the church and would have caused confusion at the corners where the façade and side elevations could be seen together. A further advantage of the mezzanine system was that it produced three ample bays of like dimensions to accommodate relief panels, and four spaces for statues between the uprights, without interfering with the architectural character as the first scheme tended to do. The solution may have been inspired by the attic design of Roman triumphal arches, such as that of Constantine.

In Pl. 3d, the better features of the preceding designs were combined, so that the outer tabernacles could be retained without abandoning the mezzanine. In this sketch Michelangelo may have been toying with the idea of bringing the central bays forward under a gabled roof to create a Pantheon-like porch. All of these ideas reach maturity in Pl. 4a, which could well be the design that won Michelangelo the commission when he went to see the Pope at the end of 1516. Cohesion is regained here by the device, already foreseen in the initial scheme, of combining a two- and three-story elevation; but here it is the upper rather than the lower Order that embraces the mezzanine. Now there is a well-distributed accommodation for ten statues in niches, as requested by the Pope, for three major reliefs in the mezzanine, and for minor ones on the lower story. Only one problem remained unsolved: in terms of the actual measurements of the church, the upper pilasters of the Order would have had to be so much taller and hence broader than the columns (?) beneath them that even Michelangelo might have paused at the affront to classical canons. Yet a design close to this one probably became the basis of the model made by Baccio d'Agnolo early in 1517.

Michelangelo would not accept Baccio's model, even after it had been altered according to his instructions. Although this can be explained by his inability to work with anyone except subordinates and by his apparently unreasonable suspicion of Baccio's loyalty, the most likely reason was that he had conceived an entirely new kind of façade, the nature of which he had kept secret even from his patron (he refused to send to Rome the clay model he had made in the spring of 1517, and even announced without any explanation that the cost would be increased by over a third).

The new design, while it retained many superficial elements of the preceding studies, was fundamentally different. It was no longer a veneer to be attached to the surface of the old façade, but a three-dimensional structure in its own right, a narthex that was to project forward one bay from the existing church and thus would have three faces rather than one. This proposal appears in the last and most impressive of Michelangelo's drawings (Pl. 5a), where the side elevations are suggested only by the projections of members on the far right. Now the lateral bays as well as the centre are three stories in height, a solution that became structurally imperative with the decision to erect a semi-independent building. The independence of the narthex also relieved the architect of the obligation to express the unequal heights of nave and aisles behind. Again the mezzanine level is accentuated; it no longer has to be embraced within the upper or lower Order of columns or pilasters because the raising of the outer bays to the full height of the façade adds sufficient vertical emphasis to counterbalance the strong horizontal (compare Pls. 4a and 5a). The mezzanine is divided by an emphatic cornice into two levels of pilaster-strips in order to urge us to read the upper level as part of the pilaster Order above, so that the proportions of this Order should not appear to be as squashed as they are in Pl. 3d or in G. Sangallo's comparable design (Pl. 3a).

This solved most of the problems that bedevilled earlier architects; it did not deny the existence of a three-aisled, three-storied basilica behind; it had no false fronts that would conflict with the side elevations; and it made legitimate use of classical vocabulary by adding to the normal superposition of Orders an adaptation of the triumphal-arch attic to solve the dilemma of the narrow intermediate Order. Furthermore, the design was ideally suited to the sculptural programme, allowing space for six statues on each of the three stories (counting those that would be placed on the side façades); for two round relief panels in the lateral bays of the upper story; and for five rectangular ones – three in the mezzanine and two above the *tondi*. These reasons, coupled with the practical fact that new foundations were required anyway, motivated the adoption of a narthex scheme; we need not search for profound philosophical or pressing liturgical causes.

There was a precedent for Michelangelo's decision in the work of Leone Battista Alberti who, after two early experiments with veneer façades (San Francesco in Rimini, Santa Maria Novella in Florence), produced narthex designs in his last years (San Sebastiano and Sant' Andrea in Mantua) because they were easier to adapt to the temple-front motif. Furthermore, Alberti, and other theorists after him, spoke of the narthex or porch as an essential element of the church.

Everyone admires Michelangelo's drawing (Pl. 5a) more than the model (Pl. 5b), which represents a revised version of the project close to the one accepted by the Pope in 1518. No doubt Michelangelo preferred it too; but the drawing has serious practical drawbacks. If the design is redrawn to scale, the total height diminishes so that the lower part of the mezzanine no longer retains well-proportioned spaces for statues and reliefs (See Pl. 4b where the disadvantages are somewhat exaggerated). Consequently, Michelangelo decided to unify the two levels of the mezzanine, thus gaining space for over-life-size seated statues.

It is not the unified mezzanine that makes the model less successful, but an arid linear quality often found in Florentine Mannerist architecture. The fault does not necessarily originate in the design, since the model could not have been very different if it had been made from Pl. 5a. It is due partly to the small scale, which inevitably changes much of the modelling into line and the apertures into dull planes, and partly to the absence of the eighteen statues and seven reliefs which justify the formal composition. On the other hand, a certain brittleness is inherent in the material; marble is bound to produce an effect sharper and colder than that of softer stones. In judging this model we might ask if a model of the Medici tombs at the same scale and without sculpture would not have been equally unexciting. There are some minor differences between the model and the measurements given in the final contract of January 1518 for the construction of the façade, so we cannot be sure that it was the one made by Michelangelo. But even if it was a copy it is a fairly good record of the design (Fig. 1).

We get closer to Michelangelo's final purpose by analysing the measurements in the contract and those on the sketches made in Carrara from the façade blocks as they were cut to measure (see catalogue, pp. 14–17). The reconstruction drawing shows the result of this analysis (Fig. 1). The major differences from the model are the broadening of the central portal-bay at the expense of the lateral ones and the raising of the mezzanine at the expense of the upper pilaster Order. Both of these solutions are anticipated in Pl. 5a, so that it may have been the model-maker, and not Michelangelo, who tried the more contracted scheme.

Whether we speak of the drawing, the model, or the reconstruction, the unique virtue of Michelangelo's design is the equilibrium of its parts; though the membering makes the façade a complicated grid of horizontals and verticals, there is still an impression of unity and, what is especially apt, the members serve a dual function of symbolizing the structure of a post-and-lintel system and of providing frames for apertures and sculptured panels. Usually when Renaissance architecture was allied

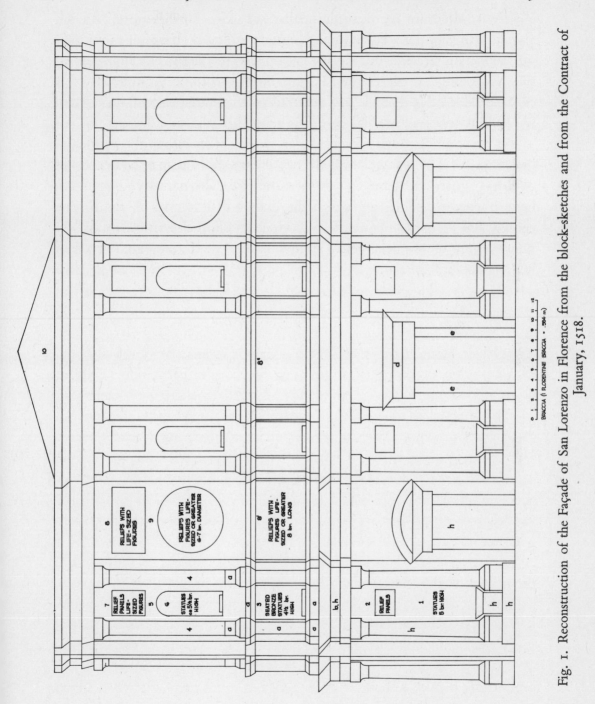

Fig. 1. Reconstruction of the Façade of San Lorenzo in Florence from the block-sketches and from the Contract of January, 1518.

closely to sculpture the tectonic quality was lost. Furthermore, Michel-angelo brings to the architectural design a sculptural character previously unknown; his façade is not a plane cut up into rectangles but an organiza-tion of bodies that project and recede. Even before he thought in terms of a narthex he had made his outer bays semi-independent forms that by their nature were suited to being echoed in the side elevations.

Yet we cannot judge the façade as we see it in either the model or drawing, for Michelangelo would not have subordinated the profusion of huge figures and panels to the architecture. The narrative might not have overwhelmed its setting to the extent that it does in the Sistine ceiling, but perhaps sufficiently to produce an effect determined more by the *terribilità* of Michelangelo's figural style than by the equilibrium of his architectural design.

CHAPTER III

The Medici Chapel

IN almost all of Michelangelo's architectural commissions there was a restricting condition – some predetermined and unchangeable factor in the design. At one time, the proportions would be fixed by existing foundations (San Lorenzo façade, San Giovanni de' Fiorentini), at another, existing buildings could not be removed (Laurentian library, Capitoline Hill); a half-finished building would be left by another architect (Farnese palace, St Peter's), or a complete structure would have to be transformed to serve a new function (Santa Maria degli Angeli). It is tempting to speculate on what Michelangelo might have done without obstacles, but apparently he liked them, perhaps even sought them out; these buildings he worked on with fervour, while not a drawing, much less a stone, remains to recall his major unencumbered commissions (Rialto bridge, Il Gesù in Rome).

Perhaps Michelangelo needed some limitation to direct and restrain his imagination just as the confines of a stone block controlled his sculptures. Some of his greatest marble figures were formed in response to confining conditions: the second-hand block given to him for the *David* was astonishingly thin. In architecture as in sculpture, he could evoke a tension between pre-existing, static boundaries, and dynamic forms that strain against them. Consciously or not, Michelangelo managed to convey in any art his view of the human body as the *carcer terreno*, the earthly prison that confines the flight of the soul.

In the Medici chapel there are two distinct architectural systems (Pls. 7a, 10). One, the masonry construction of the sacristy itself, is faced inside with white stucco and articulated by membering in the grey pietra serena of Tuscany; the other, made entirely of veined white marble, belongs to the tombs of the Medici and is fitted into recesses framed by the pietra serena members. The Sacristy system constitutes one of Michelangelo's predetermined encumbrances: the chapel was to be a sister, if not a twin of Brunelleschi's Old Sacristy on the opposite side of the transept of San Lorenzo, built in 1421–1429 (Pls. 7, 15; Fig. 3 [2–3]). In plan, it had to be roughly of the same dimensions; the materials had to be the same, and the fluted Corinthian pilaster Order, though slightly modernized, was to remain basically Brunelleschian.

Vasari, in his account of the chapel, noted the tension between the conservative Sacristy system and the unprecedented tomb architecture (VII, p. 193):

". . . and because he wanted to make it in imitation of the old sacristy which Filippo Brunelleschi had made, but with a different order of ornaments [the marble veneer, not used by Brunelleschi], he made on the interior an ornament composed in a manner more varied and novel than ancient or modern masters had been able to achieve at any time; because in the innovations of such beautiful cornices, capitals and bases, doors, tabernacles and tombs he proceeded quite differently in proportion, composition, and rules from what others had done following common practice, Vitruvius and antiquity, fearing to add anything [of their own]. This license greatly encouraged those who saw his work to try to imitate it, and shortly new fantasies appeared in their ornament, more grotesque than rational or disciplined. Whence, artisans have been infinitely and perpetually indebted to him because he broke the bonds and chains of a way of working that had become habitual by common usage."

The marble architecture of the chapel may not seem so shocking today; but Vasari, in mixing admiration with apprehension, reminds us that it was one of the first works of a generation obsessed with Roman antiquity in which the classical canon was ignored, even violated. The tabernacles and entablatures which belong to no recognizable Order appear especially peculiar in their Quattrocento framework.

In 1520, when Michelangelo planned to put a free standing mausoleum in the centre of the chapel, he may have visualized the architecture as a literal copy of the Old Sacristy. But when he was ordered to design wall-tombs early in the following year, he had to change the architecture to accommodate them. Niches were needed in the thickness of the walls, and the three-bay system that Brunelleschi had used only on the choir

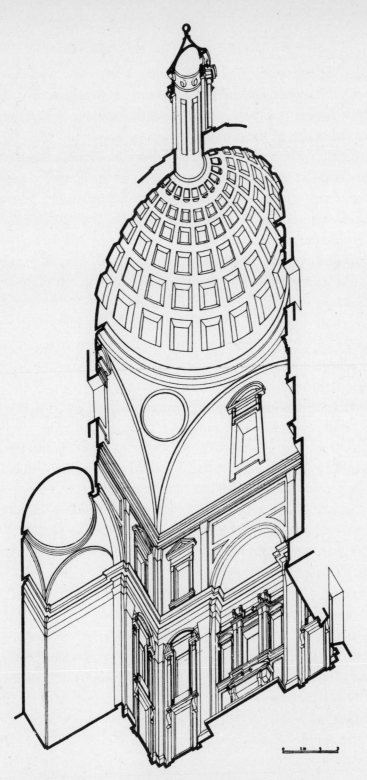

Fig. 2. Florence, the Medici Chapel (after Apolloni).

wall had to be repeated on all four walls of the New Sacristy (compare Pls. 7a, 7b). Michelangelo did not keep the proportions of Brunelleschi's bays. He shifted the pilasters nearer to the corners without, however, adding to the width of the central bays, since he added a plain pietra serena pier where Brunelleschi's pilasters had been. Characteristically, he went out of his way to squeeze the entrances without thereby gaining equivalent breathing-space for the tombs. Now both were constricted, by virtue of an innovation that increased the already confining pressure of the old architectural system upon the new.

The most important innovation was the addition of an entire story between the entrance level and the dome. While Brunelleschi had put pendentives on the entablature of the first Order, Michelangelo inserted an intermediate zone with windows flanking the arches. He elevated the pendentives to a higher zone with central windows (Fig. 2) and raised on them a coffered dome and a lantern entirely different in style from the exotic orientalism of Brunelleschi's design.

Michelangelo retained a quasi-Brunelleschian flavour in the lower portions, and asserted his individuality increasingly as the building rose. The entire pietra serena Order of the lower story is in the Quattrocento style – but closer to the nave of San Lorenzo than to the Old Sacristy. The intermediate Order is transitional: the windows, as Tolnay noted, are close to those of Cronaca (d. 1508). The only obviously sixteenth-century features at this level are the projecting strips in the spandrel above the arch, which are a new device for reducing the wall mass and breaking the monotony of plane surfaces.

Michelangelo's individuality bursts out at the third level, where the window frames were done after his drawings. They are vigorous counterparts of the frames in the Laurentian library, but they are unique in diminishing in breadth toward the top, as if in a perspective with its vanishing point at the lantern; the canted lines continue those of the cupola. The coffering of the cupola, distantly related to that of the Pantheon, is unusually small, and the ingenious pattern of recessions around the oculus helps to accentuate the grid between the coffers,

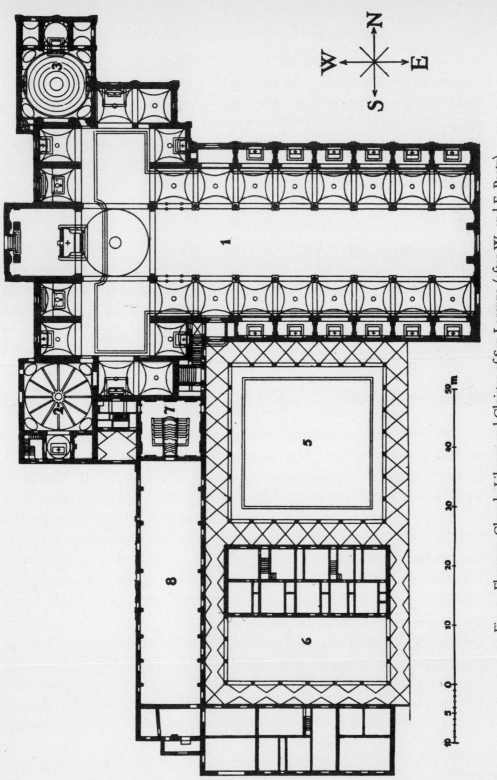

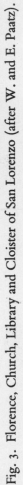

Fig. 3. Florence, Church, Library and Cloister of San Lorenzo (after W. and E. Paatz).

introducing a lively dialogue between circular and radial accents, in which the latter come to appear as structural ribs.

The lantern (Pl. 14a) is Michelangelo's only important contribution to the exterior of the chapel. Its animated fantasy inspired della Porta's lantern design for the minor domes of St Peter's. Large, simple windows attract a maximum of light, and the Order of freestanding colonnettes is one of the first in the Renaissance to carry a projection of the entablature, giving a dramatic impression of a radiating cornice in the form of a cogwheel casting varied shadows. This sharp angularity contrasts with the fleshy curves of a concave cone that holds aloft a gilded polyhedron.

It seems, in short, that Michelangelo tried to influence the design of the chapel as little as possible, though two changes were essential to his aim: the tombs had to be given enough depth, and the overall height had to be increased. Wherever these innovations permitted, he retained the Brunelleschian vocabulary as an antithesis to his own invention.

Michelangelo's metamorphosis from sculptor to architect was not fully consummated in the design of the Medici chapel. In our admiration for the sculptures and their settings we gratefully overlook the failure of the chapel to evoke a moving or even a coherent spatial experience. The power of the composition is generated by the vigour of the figures and their architectural framework, and heightened by the compression of the pietra serena members. In Michelangelo's later architecture the conflict is made more effective by the implication of tension between organically related parts. Here the marble architecture is patently of a different species than that of the chapel, and there is even a lack of coherence within the marble system: the tombs seem isolated from the lateral tabernacles by a shift in style and in scale. The upper stories might have been quite different without fundamentally affecting the tombs, and, if the projected programme of fresco decoration had been completed, the unity of the chapel would probably have been further compromised. Maybe for this reason the garlands painted on the dome by Giovanni da Udine were quickly hidden by whitewash.

In making the architectural membering of the lower Order of marble, Michelangelo associated it with the sculptured sarcophagi and figures rather than with the structure of the building (Pl. 8). Vasari rightly referred to it as ornament; it is a veneer hung onto the walls of an already self-sufficient structure and, as such, is freed of the responsibility of performing any tectonic function. Furthermore, it has no utilitarian function except to provide doors to adjoining areas – doors significantly overpowered by the more expressive tabernacles above them. The conception of a relief independent from the chapel in structure and materials was a purely sculptural one, and the extensive use of an architectural vocabulary was a matter of choice, not of necessity. But the choice was almost predetermined by the tradition of funerary wall monuments: a system of architectural niches not only offered the most convenient setting for effigies, but had carried since ancient times a symbolism, associated with the baldachin or aedicula, of apotheosis, originally the prerogative of deities and rulers.

In some of the preparatory drawings and in sketches by Michelangelo's followers, the niches alongside the effigies of the Dukes are filled with allegories, and studies such as Pl. 11a indicate that the upper portion was to have been a monumental crown, rich with symbolic figures, thrones (of which only the bases were executed, Pl. 8), and a complex composition of arms and trophies. It is difficult to judge the tombs without these important complements, which would have altered completely their effect and their relationship to the chapel. The crown, for example, projecting into the zone of the entablature, would have exaggerated the independence of the tombs from the chapel architecture.

The wall tomb in the form of a semi-independent architectural relief was the commonest type of funerary monument in fifteenth-century Italy. Michelangelo, in placing tombs into a recessed arched niche divided vertically into three bays behind an ornate freestanding sarcophagus (Pls. 10, 11a), respected a tradition that had inspired the finest efforts of early Renaissance Tuscan sculptors.[1] Many elements of the

1. C. de Tolnay, "Studi sulla Cappella Medicea", L'Arte, V, 1934, p. 5.

Medici monuments may be found, for example, in the original tomb of
Pope Paul II in St Peter's, carved by Giovanni Dalmatia and Mino da
Fiesole in the 1470's (Pl. 13a). Even Michelangelo's fantasy was hallowed
by usage, because the Quattrocento tomb was far more experimental
and unconventional in architectural detail than contemporary buildings.
But in the early sixteenth century imaginative sepulchral designs began
to give way to proper and often dull classical solutions, such as those of
Andrea Sansovino; Michelangelo must have aimed consciously to revive
the earlier freedom, which partly explains why Vasari congratulated him
for his liberating influence.

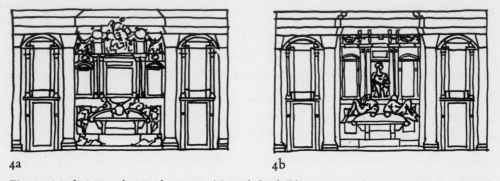

4a   4b

Fig. 4. Medici Tombs. Preliminary (a) and final (b) versions, showing the narrowing
of the central bay.

The surviving preparatory drawings for the tombs affirm a Quattrocento inspiration (Pls. 11, 12) in representing isolated reliefs designed for
a frame of given proportions and indicating nothing of the architectural
setting or flanking bays. Yet these studies aim, far more than the final
solution, to reflect in the design of the tombs the arrangement of the
wall into which they are set. In the last project for a Ducal monument
(Pl. 11a), the tomb repeats the pattern of the wall as a whole (Fig. 4a):
the relationship of the wall bays (ABA) is repeated in the tomb bays (aba);
in both, the central bay (B,b) is larger, almost a square, and the side bays
(A,a) contain tabernacles with segmental pediments; even the entrance
doors are reflected in the rectangular panels beneath the tomb-tabernacles.

This may explain the overpowering scale of the tabernacles over the doors; it is the outcome of enlarging the smaller tomb tabernacles according to the ratio established in the overall composition: B:A=b:a. A comparable proportioning of tabernacles to tombs was planned for the Magnifici monument in the entrance wall (Pl. 12a, c), but here the rhythm was changed: the side tabernacles were to be reflected in the *central* bay rather than in the lateral bays of the tomb, thus: AbAbA. Since the two sarcophagi planned for this wall removed the emphasis from the central axis, it had to be restored by accentuating the central aedicula, a solution also prompted by the project to place the *Madonna* there.

In execution, this rhythmical unity was lost; the Magnifici tomb was not built at all, and the Ducal tombs were entirely altered in proportion. In Pl. 11a (Fig. 4a), they are drawn as if to fill the entire opening between the pilasters, but in the final version (Pl. 8, Fig. 4b) pietra serena piers were crowded between the pilasters and the tombs, narrowing the whole tomb design. Michelangelo chose to subtract the lost width from the central section of the tombs, changing it from a square panel to a tall niche enclosing the effigy. This solution disrupted the continuity between the entrance bays and the tomb, and made the former seem disproportionately large. We do not know what prompted the change, since there are no studies of the wall elevation as a whole: perhaps purely structural considerations, since the piers support relieving arches over the tomb niches. But there may have been expressive motivations also: if Pl. 11a had been drawn for a two-story chapel like Brunelleschi's, the later addition of a third story might have suggested confining the tombs to a more vertical frame consonant with the higher elevation; whether the decision to put only one effigy at the centre of each tomb (Pl. 11a has two on a level with the sarcophagus), which also produced a more vertical composition, was a cause or a result of narrowing the tomb, cannot be determined. The loss of architectural coherence in the final design suggests that Michelangelo was concerned primarily with the sculpture.

It is the sculpture rather than the marble architecture that gives the interior space its three-dimensional unity. The dynamic forces generated by the figures and sarcophagi organize the two lateral walls – forces that would have been intensified had Michelangelo finished the river-gods at the base of Pl. 11a, which initiate an upward and outward movement. The side walls are bound to the entrance wall across the intervening space by the intense gazes of the Dukes and by the gestures of the allegories, which focus attention on the *Madonna* (Tolnay) (Pl. 10).

The dissimilarity in style between the architectural members of the chapel and those of the tombs is partly due to differences in material. Marble is particularly suited to sculptural refinements and may be carved with the most meticulous detail, while pietra serena does not lend itself to such finesse. Yet the sharp precision of Michelangelo's treatment is not implicit in the nature of marble, which is equally congenial to softly modelled forms, as the tomb figures show; the emphasis on line, plane, and fine detail was the outcome of a purposeful effort to accentuate by contrast the plasticity of the figures. Modelling was avoided in the architecture as far as possible: there are no columns, and mouldings are so narrow that they appear as lines, an impression that is reinforced by the soft, uniform diffusion of light from high above, which favours surfaces more than recessions. Such linearity is another indication of the revival of later fifteenth-century architectural sculpture; it is not found to the same degree in Michelangelo's subsequent work. Already in later designs for the chapel more plastic forms appear; projecting columns were used in the initial drawings for the Magnifici tomb (Pl. 12a, c); they appear more distinctly in later copies; and a mid-century plan of the chapel shows a revised version with deep niches containing encased columns comparable to those of the library vestibule (Pl. 17). Apparently Michelangelo came to re-evaluate his conservative approach to the chapel architecture in the process of designing the library in the mid-1520's.

In the light of Vasari's comments, the term "conservative" would appear to be applicable only to the treatment of the material. Yet few of the architectural elements are radical in design: the pilaster system and the flanking aediculas with segmental pediments on brackets are sober, almost canonical by contrast to the extraordinary tabernacles over the doors (Pl. 9). These tabernacles are a sign of Michelangelo's emancipation from the proprieties of Vitruvian rule and ancient models and establish a fantastic theme that was to re-appear in all his later designs for doors and windows. The fantasy, however, is always strictly disciplined by the realization that its effect depends on the variation of traditional forms and would be lost if these were abandoned for uncontrolled innovation. The tabernacle pediments are broken at the base and jut forward at the crown, and yet are adequately supported by pilasters which we recognize as such in spite of the absence of definable capitals; the niche is conventional in its deepest recession, but in a nearer plane it violates the expected independence of parts by expanding horizontally and vertically beyond its proper limits. Where the inventiveness of Quattrocento sculptors had been manifested in the free embellishment of familiar forms, Michelangelo penetrated into the nature of the forms themselves to give them unprecedented significance: the wall is transformed from an inert plane to a vital, many-layered epidermis, and elements formerly assembled – niche, frame, pediment – are now inextricably bound together by an architectural anatomy. The tabernacles signify an abandonment of traditional expression, and, by this token, a fundamental departure from the spirit of the tombs. The absence of any Quattrocento model for the entrance bays partly explains the differences, but we must also suppose a substantial passage of time between the designs of the tombs and tabernacles. The tombs were planned in 1521, when quarrying began, but drawings for the tabernacles were sent to the patron only in 1524, and even then Michelangelo refused for more than a year to send specific instructions to the quarries. The likelihood that the final tabernacle design was determined four or five years later than that of the tombs is strengthened by its similarity in style to the reading-room portals of the Laurentian library, drawn in 1526. The Magnifici tomb on the entrance wall, started only in 1533, would also have been closer in style to the library than to the Ducal tombs.

In the Medici Chapel, then, as in all of Michelangelo's later buildings, an idea changes and matures before our eyes as we glance from one part to another. Here the change is drastic, because it is the outcome of rapid development from the acceptance of an old tradition to the formulation of a new one which, while it is barely suggested in the chapel, was ultimately to create a unity of ornament and structure never surpassed in architecture.

CHAPTER IV

The Library of San Lorenzo

THE pioneers of modern architecture vigorously attacked the superficial adaptation of ancient and Renaissance forms that typified late nineteenth-century design and, in their effort to express a new technology and social order, lost interest in the Renaissance itself. Preoccupied with structural and utilitarian problems, they followed the lead of Ruskin and Viollet-le-Duc in criticizing Renaissance architecture as "dishonest", unconcerned with the practical aspects of building, and devoted solely to impressing the eye with façades of borrowed ornament. Later, as modern design gradually won acceptance, architects came to feel sufficiently secure to approach the Renaissance more sympathetically, particularly for its monumental planning, control of space, and principles of scale and proportion.

This change in attitude is partly due to the efforts of historians and critics whose discovery of new dimensions in Renaissance theory and practice has encouraged a deeper understanding. But even the apologists of the Renaissance have submitted unconsciously to the old bias; in arguing that purely visual delight is a proper function of architecture, they have tacitly allowed that Renaissance buildings could not be defended on technical or practical grounds.[1]

Criticism of the Laurentian library has been affected by this bias to an extent that the building is commonly interpreted as if it were simply an essay in sculptural form and space-manipulation. But in this case purely formal analysis is especially unjustified, for a constant and guiding concern with problems of utility and structure is documented by an extensive correspondence between the patron and the architect.

1. E.g., Geoffrey Scott, *The Architecture of Humanism*, London, 1914.

A curious mixture of medieval and modern ideas motivated the commissioning of the Laurentian library. The decision to build it in the cloister of a religious establishment was surely prompted by the role of monasteries as major centres for the conservation and acquisition of manuscripts in the Middle Ages. From monastic libraries the humanists of the fifteenth century formed their private collections by copying and ultimately by printing ancient manuscripts. When humanists were absorbed into the church, their books returned with them; to the library of Sixtus IV in the Vatican; or to the Piccolomini library in the Cathedral of Siena. The Medici library, greatly enlarged by Lorenzo the Magnificent at the close of the fifteenth century, was preserved in the family palace as one of the major embellishments of a worldly court; its removal to the cloister of San Lorenzo symbolized the shift in the roots of Medici power from mercantile to ecclesiastical activity. But the decision was more than a symbolic gesture; it also involved a change in the role of the library from a private mark of distinction to a public institution, thus announcing a transition from the Age of Humanism to the Age of the power state, in which institutions for commoners were conferred by princes as a palliative for tyranny. The new role put more emphasis on utility than had been customary before; the library had to be designed for the convenience of readers as well as for the conservation of books. It might be a civic ornament, like the great Quattrocento palaces and villas, but this no longer could be its chief function; as if to accentuate the change, its expressive effects were kept inside, for the benefit of scholars, while the exterior remained anonymous (Pls. 15–17; Figs. 3, 5).

Correspondence between Pope Clement VII in Rome and Michelangelo in Florence reveals the new approach; as in modern practice, the patron was constantly concerned with the utilitarian programme while the architect strove for a maximum of expressive effect within its confines. In the initial instructions of 1524, economy and convenience were guides to the choice of site, and preoccupation with utility moulded the plan; separation of Latin and Greek books in the first scheme, later the isolation of rare books into small studies, finally the amalgamation

of the studies into a large rare-book room. Michelangelo met the requirements readily, but constantly sought to guide decisions toward
aesthetic goals. A site on the church square, for example, he rejected in
spite of its convenience for construction because the new building would
have hampered the view of the façade.

Having selected the present site, the Pope demanded the strengthening
and vaulting (for fire prevention) of the monastic quarters beneath the
library with minimal disturbance of their customary functions. In the
Spring of 1524 Michelangelo concentrated on sustaining the weight of
the new structure without substantially thickening the walls of the old.
His solution was a buttress system applied to the exterior which may be
seen between the façade windows (Pl. 15) and on the opposite side, where
a Romanesque device of blind arcades was applied to the old building.
This method imposed two limiting controls on the design: first, it did
not greatly thicken the walls below, so that the library walls had to be
as thin as would be compatible with security, and second, its regularly
spaced buttresses established a bay-system which controlled the placement
of the windows and the interior articulation. These are major determinants in the design of late medieval buildings and Michelangelo, like
his Gothic predecessors, responded to them by submitting his expressive
forms to the discipline of structure.

This discipline is most evident in the reading room interior (Pl. 16,
Fig. 5) where the bay-system of the buttresses determines not only
treatment of the wall elevations, but of the ceiling and floor as well.
The ceiling, designed as if its decorative partitions were set within a
skeleton of longitudinal and transverse beams, appears to be supported
by the wall pilasters. Earlier Renaissance ceilings were composed in
abstract patterns of coffers independent of the supporting wall.

The Pope was aware of this difference; he started by demanding a
ceiling which would differ from those in the Vatican, and when Michelangelo sent him a drawing, he was disturbed that the skeleton did not
appear to conform to the wall membering. Though the skeleton is only
a symbol of actual structure, it must conform closely to the beams and

ties of the roof trusses above, because the walls between the pilasters are too thin for support. (Fig. 5, plan). This uncommon thinness is a response to structural imperatives which did not occur to Michelangelo in his initial designs. In an early sketch, motivated more by purely expressive impulses (Pl. 19b), he proposed a wall which may have been no thicker at the base, but which would surely have been heavier. Apparently this drawing preceded the structural solutions, since it ignores the final buttressing system. This is familiar Renaissance practice; what is remarkable is that such a marvellous invention should have been cast aside in favour of a quite different one under pressure of structural and practical requirements.

In the final design for the reading room (Fig. 5) the windows were placed closer together and brought down to a level as low as the cloister roof allowed (Pl. 15). This change, which increased the light and brought it closer to the reading desks, was prompted also by a change in the position of the desks; Pl. 19b shows the articulation starting at the floor, and was drawn with free-standing desks in mind, while the final scheme placed them flush to the wall (Pl. 16). Now even the wooden furniture was to play a part in the structural system, as a visual support for the pilasters; in response to the new relationship, Michelangelo abandoned the massive, sculptural handling of his sketch in favour of a typically Florentine delicacy of membering and emphasis on planes. The second design reduced the wall mass to a minimum. Frames for windows and niches were not the usual sculptural aediculas projecting from the surface, but were placed in rectangular recessions behind the wall plane so that a greater part of the area between the pilasters became no deeper than the window embrasure, a mere screen less than a foot thick (Fig. 5, plan). In compensation, the pilasters were not used as ornaments hung on the surface in the usual fashion, but as structural members – interior compliments to the buttresses – bracing the wall sufficiently to relieve the thin panels between them of a bearing function.

In every detail Michelangelo gave formal expression to the lightness of the structure: the window frames are composed of lines rather than

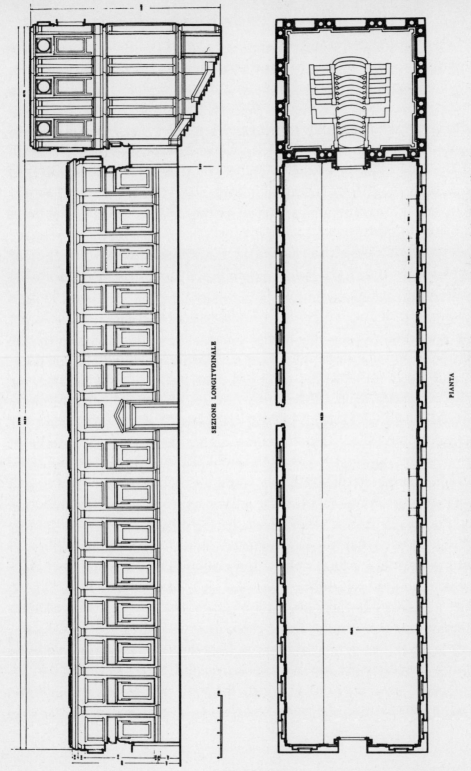

SEZIONE LONGITVDINALE

PIANTA

Fig. 5. Florence, Laurentian Library. Longitudinal section and plan (after Apolloni).

of masses; their attenuated volutes are weightless and seem to hang rather than to sustain. The baluster-like forms on the tabernacles above, though potentially sculptural, are studiously confined within the planes of the frame. There is a rococo grace in the ceiling panels, which are recessed so slightly that they have hardly more body than the sheet of preparatory sketches (Pl. 19a). The entrance door, like the walls, was first drawn in heavy, modelled forms (Pl. 25b) and later compressed into a framework composed of thin layers. In every detail, the evolution of the design tended to give the room a more calm and regular character conducive to study.

The vestibule design developed in the opposite direction, from an emphasis on planes (Pl. 20a) to a sculptural treatment resembling the first study for the reading room (Pls. 19b and 21). The ultimate contrast between the two rooms signifies their difference in purpose; the vestibule, as an area assigned only to communication, imposed fewer restraints on expression. But like the reading room, it had to be designed to a restricted wall thickness though, because it was higher, this thickness was slightly increased (Fig. 5, plan).

Michelangelo met serious practical problems from the start; an initial attempt to unify the vestibule and reading room interiors by putting the members and openings at the same height (Pl. 20a) produced a spiritless base of great height all around the vestibule. Later his hope of unifying the exterior of the two rooms under a common roof had to be abandoned, too (Pl. 21). Wittkower discovered that before the modern restoration of the exterior, when the three upper window frames were added, the masonry showed a change in plan: the vestibule cornice was started at the height of the reading room cornice and later was raised about 3m. to its present height. The early project appears in Pl. 21, where the vestibule has a flat vault the height of the reading room ceiling with small windows in the centre of each of its sides. Much of the final design is already fixed in this drawing, but because the overall height is much less, the proportions are all reduced, which made it possible to put pilasters between the columns and the tabernacles of the main Order, and to use a complete entablature. The scheme had to be changed at the end of 1525 for structural reasons, and a wooden ceiling with overhead skylights was proposed as a substitute for the heavy vault. Now lighting became a problem, because the Pope objected to the unprecedented skylights, and the only possible solution was to raise the walls to admit orthodox windows, thereby destroying the overall unity of the library design. The heightening of the vestibule changed its proportions (Pl. 17, Fig. 5): the columns were greatly heightened and correspondingly broadened, so that there was no longer room for the flanking pilasters (the pilaster motif returned, however, on the inner faces of the column niches), and the entablature was reduced to a thin moulding. Each of these alterations reduced the horizontal accents of the early design and, in combination with the tall clerestory windows, increased verticality; at this point the additional vertical motif of the volutes beneath the columns may have appeared (Pls. 17, 25a).

The restricted width and expanded height of the vestibule made an interior of a strange, irrational quality, unique in the Renaissance. It is pointless to discuss whether this compelling space was the product of practical lighting requirements or Michelangelo's abstract search for form; like all great architecture it owes its distinction to the fact that it is more than either. Michelangelo did not simply submit to the rejection of his original scheme, but used the demand for heightened proportions as an inspiration to conjure a new spirit from existing motifs. The retention of the basic forms of Pl. 21 in the final design illustrates Michelangelo's organic approach to design. Columns, pilasters, and tabernacles grew as the body grows: with the heightening of the walls, the membering expanded; and since here only upward growth was possible, vertical accents overcame the horizontal as if by biological necessity.

The most extraordinary innovation in the vestibule design is in the main Order, where columns are placed in recessions behind the surface of the wall (Pl. 17, Fig. 6). In orthodox Renaissance practice, columns project forward to sustain lintels or entablatures as they do in the San Lorenzo façade (Pl. 5b), but in the library the foundations were only as

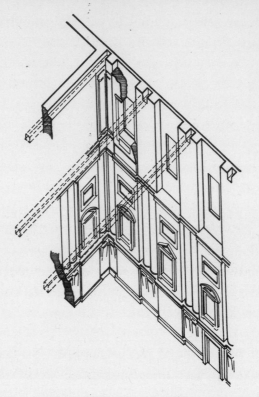

Fig. 6. Structural system of the Library vestibule.

thick as the wall, and could not have supported projecting members. Michelangelo's design alters the classical role of columns, which seem to be independent from the architecture, like statues in niches, while the projecting wall appears to support the roof. But this impression is the result of our own conditioned responses to the Renaissance: paradoxically, it is the canonical use of the column (Pl. 5b) that is entirely ornamental, while Michelangelo's invention is as essential to the stability of the structure as a Gothic pier. The isometric projection (Fig. 6) shows that the wall behind the columns is a fragile screen that could support nothing without their aid, so that they function as a substitute for the wall-mass. But they are more than a substitute; being monolithic stone shafts, they are stronger in compression than the brick masonry of the

walls, and Michelangelo capitalized on this property by making the
columns the chief support of the roof. Before the clerestory got its
deceptive facing, one could see that the columns support heavy piers
which sustain the roof, while over the tabernacles the walls recede to a
thin plane that accommodates the windows (Fig. 6). In the final design,
then, the structural function of column and wall are exactly the opposite
of their visual effects. Michelangelo disguised his technical ingenuity
because he was chiefly concerned with form, which partly justifies the
failure of modern critics to detect the nature of the structure. Like many
engineering discoveries, the recessed column device started as an expressive motive; in Pl. 19b the stresses are concentrated on the flanking
pilasters rather than on the columns, and contemporary tomb designs
(Pl. 13b) used the recessed columns for sculptural effect. But even where
it was not a conductor of major forces, the recessed column remained an
efficient substitute for the wall, and in this respect was more utilitarian
than its projecting cousins.

Everywhere in the vestibule Michelangelo's licentious use of classical
vocabulary, obscuring the actual relationships of load and support,
created paradoxes for his academic contemporaries (Pl. 17). On the lower
level, the volutes, which others used as supporting members, stand in a
plane well forward of the columns, sustaining nothing but themselves.
The pilaster frames of the tabernacles (Pl. 24) invert the traditional design
by narrowing toward the base rather than toward the top, and are crowned by "capitals" which are thinner rather than broader than the shaft;
just below the capitals appear vestigial *regulae*, motifs boldly pilfered
from the eaves of Doric Temples. These and lesser details of the tabernacles, niches, and door frames show an extraordinary fertility of invention; striking in themselves, they are given more impact by our fore-
knowledge of the ancient models from which they err.

Though Michelangelo's drawings for the vestibule are all elevations
of one wall – the west – this conventional device did not commit him
to working in line and plane: shading and the indication of projection
and recession give them sculptural mass. This consciousness of the third

dimension is what made the design uniquely successful spatially, for the room is not an assemblage of four walls but an organic unity: at the corners the elevations can be described as mating rather than meeting. Furthermore, motifs conceived for the west wall serve a different purpose on the north and south; at the entrance to the reading room the recessed columns may be read as a monumental framework for the door, and on the wall opposite the door the central bay remains blank, without a tabernacle. Though the four walls of this remarkably confined space have three different elevations, unity is enforced by the power of the insistent and continuous alternation of receding and projecting elements.

Continuity in the design of the wall heightens the shocking effect of the stairway (Pl. 18a, Fig. 5), which pours out into the vestibule as an alien intruder, a monumental piece of furniture, yet the only essential feature of the design (Michelangelo intended to emphasize this contrast by constructing it in wood). The present stairway, executed by Ammannati after Michelangelo's model of 1558–1559, in no way resembles plans of 1524; at that time two flights were placed against the side walls, mounting to a platform before the reading room entrance (Pl. 20b). The aim of the early project was to achieve tectonic and visual unity of stairs and walls so that the flights would start and end beneath the major bay divisions of the elevation. There was no sense of intrusion or of contrast at that time, and the design was quite practical because it left a maximum of free circulation space between and before the stairs. Two stairways flanking a central entrance rarely appeared earlier in Renaissance architecture, but the motif was not Michelangelo's invention; a generation before, Giuliano da Sangallo had sketched[2] exterior entrances for the Medici Villa at Poggio a Caiano in the form that appears in the uppermost drawing of Pl. 22.

The final plan (Fig. 5) departed from both utility and tradition. Since the vault beneath the vestibule was uniformly strong, no restrictions

2. Giuliano's drawing, Uffizi *Arch.*, 1640, is reproduced by G. Marchini, *Giuliano da Sangallo*, Florence, 1943, Pl. II, Fig. a.

were imposed on the placement of the stairs, and at an early date Michelangelo must have regarded this exceptional freedom as an invitation to bold expression. Once permitted to abandon the wall flights, he was able to change an area subservient to convenience to one which commands the visitor's experiences. While the wall flights, like relief sculpture, had been devised for an established framework, the free-standing stairway, like sculpture in the round, could be nearly independent from its environment. Its modelled, curvilinear motifs and irrational form signify the release from tectonic laws and actually clash with the surrounding walls. The stairway so lavishly fills the room that the limited remaining space is wasted for circulation, exaggerating a confinement already implied by the shaft-like proportions and the unattainable height of the windows. To the sense of compression which this imposes on the visitor is added a factor of frustration: he seeks to mount toward the goal, but the steps appear to be pouring downward and outward. On the side flights the upper story of each successive pair projects forward over the lower, while in the centre the softened convex treads appear to advance, spreading out, as Tolnay phrased it, like a flow of lava, which they resemble in colour. The globules emerging at their sides fortify this impression; they seem to have been forced ahead by the pressure of the balustrade. While the centre flight suggests the discomfort of ascent against the tide, the side flights, being unprotected by railings, are a more real hazard.

There is, after all, a dramatic if not a formal harmony between the stairway and the walls, because both conspire by their aggressiveness against the observer's ease; the wall planes, emerging forward from the columns, seem to exert inward pressure on the confined space in response to the outward pressure of the stairs.

To anyone familiar with Michelangelo's sculpture it should be no surprise to find the evocation of compression and frustration in his architecture as well. Here, in an enclosed space, he had the opportunity to engender in the visitor the ambivalence between action and immobility which we imagine his *Moses*, for example, to be experiencing. So we, in a sense, become the subjects as well as the observers of the work.

We may look at the *Moses* without attempting to share or even to analyse his state of mind, but we should have to muster uncommon resistance not to experience some of the conflicts that Michelangelo prepared for us in the vestibule.

As the vestibule design evolved from an initial unity of stairs and walls to an opposition of the two, so the concept of the library as a whole developed from a unification to a contrast of the reading room and vestibule. As the one was systematically sobered, the other was progressively dramatized. The two must be seen together; the vestibule does not engender frustration for its own sake, but rather to intensify the experience of relief as one passes into the reading room. The rare-book room, if it had been built (Pl. 18b; planned for the south end of the library, to the left in Fig. 5), would have added another experience mediating between the contrasting moods by its combination of static form and vigorous modelling. Its plan reveals Michelangelo's consciousness of the geometrical sequence of his scheme: square, long rectangle, triangle, and suggests the psychological as well as the utilitarian aptness of his decision to articulate the upright, vertical vestibule actively, and the recumbent, horizontal reading room passively.

We can gain from the history of the Laurentian library a singular insight into the relative significance of "commodity, firmness, and delight" in Renaissance architectural design. The aim of this analysis has been to emphasize the neglected factors of utility and technique without sacrificing awareness of Michelangelo's constant preoccupation with expressive and commanding form. If this preoccupation was dominant in the sixteenth century, it was not exclusive; Renaissance architecture, like that of any other period, was a product of social and technological forces as well as of ideals. Michelangelo himself justified the fantastic design of his stairway by explaining that the central flight was for the ruler and those on the side for retainers.[3]

3. Letter to Vasari in Florence of Sept. 28, 1555 (*Lettere*, p. 548; *Nachlass* I, pp. 419 f.)

CHAPTER V

The Fortifications of Florence

WAR was considered an art in the Renaissance. The Quattrocento *Condottieri* fought for fame and money and aimed to
outwit rather than to destroy one another; they were colleagues in an honourable profession. But by the mid-sixteenth century
the aggressive politics of great states and the increasing efficiency of
firearms turned war into the deadly science that it has been ever since.
So, for a century after the introduction of heavy artillery (*ca.* 1450),
military installations were designed by artists; but when technical
knowledge of arms and tactics became more important qualifications
than imagination and improvisation, military engineers pre-empted the
field.

Art historians rarely have made the distinction between the aesthetic
and the technical age of warfare, and have set aside the military treatises
and designs of the Renaissance as if they were irrelevant to the study of
artistic personality. But for many artists of the century 1450–1550,
military design was not only a major source of income, but a major
preoccupation. Leonardo da Vinci recommended himself to Lodovico
il Moro in 1482 as a civil and military planner, suggesting only cas-
ually that he was a competent painter. And over a half century later
Michelangelo said that while he knew little of painting and sculpture,
his long study of and experience in fortification qualified him as an
expert.[1]

Medieval fortifications with their long walls interrupted at regular
intervals by high, square projecting towers (Pl. 25c) became obsolete
after the introduction of heavy mobile siege artillery in the mid-fifteenth

1. See the conversation quoted Vol. II, p. 113.

century.[2] Early cannon were powerful enough to destroy defences made vulnerable by thinness, height, and sharp angles. And the artillery of the defenders could not be manoeuvered on the narrow parapets designed for small arms. The need for a drastic change in design was demonstrated to the Italians by the French invasions of the 1490's, the success of which was not due so much to superiority of arms as to an earlier grasp of the tactical potential of large batteries of artillery. (An Italian military treatise of 1476 advised using one cannon for a force of 18,000 men.)

It was a long time before cities could afford to do more than to lower old walls and towers and to remove crenellations; the chief problem for early designers was to strengthen angles and gates or to build compact fortresses at strategic points. At the turn of the fifteenth century, the favoured solution was a fortress of square or triangular plan with low, heavy round towers at the corners having gun emplacements in vaulted interior chambers and on the roof.

Variations of this method are found in the theoretical studies of Leonardo and of Dürer[3] and were built at the Fortresses of Ostia (1483–1486 by Giuliano da Sangallo and Baccio Pontelli), the Castel Sant' Angelo in Rome (1490's, Giuliano and Antonio da Sangallo the Elder), Sarzanello in Tuscany (1490's, designer unknown), the Port of Civitàvecchia (1508, Bramante) and, via Leonardo, influenced the design of the Château of Chambord.

The round tower had two advantages over the square; it was less vulnerable to missiles and it had an unimpeded coverage of a wide arc.

2. On the development of Italian fortifications in the fifteenth and sixteenth centuries, see N. Machiavelli, *L'arte della guerra e scritti militare minori* (Florence, 1929); A. Guglielmotti, *Storia delle fortificazioni nella spiaggia romana . . .* (*Storia della marina pontificia, V*), Rome, 1887; E. Rocchi, *Le piante . . . di Roma del secolo XVI*, Turin and Rome, 1902; *Idem, Le fonti storiche dell'architettura militare*, Rome, 1908; B. Eberhardt, *Die Burgen Italiens*, Berlin, 1908–1918; F. C. Taylor, *The Art of War in Italy*, Cambridge, 1921; J. W. Wright, *The Development of the Bastioned System of Permanent Fortifications*, 1500–1800, Washington, D.C., 1946 (mimeographed volume); A. R. Hall, "Military Technology", *A History of Technology*, III, Oxford, 1957, pp. 347–376; H. A. Delacroix, *Problems in 16th Century Italian Urbanism: the Radial Plan from Sforzinda to Palmanova*, Thesis, U. of California, Berkeley, 1958; J. R. Hale, in *The New Cambridge Modern History*, Cambridge, 1958, Vol. I, Ch. IX; Vol. II, Ch. XVI. On Michelangelo's fortification drawings, see Tolnay, 1940.
3. *Unterricht der Befestigung*, Nürnberg, 1527.

But the interior chambers were made impractical by fumes from the cannon, and the forward faces of the towers could not be protected from the curtain walls behind, so that the enemy might take cover directly before the towers. This was such a serious drawback that the tower system was abandoned a few years after the first experiments; it was already extinct in Italy by the time of Dürer's publication.

The alternative was the bastion (Fig. 7), which became the basis of modern systems of fortification. It was not a tower but a projecting platform, level with the walls; its basic form was triangular, since this shape allowed all its surfaces to be flanked by fire from the curtain walls behind. At the base the triangle was modified to provide emplacements for gunners to shoot parallel to the curtain walls in case the enemy came close.

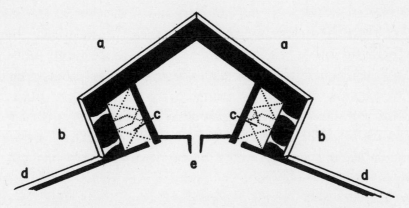

Fig. 7. Typical early bastion trace ("Delle Maddalene", Verona, 1527)
a. face   b. flank   c. casemate   d. curtain walls   e. gorge.

The bastioned system probably developed out of drawings and fortresses by the Sienese artist Francesco di Giorgio Martini, whose manuscript *Trattato di Architettura civile e militare* (after 1482?) was written with the assistance of the most learned of Quattrocento *condottieri*, Federigo da Montefeltre. Francesco, though a partisan of the round tower, produced a number of fortress plans including triangular salients also. Perhaps the success of such salients, built by Francesco in late fifteenth-century fortresses in the Duchy of Urbino and adopted by Leonardo, accelerated the development of the bastion.

In view of the historical importance of the bastion, it is curious that the effort to determine when and where it was first used was abandoned after the initial researches of nineteenth-century military writers. It may have been invented by members of the Sangallo family in the service of the papacy at the turn of the sixteenth century; primitive versions appear in the Siena sketchbook of Giuliano da Sangallo dating before 1503; and two small coastal forts in papal territory – at Civita Castellana (1494–1497) and Nettuno (1501–1502) – reveal successive stages in the evolution of the form. A few years after the French invasions, the flurry of fortress building subsided, and until the eve of the Imperial invasion of 1527 that ended with the Sack of Rome, we know of only two major defensive systems raised in Italy at Ferrara in 1512 and at the Port of Civitàvecchia in 1515-1519. The Ferrara enceinte, which Michelangelo inspected in preparation for defending Florence, was modernized later in the century, and no earlier plans have been published; but projects for Civitàvecchia by Antonio da Sangallo the Younger are preserved in the Uffizi and show an irregular enceinte in which the bastioned system appears to be fully developed. The younger Antonio subsequently became a leading Italian authority on fortifications; in 1526; with Michele Sanmichele, he surveyed the defences of the papal territories in the Marches and the Po Valley for Clement VII, and was invited by Machiavelli to consult on the Florence fortifications; three years later, as chief engineer of the Imperial forces, he was pitted against Michelangelo in the siege of Florence and afterwards was commissioned to build the permanent defences and the Fortezza d'Abasso (1534–). Sanmichele, who was probably a disciple of Sangallo, was credited by Vasari with the invention of the bastion and with the design of the earliest surviving example called "delle Maddalene" in Verona, in 1527 (Fig. 7). Recently the engineer Michele da Leone was found to be the designer; round tower-bastions had been raised at Verona as late as 1525, and Leone's innovations were refined by Sanmichele in completing the city's enceinte after his arrival in 1529–1530.[4] These bastions remained for decades the most advanced in Italy because of their large vaulted and ventilated interiors, covered passages and retired flanks. In the year that Verona changed to the modern system, Siena also built six bastions on designs by Baldassare Peruzzi. In the 1530's many of the major cities in Italy followed the lead: Ancona (1532), Turin (1536), Castro (1537), Naples (1538), Perugia and Nepi (1540).

The little we know of the early history of the bastioned system is enough to show that a lethargic development in the first quarter of the sixteenth century was suddenly accelerated throughout Italy in the years 1526–1530. This places Michelangelo's fortification projects among the incunabula of modern military architecture, just at the most fluid and inventive moment in its history, at a time when experience had established no proven formula of design. Unlike the situation in other arts, the lessons of antiquity and of preceding generations were of little account; this is one of those rare events in the history of architecture when technological advances altered the basic precepts of design. As a rule, technical discoveries that most affect buildings are in the field of structure – such as the invention of concrete in ancient Rome or of structural steel in the last century – but the challenge encountered by Michelangelo and his contemporaries was more comparable to that of the modern architect in planning for the requirements of the automobile. Artillery, like motor transportation, is a mechanical innovation which is not a part of a building but which affects the way it is used, and consequently the way it must be built.

The foremost problem of fortification is to reconcile two exigencies of artillery warfare that are incompatible: defence and offence. A design with maximum security against enemy missiles is likely to allow the defenders only a minimum of manoeuvrability and range, and *vice versa*. In the Renaissance a satisfactory equilibrium was reached only after a long period of experimentation. The early solutions discussed

4. See the important study of Sanmichele's fortifications, E. Langenskiöld, *Michele Sanmichele*, Uppsala, 1938, Ch. VIII.

here were overbalanced on the side of defence; Michelangelo's designs were the first to suggest the full potentialities of offensive planning.

The drawings eloquently testify to Michelangelo's concentration on the power of the defenders; his bastions spring from the walls like crustacean monsters eager to crush the enemy in their claws (Pls. 26a–28a). Compared to the blunt and massive blocks of the Sangallos and Sanmichele (Pl. 3b), they seem to be fantastic visions created rather to symbolize than to implement the terrifying power of firearms. Apparently this is the impression they made on contemporaries, for further evolution of sixteenth-century fortification followed the path of the other architects; but the fact that Baroque fortification ultimately produced designs similar in many respects to Michelangelo's impels us to find in these drawings not only their unparalleled expressive force but the special grasp of military functions that made them prophetic if not influential.

Part of the motivation for the aggressive biological forms in these drawings is certainly purely formal: the curved orillons of some of the bastions (Pl. 27a) are monumental versions of the stairway motifs in the Laurentian library; in other designs what Scully has aptly called the "reflex diagonal" has the dynamic spirit of the Medici tomb sarcophagi allegories and of the stairways of the Capitoline Hill and Belvedere. But an analysis of the nature of artillery defence reveals a peculiar practical justification for such forms.

While civil and religious buildings are planned to suit the people who use them, fortifications must be planned to suit guns. The architect may visualize people in motion or at rest, and in the Quattrocento he chose the latter; but he *must* visualize guns in action, since they are no use unless constantly propelling missiles. On this account, the development of modern fortifications aided the radical change from a static to a dynamic conception of architecture which came about in the course of the sixteenth century. Though most military architects were slow to see the special implications of planning for artillery, Michelangelo was prepared to grasp them immediately, because his projects for the Laurentian library represent the first dynamic planning of the Renaissance in that they urged the visitor to pass through the building rather than to seek a static vantage point.

The uniqueness of Michelangelo's fortification drawings is the result of his concentration on the aggressive action of heavy missiles as they explode outward from a defensive nucleus. These are the only military designs of the age – with the exception of a few of Leonardo's sketches – that consistently specify the trajectories of cannon; they are stroked with a vigour that evokes their spread and power; the structures themselves take shape around them. The peculiarly organic character of Michelangelo's bastions is due to the fact that they are envisaged as a framework to house and to release dynamic forces. A comparable adjustment of form to mechanical forces is found in the "streamlining" of modern airplanes, which also produces certain zoomorphic suggestions.

What Michelangelo did not consider in his plans was the equally powerful artillery of the enemy: the fact that cannon balls would be hurtling into, as well as away from the bastions seems to have played little part in his thinking. Had he given more attention to this inescapable condition of defensive action, prudence might have dictated a more sober expression.

His many sharp and attenuated salients are comparable to small and lightly armed commando units; they provide maximum range and versatility but are not calculated to sustain prolonged attack from concentrated forces. Since bastions are devices by nature more defensive than offensive, Michelangelo's ideas were not destined to be accepted; but his contemporaries, who thought almost exclusively of defence, would have found better balanced solutions had they studied his drawings.

In the most zoomorphic of the projects (Pls. 26a, 27b) there are curves on the faces of the bastions which cannot be flanked by fire from other positions and so give cover to an enemy close to the walls. In some of the later (?) drawings (Pl. 28a) these blind spots are eliminated, which may be due both to criticism from military experts and to Michelangelo's habit of starting with a formal statement and later adjusting it to structural and functional conditions.

It is in these "later" drawings that Michelangelo anticipates the forms of Baroque fortifications. Plans such as Pl. 28a are strikingly similar to ideal bastions suggested in the *Manière de Fortifier* (1689) by the great French military engineer Vauban (Pl. 28b), particularly in the use of ravelins, the isolation of the several salients, and the acute, attenuated triangular trace. But in comparing isolated bastions by Vauban and Michelangelo we may fail to detect a crucial difference between the two which explains the obscure fate of the latter: Vauban's system is part of an overall fortress plan in which every bastion is supported by flanking fire from adjacent salients and bastions, while Michelangelo's is an isolated unit, added to the curtain wall, which must fend for itself. The attitude of contemporaries toward this deficiency is expressed by Bonaiuto Lorini in criticizing his French colleagues:[5] "Since (the bastions) were small in size and the curtain walls were long, the defenders were hampered both by the distance between bastions and by the restricted space, which easily became congested; thus the faces of the bastions remained undefended . . .". In the perfected late Renaissance system the mutual support of all salient elements was taken for granted.

We do not know whether the temporary earthworks that Michelangelo hurriedly erected for the Siege of Florence in 1529–1530 resembled his drawings, which were projects for permanent installations, probably done a year earlier. Antonio da Sangallo the Younger, who replaced the earthworks with masonry in the later 1530's could not have retained much of Michelangelo's system, since the permanent installations were typical examples of his more cautious style. It is ironic that Michelangelo's remarkable experiments should have reached posterity filtered through the hands of his worst enemy and most unsympathetic compatriot, and that Vauban himself should have studied the later defences of Florence as authentic documents of Michelangelo's work.

The drawings never were circulated. Military historians have not discovered them yet, and have interpreted Michelangelo on the grounds of his dubious contribution to the defences of the Vatican and the papal

5. *Delle Fortificationi*, Venice, 1597, pp. 140–141.

ports, and from literary chronicles of the Siege of Florence. But the chroniclers, brief as they are, left a record of Michelangelo's temporary defences that adds a dimension to the data in the drawings. They describe curtains and salients of packed earth and straw covered with unbaked bricks made of organic materials, the principle of which was to nullify by absorption the shock of missiles on exposed surfaces. The theory of elastic defence opposed the current preference for massive rigid walls, and was conceptually attuned to the supple, zoomorphic character of the drawings which, in fact, have frequent indications of earthen escarpments serving the same purpose along the curtains (Pls. 27a, 28a marked "terra"). Thus Michelangelo applied his organic theory of design both to the offensive and defensive problems of military architecture.

If the drawings had no chance to affect the future history of fortifications, they were an important factor in the formation of Michelangelo's mature style. The necessity to find an architectural solution for projectiles in constant radial motion along infinitely varied paths must have helped to remove from his mind the last vestiges of the static figures and proportions of the Quattrocento. The experience was a catalyst to ideas tested in the Laurentian library, where the visitor was impelled to move, but still along a fixed axis and through independent spaces; the next stage, represented by the Capitoline Hill and the projects for San Giovanni dei Fiorentini, imposed a variety of radial axes on a unified space, allowing the visitor a multiple choice of movements (compare Pls. 28a and 36b). Perhaps the study of artillery suggested this new way of dealing with human motion.

CHAPTER VI

The Capitoline Hill

MEDIEVAL Rome had no centre. Other Italian towns that had been smaller in antiquity grew in clusters about their ancient squares, while Rome gradually shrank until its fora and major churches were on the outskirts, and the remnants of a metropolis settled in compressed disorder along the banks of the Tiber. When the city government decided to raise a communal palace in the twelfth century, it chose the deserted site of the Tabularium on the slope of the Capitoline Hill overlooking the Republican Forum. The decision must have been dictated by the dream of *renovatio* – the restoration of ancient glory – as the hill had been the site of the *Arx* of the earliest settlers and of the major temples of Imperial Rome.[1] Isolated from the everyday life of the city on a summit without paved accesses, the Capitol, or Campidoglio as the Romans called it, failed until the sixteenth century to arouse sufficient civic pride to foster the construction of a monumental communal piazza such as nearly every major Italian city had produced in the Middle Ages. We owe to this delay one of the most imposing architectural compositions of all time; nowhere but in Rome had a Renaissance architect been given the opportunity to create a grandiose environment for the political life of a great city.

It was lack of opportunity rather than of desire that deterred early Renaissance designers from executing ambitious civic schemes. Every architectural theorist of the Renaissance was a philosopher of urbanism; Alberti and Leonardo thought primarily of improving the appearance and convenience of existing towns; Filarete and Francesco di Giorgio

---

1. A. Graf, *Roma nella memoria e nelle immaginazioni del medio evo*, 2nd ed., Turin, 1923; P. Schramm, *Kaiser, Rom u. Renovatio*, Leipzig, 1925; F. Schneider, *Rom und Romgedanke im Mittelalter*, Munich, 1926.

drew ideal, geometrically perfect projects to be raised anew. But their schemes remained on paper, and only in occasional provincial villages, such as Pienza, Cortemaggiore, or Vigevano, or in the refurbishing of existing squares, could modern ideas be tested. Unfortunately, the largest planning project of the sixteenth century was totally destroyed: the town of Castro, redesigned by Antonio da Sangallo the Younger for Pope Paul III as the capital of a Duchy fabricated for the Pope's son.[2]

The square at Pienza, of 1456/1458 – 1464 (Pl. 34a), is the only Quattrocento scheme comparable to the Campidoglio. Built for Pope Pius II by Alberti's follower Bernardo Rossellino, it was the core of the town's life, containing the Cathedral at the centre, and on three sides, the palaces of the Bishop, the Piccolomini family, and the Commune.[3] By chance, the plan is trapezoidal, like Michelangelo's (Pl. 36b), because of the axes of the pre-existing streets on either side, and because the expansion in width opened prospects past the Cathedral transepts over a panorama of Tuscan valleys and hills. Though the major street runs through the base of the trapezoid, a lesser one enters, like the Capitoline cordonata, on the principal axis. Rossellino divided the piazza into rectangles by horizontal and vertical bands which help to draw together the façades and lead the eye toward the Cathedral. The projects of Rossellino and Michelangelo have similar devices: the regular plan, symmetrically organized about the entrance axis of the central building; the systematization of the entrance ways into the piazza, and the pavement pattern calculated to integrate the several buildings. But the effect is quite different; the Pienza buildings are diverse in size and scale, and above all, in style; the sole monument within the square – a wellhead – is eccentrically placed on the right edge. The harmonious relationship among independent units, characteristic of the Quattrocento (cf. Ch. I), focused attention on the individual buildings, and spatial effects were a by-product of

2. On Renaissance urbanism, see G. Giovannoni, *Saggi sull'architettura del Rinascimento*, Milan, 1935, pp. 265–304; on Medieval planning, see W. Braunfels, *Mittelalterliche Stadtbaukunst in der Toskana*, Berlin, 1953.

3. L. Heydenreich, "Pius II als Bauherr von Pienza", *Zeitschrift für Kunstgeschichte*, VI, 1937, pp. 105–146.

the design of the enframing masses. Only in the last generation of the fifteenth century did architects begin to think of single elements as a function of the whole – to regard a given environment not merely as a neutral repository for a work of art, but as something that might be formed and controlled by the manipulation of voids and the co-ordination of masses. The difference in approach is illuminated by a similar change in the music of this generation; the polyphonic structure which produced harmonies through the superposition of independent melodies began to give way to homophonic forms in which the several lines were subordinate to harmonies constructed vertically, in chords; a concordance of voices became primary.[4]

The new spirit, foreseen in certain sketches of Francesco di Giorgio, appeared in the planning schemes of Leonardo and Giuliano da Sangallo, but was first applied in practice by Bramante. In his plan of 1502 for the precinct of the Tempietto of San Pietro in Montorio, the central building was not intended to stand isolated in a neutral space as it does today, but to be the nucleus of a scheme which controlled the total environment, which formed palpable spatial volumes as well as architectural bodies, in such a way that the observer would be entirely enveloped in a composition that he could grasp only as a whole. Two years later Bramante applied the principles of environmental control to the most monumental programme of the age, the Cortile del Belvedere (Pl. 65c). Here his raw material was an entire mountain side; his design had to impose the authority of intellect upon nature. Inspired by antique precedents, he devised a sequence of rectangular courts on ascending levels, bound by stairways and ramps of varying form and framed by loggias. His principles of organization were: first, emphasis on the central axis (marked by a centralized monumental fountain in the lowest court, a central stairway and niche in the central court, and a focal one-story exedra in the garden at the upper level, the last already destroyed by Michelangelo in Pl. 65c; second, the symmetrical design of the lateral façades; and

---

4. See E. Lowinsky, "The Concept of Musical Space in the Renaissance", *Papers of the American Musicological Society Annual Meeting, 1941*, Richmond, 1946, pp. 57 ff.

third, a perspective construction in three dimensions devised for an observer in a fixed position within the Papal *Stanze*, and reinforced by the diminishing heights of the loggias as they recede toward the "vanishing point" at the rear.[5]

Michelangelo must have borrowed certain elements of his composition from the Belvedere; the fact that he used a replica of the Senatore staircase in remodelling Bramante's exedra in 1551 (Pls. 29 and 65a) indicates his awareness of the similarity of the two plans. Both required the regularization of rolling hillsides, the integration of pre-existing buildings, and covered porticoes on either side. Several of Bramante's devices were applicable to the Campidoglio, particularly the central monument and stairway used for axial emphasis, and the niche centred in a triangular plane formed by ramps. Bramante's static perspective construction was unsuitable to the Capitoline topography, and was anyhow uncongenial to Michelangelo's interest in movement through space; but the Campidoglio plan does fix the observer's viewpoint momentarily by forcing him to enter the piazza on the central axis at the only point from which the composition can be viewed as a whole.

The common feature of the two plans is a unity achieved by the organization more than by the character of the component parts, a unity imposed by general principles – axis, symmetry, convergence – which command the voids as well as the architectural bodies. The actual form of certain elements might be changed without disturbing the organization – for example, the Marcus Aurelius monument could be a fountain; and this illuminates what Michelangelo meant when he said in speaking of axial compositions (p. 1): "the *means* a_ie unrestricted and may be chosen at will". What distinguishes Michelangelo from his predecessor is that his choice of means more effectively reinforces the principles of organization and binds the Campidoglio into a coherent unity. His individuality emerges in dynamic composition; the elements in the

<hr>

5. See J. Ackerman, *The Cortile del Belvedere*, Vatican, 1954, pp. 121 ff.; and the broader treatment of planning concepts by B. Lowry, "High Renaissance Architecture", *College Art Journal*, XVII, 1958, pp. 115 ff.

Campidoglio do not produce the restful progression of the Belvedere, but are directed toward a dramatic climax at the portal of the Senators' palace. Internal tensions built up by contrasts of equally potent forms – horizontals and verticals in the façades; oval and trapezoid in the pavement – offer diversions and ambiguities that only amplify the ultimate confluence toward the goal. This crescendo of forms was destined to become archetypal in civic planning; though the vigour and ingenuity of the Campidoglio have rarely been equalled, the U-shaped plan, the convergence of low wings toward a dominant central accent, the double-ramped stairway and the centralized monument were to become characteristic components of urban and villa design in the following centuries.

On December 10, 1537, "Master Michelangelo, sculptor", appeared on a list of foreigners awarded Roman citizenship in a ceremony at the Capitol;[6] in the same month, he probably started designing for the statue of Marcus Aurelius – which Pope Paul III had brought to the hill against his advice – a pedestal, the shape and orientation of which implies the conception of the entire plan. No more is known of the circumstances leading to his project for the piazza; but certain conditions of the commission may be deduced from knowledge of the site in these years. The statue had been placed in an uneven plateau in the saddle of the hill between the northern peak occupied by the church of Santa Maria in Aracoeli and the southern rise toward the Tarpeian Rock (Pl. 30a). Two structures bordered the plateau: the medieval Senators' palace on the east, and the Quattrocento Conservators' palace on the south. The only paved access was a stairway decending from the transept of the Aracoeli; toward the city the slope of the hill, creased by muddy footpaths (Pl. 31b), fell sharply off to the west. Michelangelo must have been asked to submit proposals, first, for an entrance from the city, second, for the conversion of the plateau into a level paved area, and third, for a modest restoration of the dilapidated palaces.

6. Document published by F. Gregorovius, in R. Accad. dei Lincei, cl. di scienze morali etc., Atti, III 1876–1877, pp. 314 ff.

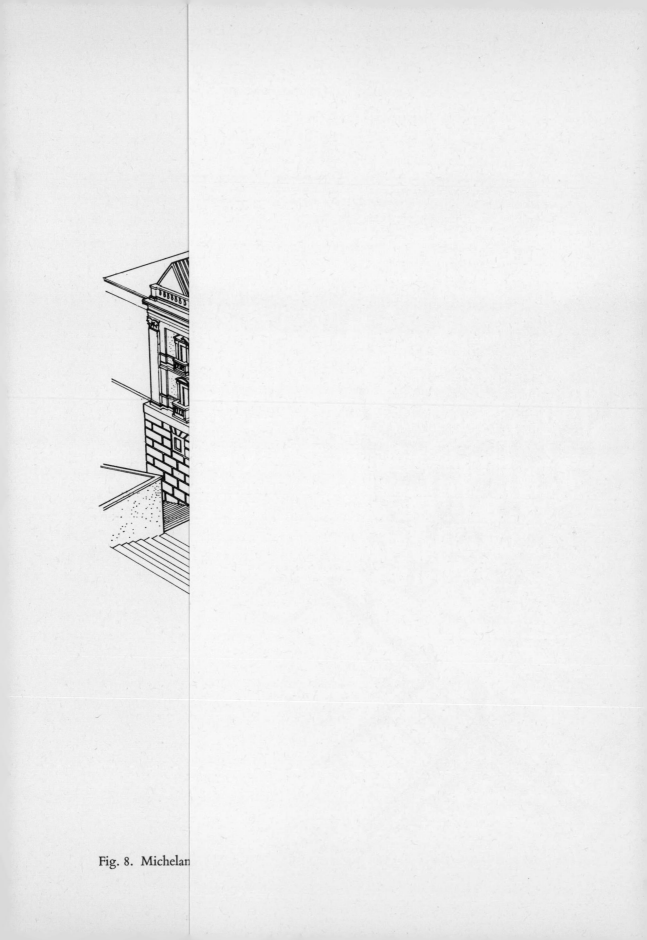

Fig. 8. Michelan

The plan that transformed the disorderly complex into a symmetrical composition unifying five entrances, a piazza, and three palace fronts (Pls. 36b, 37; Fig. 8) was too extraordinary to have been foreseen by lay administrators; Michelangelo must have found in their mundane programme an inspiration for a design the grandiose character of which persuaded them to raise their goals. The Conservators may not have assented easily: their budget was restricted throughout the sixteenth century, and they cannot have anticipated proposals to build a new campanile simply to emphasize the axis, and to raise a third palace along the left side of the square the function of which was to be purely aesthetic. Yet without the "Palazzo Nuovo" (the name indicates the absence of a practical purpose), no order could be imposed on the scheme; it achieved precisely the goal that Michelangelo so vigorously defined in the letter quoted on page 1, where he affirmed the relationship of architecture to the human body in the sense that necessary similarity of the eyes and uniqueness of the nose implies that architectural elements to the left of a central axis must be mirrored by those on the right, while the central element must be unique. Aside from the gratuitous addition of a palace front, economy was a major determinant in Michelangelo's solution; he accepted the condition that the existing palaces were to be retained intact and merely to be covered with new façades. This gave his patrons the freedom to execute the project in stages, according to their means; the Senators' stairway could be finished fifty years before the façade, and the Conservators' façade be built in one-bay sections without demolishing the earlier façade or interrupting the normal functions of the offices inside.

In accepting the existing conditions, Michelangelo had to rationalize the accidental orientation of the two palaces, the axes of which formed an 80-degree angle. An irregularity that might have defeated a less imaginative designer became the catalyst that led Michelangelo to use a trapezoidal plan and to develop from this figure other features of his scheme; he so masterfully controlled this potential disadvantage that it appears quite purposeful.

In the engraved plan and perspectives after Michelangelo's design (Pls. 36b and 37) only those elements are specified that may be seen by an observer within the square: of the five access stairways only the first steps are indicated, and nothing is shown of the palaces except the façades and porticoes. Obviously the project was not envisaged as a complex of individual building blocks, but as an outdoor room with three walls. This is a response to topographical conditions that are falsified by engravings and modern photographs (Pl. 29) where the observer is artificially suspended in mid-air. In actuality, one cannot grasp the composition from a distance; it unfolds only upon arrival at the level of the piazza, as upon entering a huge *salone*. So Michelangelo did not continue the palace façades around the buildings; they stop short at the corners as if to indicate that they belong properly to the piazza. Consequently, the Palazzo Nuovo was planned simply as a portico with offices; the present interior court is a seventeenth-century interpolation. Michelangelo built the niched wall that appears in Pl. 31b just at the rear of the offices (note the shallow roof in Pl. 37).

Another explanation for the apparent artificiality of the solution is the immemorial function of the Campidoglio as the site of solemn public ceremonies performed in the open air. The piazza was to be the chief locus of civic events, rather than the conference halls, prisons, and tribunal within the palaces. The average citizen would come to the hill only to witness some ritual that demanded an awesome and spectacular setting. Perhaps the project was visualized as a translation into permanent materials of those arches, gates, and façades of wood and canvas erected in the sixteenth century for the triumphal entries and processions of great princes. Indeed, an occasion of this kind prompted the renovation of the Capitol; when the Emperor Charles V entered Rome in 1536, the lack of a suitable access to the hill forced his cortège to detour around it, and frustrated the enactment of the traditional climax to an Imperial triumph. The Pope's determination to acquire the statue of Marcus Aurelius for the Campidoglio in 1537 appears to have been the initial reaction to the embarrassment of the previous year.

In order to place the equestrian statue properly when it arrived in 1538, an over-all plan was needed, since it had to be purposefully related to the existing buildings. Michelangelo's plan must have been produced at that time since the oval statue pedestal, which mirrors the proposed form of the piazza, appears in the sketchbook of Francisco de Hollanda (Pl. 32). The oval area, with its vigorous stellate pattern (Pl. 36b), is one of the most imaginative innovations of the Renaissance; set off by a ring of three steps descending to its depressed rim, it rises in a gentle domical curve to the level of the surrounding piazza at the centre. The oval was almost unknown in earlier architecture: Michelangelo had proposed it in projects for the interior of the tomb of Julius II, and it appears in church and villa sketches by Baldassare Peruzzi; but humanistic distaste for "irregular" figures discouraged its use.[7] Further, it was traditional to treat pavements – particularly in outdoor spaces – in rectilinear patterns, either in grid form (Pls. 34a and 41) or, in the courts of large palaces, as bands radiating out from the centre. But neither solution was adaptable to the trapezoidal boundary of the Campidoglio. The problem, so elegantly solved by the oval, was to find an organizing figure that would emphasize the centre where the statue was to be set, and yet not counteract the longitudinal axis of both the piazza and the statue itself. While the circles, squares, and regular polygons that formed the vocabulary of the Quattrocento could meet only the first condition, the oval combined in one form the principles of centrality and axiality; it was this dual character that later made it so popular in church design. As a pure oval, however, Michelangelo's figure would have conceded nothing to its trapezoidal frame, but it contains a further refinement: three concave recessions formed in the surrounding ring of steps suggest to the visitor entering from the cordonata the expansion of the piazza toward the rear, and at the same time introduce him to the choice of two ascents to the Senators' palace.

The offer of alternative routes imposes an unclassical ambivalence: while the visitor enters the piazza, and later the Senators' palace, on axis,

7. For a general discussion of the oval in Renaissance architecture, see W. Lotz, "Die ovalen Kirchenräume des Cinquecento", *Röm. Jhb.*, VII, 1955, pp. 9 ff.

his direct progress is barred first by the statue, and then by the entrances to the double-ramped stairway. He is not only forced to choose between two equally efficient routes, but is distracted by an emphatic stellate pavement that suggests movement of a different sort, along curvilinear paths toward and away from the centre. He thereby becomes intensely involved in the architectural setting to a degree never demanded by earlier Renaissance planning. By forcing the observer into a personal solution of this paradox, Michelangelo endowed the practical function of movement in architecture with aesthetic overtones.

The stairway to the Senatore palace (Pl. 37), though also anticipated in Peruzzi's sketches, was the first of its kind to be adapted to a palace façade. Like the oval, this form solved several problems at once: it pre-empted a minimum of space in the piazza, it gave direct access to the great hall on the *piano nobile*, and it was the perfect setting for the reclining river gods that had previously blocked the entrance to the Conservators' palace (Pl. 30a). Its purpose was expressive as well as practical; the dynamic effect of the triangular form, which so powerfully co-ordinates the three façades and masks their inequality in height, had been evoked by Michelangelo in organizing the figures of the Medici chapel and in his fortification drawings (Pls. 8 and 27a); perhaps it was initially suggested by the analogy of the river gods to the reclining allegories in the chapel. The baldachin at the summit of the flights, which may have been devised as a ceremonial setting for the appearance of dignitaries, diverts the angular accents of the stairway into the mainstream of the central axis, echoing the form of the campanile above.

As the stairway covered most of the lower story behind and raised the entrance to the level of the *piano nobile*, the façade could not conform to the three-story Florentine tradition exemplified by the Farnese palace (Pl. 39). The lower story had to be treated as a basement distinct from the upper floors; its drafted facing emphasized this distinction and also expressed the rude character of the prisons behind. In effect, the palace became a two-story structure like those on either side, so that it proved possible to harmonize the composition by adapting to all three palaces the colossal Order with its heavy cornice and crowning balustrade; within this syntax the central palace could be differentiated by the design of its apertures.

The open porticoes of the lateral palaces belong, like the loggia of Brunelleschi's Foundling Hospital in Florence and the Procuratie of St Mark's Square in Venice, as much to the square as to the buildings. They even favour the piazza by screening the entrance portals within, so as to increase the dominance of the longitudinal axes over the cross-axes. They are extraordinary in structure as well as in form. Early Renaissance porticoes had been a succession of vaults supported by arches. Though Alberti insisted that antique precedent demanded that arches be sustained by piers while columns should carry only lintels, his advice was ignored before 1500; Quattrocento arcades are generally columnar. Bramante reintroduced the column-and-lintel system in open loggias in the Cloister of Santa Maria della Pace and in the Vatican façade (now Cortile di San Damaso), but only in upper stories, where the interior could be spanned in wood. Peruzzi's entrance to the Massimi palace of 1535 was perhaps the first revival of the ancient technique of spanning a portico with stone beams, though on a much more modest scale than at the Campidoglio. Michelangelo's combination of column and pier provided sufficient bracing to allow expansion of the system to monumental scale. The scale actually precluded the use of arches; openings as broad as those of the Conservators' palace could not have been arched without penetrating into the pre-existing second story. Furthermore, Michelangelo preferred the effects of post-and-beam construction; in 1548 he walled up Sangallo's arch over the central window of the Farnese palace to replace it with a lintel (Fig. 10 and Pl. 42a), and on the one occasion when he used structural arches on the exterior of a building – at the Porta Pia, where they were imperative – he disguised the form (Pl. 74). Semi-circular arches have a static effect uncongenial to Michelangelo's powerful interplay of horizontal and vertical forces.

In the Conservators' palace, this interplay recalls the effects of a framed structure; the façade construction is as close to a skeletal frame as it is possible to attain in stone. Where the columns, pilasters, and entablatures of San Lorenzo and St Peter's (Pls. 5a and 63) merely express stresses of load and support that actually are absorbed by the wall mass, here they really do the work that they appear to do. The cornice is supported by the pilaster-piers and the lower entablature by the columns; the façade wall is no longer a major bearer of loads; it is itself supported on beams and takes so little stress that della Porta was able to replace almost an entire section with glass (Pl. 35b). Consequently, so little wall is left that attention is drawn to the members, where it is held by the contrast of their rugged texture and light, advancing colour to the smooth surface and receding colour of the brick wall-plane. But the stability of the portico and façade is not wholly due to the "skeleton"; it requires stiffening by internal walls perpendicular to the principal axis – those in the rooms above, and especially by those of the lower floor (Pl. 36b), which Michelangelo ingeniously calculated to work both as buttresses and as partitions between the guild offices.

Because the Conservatori design gives the antique Order a structural as well as a decorative function, it may be used profitably to illustrate the relationship of building techniques to expression in Michelangelo's architecture. The decision to unify the three palaces by a continuity of horizontal accents indicated lintel construction and emphatic cornices. In the final design it appears that Michelangelo intended to keep the potentially overwhelming horizontal accents in check by applying verticals of equal power: the colossal pilasters which, in embracing two stories, interrupt the continuity of the lower entablature and, together with the columns, window-colonnettes, and balustrade figures, establish a tense equilibrium of forces. But a structural analysis reverses the process proving that ingenious devices were necessary to prevent *verticals* from dominating the façade. The vertical loads are concentrated in heavy masses of masonry extending from the foundations to the cornice, out of which the pilasters are carved (Pls. 35b and 36b). To de-emphasize these, Michelangelo made it appear that the pilasters alone sustain the weight. The remaining surfaces of the pier-mass on either side of the pilasters he disguised as superficial decorative bands – first, by covering them with horizontal relief elements that make them seem discontinuous, and second, by applying to the wall-surface above the windows horizontal bands of the same dimensions, so that the recessed pier-surfaces should be read as part of an applied wall-frame. So the colossal pilaster Order functions as a means of diminishing rather than of emphasizing the preponderant verticality of the piers; perhaps Bramante had a similar purpose when he first used the colossal Order on the piers of St Peter's. Conversely, the horizontals had to be exaggerated to maintain an equilibrium, and again Bramante's inventions were called into service: the crowning balustrade, which appeared first in the Tempietto of 1502, augments the crown of the building to nearly six metres without substantially increasing its weight; the window-balconies, which Bramante had used in the House of Raphael, diminish the verticality of the apertures without obstructing light.

When the vocabulary of the Conservators' palace was adapted to the Senators' façade it became purely expressive, since there were no structural problems in facing the existing medieval structure (Pl. 31b). Now the pier surfaces, which had originally masqueraded as ornament, became honestly ornamental; and it is this change in function which suggests that the design of the lateral palaces preceded that of the Senators'. Moreover, it strengthens the hypothesis that the Campidoglio façades were at least partly designed before the apses of St Peter's (1546/1547); a similar motif appears there in a context that must be ornamental, since the structure depends wholly on wall-masses and not on surface members.

To appreciate fully the significance of the Campidoglio design we must understand what might be called its subject matter as well as its architectural character. Like the Cortile del Belvedere, which was built to rival the great villas of antiquity, the Campidoglio was a monumental symbol in which the haunting dream of ancient grandeur became concrete. Like paintings of their time, both were designed to be looked at more than to be used, and both communicated a specific content of a more complex sort than is usually found in architecture.[8]

Sculpture played a peculiarly formative role in the evolution of the Belvedere and the Campidoglio. Distinguished collections of antiquities assembled in the fifteenth and early sixteenth centuries stimulated the urge to build; the statues had priority, and the architecture took shape around them. The Belvedere was planned as a setting for and approach to the Papal museum, and the resurgence of the Capitol awaited the arrival of its equestrian centrepiece.

The ancient bronzes donated to the people of Rome by Sixtus IV and Innocent VIII in the fifteenth century were chosen more for their associations than for their beauty. They were objects of almost totemic power which the medieval mind had endowed with the responsibility for sustaining the legal and imperial symbolism of antiquity. A figure of the mother wolf which had nursed Romulus and Remus, mythical founders of Rome, was placed over the entrance of the old Conservators' palace (Pl. 30a) – and to emphasize her significance, a pair of suckling infants was added by a Quattrocento sculptor. A colossal Constantinian head, and a hand from the same figure bearing a sphere, were placed in the portico (Pl. 30b); the medieval pilgrim's guidebook called the *Mirabilia Urbis Romae* identified these as the remains of a colossal "Phoebus, that is, god of the Sun, whose feet stood on earth while his head touched heaven, who held a ball in his hand, meaning that Rome ruled the whole world". Both stood by the Lateran, near the *Marcus Aurelius*, throughout the Middle Ages, in a spot of which the *Mirabilia* says "There the law is final". A third figure of Hercules, whose relation to the city was less firmly established, was installed on a base pointedly inscribed "IN MONUMENTUM ROMANAE GLORIAE". Further additions were made in the

8. On the iconography of the Capitol, see note 13; H. Sedlmayr, "Die Area Capitolina des Michelangelo", *Jhb. d. Preuss Kunstslg.*, LII, 1931, pp. 176 ff.; H. Siebenhüner, *Das Kapitol in Rom. Idee und Gestalt*, Munich, 1954, *passim*; W. Hekscher, *Sixtus IV . . . Aeneas Insignes Statuas Romano Populo Restituendas Censuit*, The Hague, 1955; J. Ackerman, "Marcus Aurelius on the Capitoline Hill", *Renaissance News*, X, 1957, pp. 69 ff.; F. Saxl, "The Capitol during the Renaissance: A Symbol of the Imperial Idea", *Lectures*, London, 1957, pp. 200 ff.

sixteenth century: Leo X installed the colossal statues of two river gods before the Conservators' portico (Pl. 30a), and donated reliefs depicting the triumphal procession of Marcus Aurelius onto the hill.

Some of these pieces were integrated into Michelangelo's scheme, and others were moved indoors, but the theme *Romanae gloriae* was reinforced by new acquisitions, and made explicit by inscriptions. A tablet alongside the portal of the Conservators' palace reads: "s.p.q.r., imitating as far as possible its ancestors in spirit and deed, restored the Capitolium decayed by the ravages of time, the year 2320 after the founding of the city". But on the opposite side of the portal, a similar inscription, dated "in the year of our salvation 1568" consigns "to Jesus Christ, author of all good" the care of the people of Rome and of the Campidoglio "once dedicated to Jove". The twin tablets are a clue to hidden meanings in the design of the Campidoglio and a reminder that a Christian motivation underlies the pagan splendour.

It was Pope Paul III rather than the city fathers who insisted that the statue of Marcus Aurelius be brought to the hill against the wishes of its proper owner, the Chapter of St John in the Lateran. Michelangelo opposed the project, but managed only to dissuade the Pope from expropriating the statues of Jupiter's twin sons, Castor and Pollux, with their rearing horses, that had stood throughout the Middle Ages on the crown of the Quirinal Hill (Pl. 76a). It is difficult to explain the choice of the *Marcus Aurelius*, not because the meaning of the transfer is unclear, but because it had so many meanings. The most important, perhaps, is that the statue, one of the finest and best preserved ancient bronzes known to the Middle Ages, had grown, rather like the *Wolf*, into a symbol of law and government, so that executions and punishments regularly took place before it. Consequently, once it was in place, two hallowed legal symbols were removed from the piazza: the *Wolf*, and the group with an attacking Lion on the steps of the Senator's palace which marked the spot for the sentencing of criminals far back into the Middle Ages. In this penal role, the equestrian group was known from the earliest records in the tenth century as the *Caballus Constantini*. The convenient misnomer, which combined imperial power and Christianity, survived throughout the Renaissance.

But another legend, nearly as old, identified the rider as *il gran' villano* ("villein," in English); it was fostered for political reasons in the twelfth century, at a moment when the Holy Roman Emperor was in bad repute in Rome. It told of a low-born folk hero in Republican – not Imperial – days who, singlehanded, captured a besieging army and its royal general and was honoured with a statue. So the figure came to symbolize a mixture of Republican, anti-monarchical *virtù* and romantic heroism that reminds one of the iconography of the French Revolution. The *villano* tradition may have led to the type of early Renaissance equestrians: Simone Martini's *Guidoriccio*, Uccello's *Hawkwood*, Donatello's *Gattamelata*, Verrocchio's *Colleoni*, and others – all soldier adventurers of low birth rather than prelates or princes.

The inscription designed for the statue by Michelangelo identifies the rider as Antoninus Pius (Pl. 32); though the correct identification had been made in the fifteenth century, it still was not accepted generally, and mattered only to antiquarians. Paul III must have stolen the statue because it bristled with symbolic significance, recalling at once the power of the Roman Empire and of Christianity, republican liberties, and the romantic hero popular in the Italian literature of the time. This may explain why there was no thought of commissioning a new statue from Michelangelo or another contemporary sculptor, and why *Marcus Aurelius* was not merely set into the piazza but inspired its very shape.

In Michelangelo's design (Pls. 36b, 37) the two river gods were given a more imposing setting before the triangular stairway, the form of which must have been influenced by their characteristic attitude of fluvial repose. Yet, if the decision to use the pair was made for formal reasons, it was essential to give it an iconic rationale. One was the Nile, supported by a sphinx; the other was the Tigris, identified by his crouching tiger; but before being reinstalled by the steps, he became the Tiber, Rome's own river, by the ingenious expedient of replacing his Mesopotamian prop with a new wolf suckling the two founding fathers. According to

Pirro Ligorio, the exchange was made "through the ignorance of a poor councillor", meaning Michelangelo, one supposes. Its purpose, however, was not to please such testy antiquarians as Ligorio, but to suggest the scope of Roman culture by linking great rivers at home and abroad.

If Rome is symbolized as the Tiber, it is incongruous that the figure in the central niche should be *Roma*, an ancient *Minerva* supplied with urban attributes. Her presence is, in fact, a makeshift solution; Michelangelo's plan was to place a *Jupiter* in the niche. The statue would have called to mind the temple of Jupiter Optimus Maximus which had stood on the Capitoline in antiquity, and which appears in the background of the triumphal relief displayed in the Conservators' palace. Had the god been in the centre of a triangle flanked by the two rivers, the composition might have suggested the temple pediment, with the titular deity in the dominant position.

Attention is also attracted to this area of the piazza by a baldachin or canopy over *Jupiter's* head at the top of the stairs, a curious appendage to a Renaissance façade. In late antiquity and in the Middle Ages it was one of the most universally used symbols of Imperial power. But it could be Christian, too: in the sixteenth century one would have seen such a baldachin only over the main altar of a large church.

A visitor's first impression on ascending the hill is of the statuary along the forward edge. In the earlier engraving of Michelangelo's project (cf. Fig. 8) four male figures adorn the balcony: they are all Imperial state portraits, and the two in the centre, who carry spheres, are Constantinian figures found for Paul III in about 1540. The second version (Pl. 37) replaces two emperors by a pair of horse-trainers. They appear to be the Quirinal *Castor and Pollux* (Pl. 76a) sought by the Pope thirty years before; but in this respect the engraving is inexact. A second, more relaxed version of the twins, found near the Capitol in 1560, was ready for mounting (Pl. 29). So the Pope's wish came true posthumously without despoiling the Quirinal of its traditional monuments. We may ask why Paul had coveted the Dioscures and why his successors respected his wishes? Two answers will be found in any contemporary account:

first, statues of the twins were known to have been on the Capitol in antiquity, and, second, they were protectors of Rome who had always been symbols of Liberty, as practised particularly in the overthrow of tyrants. But the sixteenth century affixed a new meaning to the old symbol, for at the coronation of Emperor Charles V in Bologna in 1532 by Paul's predecessor Clement VII, the Emperor and the Pope were represented as the mythical brothers.[9] In planning the Capitol six years later, this would be kept in mind, particularly since the Pope, who was the patron, had not given himself the customary publicity elsewhere in the scheme.

We cannot be sure that the figures found in 1560 – or even the Constantinian statues – were selected by Michelangelo, since they appeared first in engravings made after his death, and since his late poetry shows a distaste for humanistic themes. Part of the iconographic scheme may be attributed to contemporary scholars, particularly the additions made after the publication of the engravings, including the two still-lifes on a military theme, of Imperial origin, taken from an aqueduct near the city walls (Pl. 29). These were acquired because they were believed to be trophies of the victories of the Republican leader Marius, which ancient sources located on the Capitoline. The spurious trophies would have reminded contemporaries that the original Capitoline had been the goal of all great triumphal processions. The tradition was revived in 1571, when Marcantonio Colonna, the victor over the Turks at Lepanto, was given a glorious triumph in the antique mode which ended in ceremonies on the piazza.[10]

The outermost decorations of the balcony crowd together as many symbolic overtones as is possible in so little space. They are columns, symbolic of power, carrying spheres, symbolic of Rome's world-wide rule. To clarify the point, the columns are mileposts from the Via Appia. The theme so abundantly illustrated on the piazza was continued in the

9. This association was discovered (in the 1612 ed. of Alciati, *Emblemata*) by Leonard Olschki, *Dante poeta veltro*, Florence, 1953. Cf. C. de Tolnay, "Michelangelo Architetto", *Il Cinquecento*, Florence, 1955, pp. 16 f.

10. G. Borino, A. Galieti, G. Navone, "Il Trionfo di Marc'Antonio Colonna", *Misc. della R. Dep. rom. di storia patria*, XII, 1938.

palace courts, and in the halls of the Conservators' palace, frescoed with scenes from Roman history.

To support the foregoing analysis, which may appear to discover more allusion than the Cinquecento intended, we may call on a contemporary witness whose interpretation took the form of a frescoed vignette in the *salone* of a Roman palace (Pl. 38b).[11] The painter of about 1550–1560 depicted the oval piazza with Marcus Aurelius in the centre, the cordonata and the rear stairway as Michelangelo had planned them. But in place of the Senators' palace are three huge chapels of pagan divinities, the central one in baldachin form. There the herm of Jupiter is the object of unreserved adoration on the part of two Romans not yet imbued with the spirit of the Counter-Reformation. Yet it is inconceivable that Christian imagery was absent from the iconographic programme. Our knowledge of Michelangelo's deep religious convictions following the period of his association with Vittoria Colonna tempts us to see the central Jupiter figure as an anagogical reference to Christ; the presence of the baldachin overhead and the absence of any other member of the Roman pantheon admits such an interpretation.

Furthermore, the arrangement of the piazza unites the ancient Rome of the Forum and the New Rome of the church, a connection suggested in the inscriptions quoted above as well as in the engravings which pointedly show the ruins behind the Senators' palace (Pl. 37), although they are not actually visible from any standpoint in or before the piazza (Pl. 29).[12]

We come finally to the most intriguing and original feature of Michelangelo's design, the central oval which supports *Marcus Aurelius* at the apex of a gentle domical mound. Tolnay has persuasively suggested that the design may be connected with the medieval designation of the Campidoglio as the *umbilicus* or *Caput Mundi*;[13] but his belief that the convex form is intended to represent the curve of the terrestrial globe is not similarly supported by tradition or texts. The curvilinear grid

11. I know of this painting through Wolfgang Lotz, who supplied the photograph.

12. This interpretation of the siting was suggested by Richard Krautheimer.

13. "Beitrage zu den späten architektonischen Projekten Michelangelos", *Jhb. d. Preuss. Kunstslg.*, LI, 1930, pp. 25 f.; LIII, 1932, pp. 245 f.

dividing the pavement into twelve compartments recalls a symbolism commonly used in antiquity on the interior of cupolas, where the twelve signs of the zodiac were used to suggest the Dome of Heaven or the Music of the Spheres;[14] in Christian architecture the twelve Apostles surrounding a central figure of Christ sometimes took the place of the signs. The twelve-part division appeared almost as often in circular pavements as a kind of counter-dome. Vitruvius (V, 6) advised that the circular pavement of theatre orchestras be inscribed with four inter-locking triangles forming a twelve-pointed star, since "in the number twelve the astronomy of the celestial signs is calculated from the musical concord of the stars". These parallel traditions were fused in Cesariano's Vitruvius edition of 1521, where an entire theatre is reconstructed as a round, domed "Tholos" inscribed within a twelve-pointed star.[15]

While the duodecimal division in these examples is usually formed by radiating lines or by triangles, Michelangelo's complex curvilinear con-struction is found among a class of medieval *schemata* in circular form used to co-ordinate the lunar cycle with other astronomical inferences of the number twelve, such as the Hours and the Zodiac. Pl. 38c is only one of many, from a tenth-century (?) manuscript of *De Natura Rerum* of St Isidor of Seville, in which the lunations and signs appear in a form that differs from Michelangelo's chiefly in not being oval. The manu-script *schemata* of Isidor were reproduced in early printed books, estab-lishing a contact with the sixteenth century.[16]

The fact that the prototypes were round, rather than oval, may be explained as an aesthetic prejudice: the circle was preferred in architec-ture prior to the sixteenth century – and in astronomy, until Kepler's time; Michelangelo introduced the oval in a project of the early years of the century, and the first oval dome was built by Vignola shortly after the foundation of the Campidoglio.[17]

14. K. Lehmann, "The Dome of Heaven", *Art Bulletin*, XXVII, 1945, pp. 1 ff., with rich biblio-graphy.

15. Cf. R. Bernheimer, "Theatrum Mundi", *Art Bulletin*, XXXVIII, 1956, pp. 225 ff.

16. Harry Bober kindly supplied the photographs and much information on medieval *schemata*.

17. See note 7 and E. Panofsky, *Galileo as a Critic of the Arts*, The Hague, 1954, esp. pp. 20 ff.

The cosmological pavements and schemata do not explain the mound-like rise of Michelangelo's oval; its convexity adds a new dimension to the tradition in meaning as well as in form. The exception to the ancients' distaste for the oval may be found in a type of military shield that was well known to Michelangelo since it was represented not only in the vault stuccoes of the Conservators' portico and on the *"Trofei di Mario"*, but had been adopted by the Commune as the coat of arms of the S.P.Q.R. – it appears in wooden ceilings of the Conservators' palace dated 1516–1518 and 1544.[18] As was customary with the ornamental arms of the sixteenth century, these ovals are convex in shape. While ornamental shields cannot be associated with the twelve-part division of Michelangelo's pavement, there was a type of ancient shield upon which the zodiac was represented. The legendary shield of Achilles was adorned with the celestial signs, and Alexander the Great adopted the Achillean type along with the epithet Kosmokrator – ruler of the Universe.[19] The title, and the shield along with it, was transferred to Roman Emperors. Another attribute of certain Kosmokrator portraits is a corona simulating the rays of the sun, indicating the resplendent powers of Apollo; and armoured Imperial portraits where the corona is not used have images of Apollo on the breast-plate.

Usually the snake Python appears at the centre of these shields, as it does in non-military representations of the zodiac. The myth of Python is associated with the shrine of Apollo at Delphi, where the snake reportedly dwelt under a moundlike stone known as the *omphalos* or *umbilicus*, which marked the centre of the cosmos.[20] (So the central boss on military shields came to be called the *umbilicus*). The *omphalos* stone

18. C. Pietrangeli, "Lo Stemma del Commune di Roma", *Capitolium*, XXVII, 1952, pp. 41 ff., 143 ff.; XXVIII, 1953, p. 61.

19. O. Brendel, "Der Schild des Achilles", *Die Antike*, XII, 1936, pp. 273 ff.

20. G. Karo, "Omphalos", *Dict. des antiquités grecques et romaines*, IV, 1, Paris, 1904; J. Fontenrose *Python*, Berkeley, 1959, pp. 374 ff., and Fig. 27, a fresco from the House of the Vetii, Pompeii, showing Python on an *omphalos* inscribed with intersecting bands forming lozenges like those of the Capitoline pavement. My attention was first drawn to the relationship of the Zodiac and the *omphalos* by E. R. Goodenough, "A Jewish-Gnostic Amulet of the Roman Period", *Greek and Byzantine Studies*, I, 1958.

became an attribute of Apollo, who appears seated upon it in Greek vases and Roman coins.

The ancient Romans moved the *umbilicus mundi* figuratively from Delphi to the Forum, where it remained until medieval legend shifted it once more to the Campidoglio.[21] Here it was permanently fixed in Michelangelo's pavement, which combined its zodiacal inferences with its moundlike form. *Marcus Aurelius*, mounted at the centre, might have been a foreign element if iconic tradition had not permitted his association with the *umbilicus*. As Kosmokrator, he succeeded to Apollo's position upon the mound, and since the ancient sculptor had not equipped him with the requisite attributes, Michelangelo placed around his base the corona of Apollo: the twelve pointed rays which also serve as the starting points of the zodiacal pattern[22].

21. B. Gamucci, *Le antichità della città di Roma*, Venice, 1569, Fol. 10ᵛ: "Il qual colle, nell'accrescimento della città essendo restato come umbilico di quella . . ."

22. I regret that I was unable to consult the important new publication of G. de Angelis D'Ossat and C. Pietrangeli, *Il Campidoglio di Michelangelo*, Milan, 1965, before completing my emendations.

CHAPTER VII

The Farnese Palace

WHEN Cardinal Alessandro Farnese became Pope Paul III in 1534, the palace that he had been building for seventeen years on the Tiber bank seemed incommensurate with his elevated position; as Vasari said, "he felt he should no longer build a cardinal's, but a pontiff's palace". He immediately had his architect Antonio da Sangallo enlarge the building from three to five bays in the court, and from eleven to thirteen on the façades: the rows of shops on the street were suppressed as unsuitable to his eminence; and the narrow

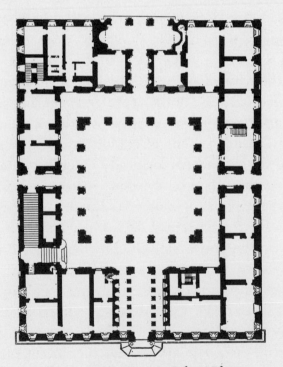

Fig. 9. Rome, Farnese Palace. Plan.

entranceway was transformed into a colonnaded triumphal "atrium" (Fig. 9). Paradoxically, the "pontiff's palace" was to be occupied not by the Pope, who had moved to the Vatican, but by his illegitimate son Pier Luigi, for whom he fabricated the Duchies of Castro and Nepi (in 1537) and of Parma (in 1545). The palace was to become a symbol of the temporal power which the pontificate had brought to the Farnese dynasty – not so much a home as a monumental instrument of propaganda.

A century earlier a new fashion in urban domestic architecture had been formed by the rising élite of commerce and politics. Florentine merchants of the mid-fifteenth century – the Pitti, the Rucellai, and especially the Medici – grasped the potential of monumental classicizing architecture as a symbol of power and of progress. The Medici palace was the earliest and most grandiose of all; towering over medieval Florentine streets and low dwellings and crowned by a huge antique cornice, it announced a new era in the evolution of the city. Contrary to popular belief, early Renaissance architecture marked the end rather than the beginning of an orderly system of town planning. Medieval ordinances had severely restricted the height, placement, overhangs, and general design of private houses and palaces in order to gain a uniformity that may be appreciated still in the streets of Siena. The new palace style violently disrupted communal controls to substitute an aesthetic of maximum individuality for one of conformity. The Renaissance palace succeeded in so far as it was dramatically unique in its environment.

The economic revolution of the Quattrocento benefited churchmen as well as merchants; like the Florentine families, high ecclesiastics vied with one another for architectural distinction. At Pienza, Pius II Piccolimini actually had his palace built in imitation of the Rucellai Palace in Florence, but he outdid his predecessors in creating an entire city square, complete with Bishop's palace, town hall, and a cathedral too large for the small rural diocese (Pl. 34a). Rome remained a feudal city in the early Renaissance, but Popes and Cardinals from the richer northern centres began at an early date to challenge the ancient emperors with the size and pomp of their palaces. The fashion started in the 1450's when the Venetian Cardinal Barbo, later Pope Paul II, started the Palazzo Venezia; and the greatest challenge to the resources of sixteenth-century competitors was Cardinal Riario's huge palace of the Cancelleria, begun in the 1480's in the neighbourhood later chosen by the Farnese. Shortly after the turn of the century, Pope Julius II made an unsuccessful attempt to build the still larger Palazzo de' Tribunali on Bramante's design, but the project was too ambitious even for his great fortune, and we know it only from drawings and remains of the rusticated ground floor.

The significance of palace design in the social and political struggles of the Renaissance is emphasized in a contemporary description of the planning of the Strozzi palace in Florence during the 1480's, which explains how "Filippo [Strozzi],[1] having richly provided for his heirs, and being eager more for fame than wealth, and having no greater nor more secure means of memorializing his person, being naturally inclined to building, and having no little understanding of it, determined to make a structure that should bring renown to himself and to all his family in Italy and abroad". Filippo's great fear, however, was that he might arouse the envy of his fellow citizens, prompting them into competition. He therefore "astutely feigned to everyone his wish and goal for no other reason than better to pursue it, saying all the while that a comfortable, everyday house was all he needed. But the masons and architects, as is their habit, enlarged all his projects, which pleased Filippo for all his protestations to the contrary". But the palace was to play more than a private role, for "he who was ruling [Lorenzo de' Medici] wished that the city might be exalted by every kind of ornament, since it seemed to him that just as the good and the bad depended upon himself, so the beautiful and the ugly should be attributed to him. Judging that an undertaking of such grandeur and expense could be neither controlled nor exactly envisaged and that it might [if not supervised] not only take credit from him as often happens to merchants, but even lead to his ruin, he therefore began to interfere and to want to see the designs, and having seen and studied

1. "Ricordo di Lorenzo di Filippo di Matteo Strozzi" (*ca.* 1500), in Gaye, *Carteggio* . . ., I, Florence, 1839, p. 354.

them, he requested in addition to other expenses that of rusticated masonry on the exterior. As for Filippo, the more he was urged, the more he feigned irritation, and said that on no account did he want rustication, since it was not proper and too expensive, that he was building for utility, not for pomp, and wished to build many shops around the house for his sons"; in both cases he was grateful to be overruled, with the result that "one may say that Filippo not only succeeded magnificently, but surpassed the magnificence of every other Florentine".

Naturally, these structures were built to be looked at more than to be lived in: the splendours of the Medici palace, for example, except for an elaborate but tiny chapel, were reserved for the street façades and ample courtyard. This gave the architect an opportunity to design regular and stately elevation without much regard for internal arrangements, and at a scale so monumental that the inhabitants had to climb stairs to peer over the window sills. The typical elevation was of three stories, usually varied on the exterior in the treatment of wall surfaces and windows. The lower story was devoted to business affairs, storage, kitchens and other practical requirements; the second story, or *piano nobile*, to reception halls, public ceremonies, and living quarters for the head of the family; the uppermost housed lesser members of the family and more distinguished members of the huge retinue of retainers. Servants were given dark chambers in mezzanines between the floors or under the roof. The rooms were mostly grandiose stages for the performance of the rites of commercial and political leadership, and it is hard to imagine where one slept, washed, or found privacy. Medieval palaces were often far more comfortable, and the most congenial residence of the Quattrocento, the Ducal Palace at Urbino, has a characteristically Gothic air in spite of its Renaissance ornament; there the rooms were designed first and the façades took shape around them.

Renaissance domestic architecture has been criticized frequently in recent times for the fact that an emphasis on the symmetry and regularity of the façade made it impossible to achieve a "functional" interior plan. The criticism is justified so long as we assume that the essential function of a dwelling is invariably to accommodate the day-to-day activities of family life. But where the purpose is to awe and to impress, an imposing façade and court are far more "functional" than a warm and well-lighted bed chamber. Like the *nouveaux-riches* of all ages, the Medici and the Farnese found security in the expression of their power – a security that they would not compromise to gain comfort or privacy. This is perhaps less difficult to understand today than it might have been a generation ago in the heyday of functionalist criticism, since the situation is closely paralleled in contemporary architecture, though it has shifted from the domestic to the commercial stage. In the past decades leading industrialists who were once committed to architectural conservatism have become aware of the propaganda potential of "progressive" monumental architecture and, like the Renaissance dynasts, have called upon the most advanced architects to design huge structures without regard to expense or convenience.

The colossal scale of Quattrocento enterprises was beyond the reach of a private family in the early sixteenth century, though imposing plans and unfinished palaces and villas survive to prove that ambitions, at least, were not hampered by lack of funds. Sangallo's project for the Cardinal's palace of 1517 was an enlarged version of a house type based on antique models which Bramante and Raphael had popularized in the preceding decade. With the expanded plan of 1535, the era of moderation in Roman domestic architecture was brought to a close; the new palace, a magnificent version of the Florentine type, was the first to challenge the Cancelleria and the Vatican in size and elegance.

Vasari, who left Rome shortly after Sangallo's death, in the autumn of 1546, wrote that there appeared to be no hope that the Palace would ever be finished or seem to be the work of one architect (Fig. 10). He erred on both counts; forty years later it was completed so homogeneously that observers were unable to distinguish the work of the four architects who contributed to the design. Michelangelo, though noted for his inability to collaborate with colleagues, showed remarkable skill in harmonizing his own dynamic style with the portions already built by

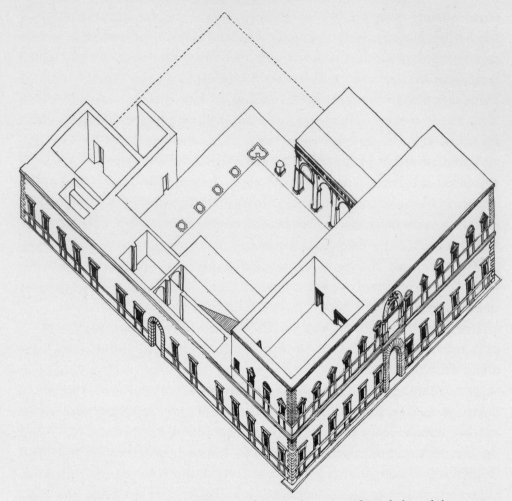

Fig. 10. Reconstruction of the Farnese Palace at the time of Michelangelo's appointment as architect (1546)

Sangallo. No two architects of the mid-sixteenth century were less congenial than these; it is symptomatic of their relationship that at St Peter's Michelangelo erased almost every trace of Sangallo's Basilica. Perhaps he would have done the same at the Farnese palace if it had not been so far advanced when he started, but economy must have forced him to keep what was there and even to make use of members that had been carved but not put in place, such as the uppermost façade windows.

Consequently the palace has a Sangallesque personality throughout. Michelangelo enhanced and gave vigour to this personality, and at essential points rescued it from dull propriety; in doing so he created Sangallo's masterpiece.

Fundamental differences in the style of the two architects are illustrated in the façade (Pl. 39). Sangallo's scheme, influenced by Raphael's Florentine Palazzo Pandolfini, is the antithesis of Michelangelo's organic design, and also represents a revolt against the richly articulated and pictorial Roman façades of Bramante and Raphael. Sangallo treated the façade as a neutral two-dimensional plane of brick upon which the stone frames of windows and doors could be set as sculptural relief. The relief is frankly applied to the surface, and we can imagine it stripped away without damage to the wall. But the frames are not mere ornament; Sangallo made them the basic vertical module of the design, applying them symmetrically about the central axis like links in a chain. This system, which might be called the additive module, supplants earlier principles of proportion in determining the overall form; the palace could be one window longer or two shorter without appearing misshapen, and indeed its early history shows that it was not essential to determine either the height or width before construction started. This thoroughgoing reaction from the geometrical and harmonic planning of the fifteenth century made it easier for Michelangelo and his followers to alter the design of unfinished portions without noticeable breaks.

In this sense, Sangallo's palace again recalls the modern structures whose neutral, two-dimensional curtain-walls are articulated by modular relief elements which determine the scale and which may be repeated at will to the desired height or width. This parallel suggests further that Sangallo's method may be explained partly by the huge scale of mid-sixteenth-century Roman programmes, in which subtleties of design would be lost on the observer. It represented, moreover, a step toward mass production: Sangallo found it unnecessary to draw the Farnese façade as a whole: he had only to sketch the central openings and four different window frames, which the carvers then executed in quantity.

The neutral brick wall could be raised without supervision and far more rapidly and inexpensively than the façades of drafted masonry and pilaster orders of the earlier generation: we might even conclude from the way in which the masonry of the corner quoins and central portal spreads over onto the wall behind that the failure to extend it over the whole surface was due chiefly to the necessity to save time and money.

What differentiates Sangallo's approach from Michelangelo's is the absence of the metaphorical expression of the stresses in the structure. The neutral plane of the wall veils any intimation of the equilibrium – or as Michelangelo would have it, the struggle – of load and support. There is nothing to suggest the ponderous downward pressures of the building, since the horizontal accents overwhelm the vertical, and this is particularly noticeable at the corners, where stone quoins are carved so as to counteract the effect of the only continuous vertical in the elevation. This imparts a calm and ease to the façade unknown in Michelangelo's work, and to complete the effect, Sangallo envisaged a thinner and lighter cornice; one which would be less calculated to suggest compression than Michelangelo's.

A contrast to Michelangelo is implicit in Sangallo's drawings, which are mostly carefully measured studies of relief elements such as window aediculas, rather than of compositions. The plain paper represents the neutral wall surface, and there is rarely an indication of masonry, texture, or light and shadow. An avid student of ancient architecture, Antonio constantly drew in the ruins, concentrating of necessity on the relief details, since the total structure was seldom preserved and nothing but the brick and rubble core remained to indicate how the Romans had originally faced their walls. This experience must have reinforced Sangallo's tendency to visualize the whole in terms of the parts.

At Sangallo's death the façade had been completed to the base of the third story, and possibly some of the uppermost windows were under construction. Michelangelo was immediately put in charge of the design and instructed to complete the façade before continuing with the unfinished side and rear wings. He made only three changes in Sangallo's project, designing a new cornice, raising the height of the third story and altering the form of the central window. The first two were closely related; we know from the complaints of Sangallo's supporters that Michelangelo substantially increased the size of the cornice; in order to avoid an oppressive effect, he increased the distance between the window pediments and the top of the wall to a height equal to that of the cornice itself. The third story now became equal in height to those below.

The massiveness of Michelangelo's cornice (Pl. 40) lends the façade a gravity, in the sense of seriousness as well as weight, that Sangallo's lower and lighter crown would have lacked. The cornice sketched by Sangallo in an early project for the façade contains many of the same elements, and appears similar to a modern eye unpractised in the subtleties of Renaissance design. But important differences are revealed in a contemporary criticism of the existing cornice on Vitruvian grounds preserved in a copy by Michelangelo himself.[2] The anonymous author complains, in effect, that the cornice is far too heavy for the façade, while the membering is too small and confused; that the ornament, moreover, is pure caprice, and mixes elements of the Doric, Ionic and Corinthian Orders. It is precisely these affronts to academic propriety that give Michelangelo's design its unique force. The massiveness of the form is mitigated by an overall pattern of ornaments calculated to produce a flickering arpeggio of highlights within the bold shadows of the overhang. Michelangelo's superiority in the handling of light and texture produces a vitality which alleviates the dry precision of Sangallo's relief.

Michelangelo's desire to give the façade a more sculptural character also prompted the revision of the central window. His changes affected only the portion above the entablature, where Sangallo had spanned the opening with concentric arches resting respectively on the free-standing and on the applied columns and enclosing a small papal coat of arms attached to a central tympanum (Fig. 10). Michelangelo walled over the arches, extended the entablature to form a flat lintel, and filled the void

2. See S. Meller, "Zur Entstehungsgeschichte des Kranzgesims am Pal. Farnese in Rom", *Jhb. d. k.-Pr. Kunstslg.*, XXX, 1909, pp. 1 ff.

with a colossal arms over three metres high (Pl. 39). The lintel accentuated the horizontal façade members and the arms the vertical ones, to substitute an equilibrium of opposing forces for Sangallo's equilibrium of rest. The stability of the complete arch had little appeal for Michelangelo, who never used it on doors or windows, and he must have found the form particularly incongruous in the Farnese façade where it was flanked by two segmental window pediments. But his main purpose in suppressing the arch must have been to gain space for arms of an adequate scale; he was confident, as Sangallo could not have been, of his ability to make a sculptural climax to the façade design more effective than an architectural one.

The great court of the palace (Pls. 43a, 44) is one of the most stately and impressive of the Renaissance; it encloses a perfectly cubic space and, by contrast to the façade, achieves its effect through an equilibrium of tangible horizontals and verticals. Its effectiveness is the paradoxical result of a chaotic and unpremeditated growth; the ground floor arcades were founded by Sangallo for the three-bay court of 1517 and later elevated by the addition of impost-blocks at the base of the arches;[3] when Sangallo died after completing the arcade, Michelangelo adopted his designs for the Ionic columns and arches of the second story, but altered the windows (which may have been designed by Vignola), balustrades and frieze; he then changed the entire upper story (Pl. 45). Further innovations were made by Vignola and della Porta, who ignored Michelangelo's project for the rear elevation (Pl. 43b) to build both the front and rear wings as shown in Pl. 43a; finally, nineteenth-century restorers equalized the four sides by closing off the open galleries of the second story and substituting replicas of the windows on the side wings (Pl. 45).

What is preserved of Sangallo's programme differs from the façade in emphasizing relief rather than surface; the massive members were conceived in three dimensions and convey a sense of the weight of the structure. The Tuscan and Ionic orders, inspired by Bramante's unexecuted Tribunal Palace plan and by the Theatre of Marcellus, are the most

3. Wolfgang Lotz kindly permitted me to make use of these results of his research.

monumental in Renaissance domestic architecture and the most powerful expression of Sangallo's classic style.

Sangallo's distinctive court design was a greater challenge to his successor than the façade, since it promised to emphasize any change in style. Michelangelo ingeniously solved the problem by using the second story as a transitional passage of a kind that composers use in changing key (Pl. 45). Retaining the original Ionic Order, he (or Vignola?) added windows which subtly fuse Sangallo's classicism with a new fantasy, and on the chaste entablature he imposed his characteristically rich frieze of masks and garlands.

Having effected the transition, Michelangelo was unimpeded in the design of the upper story, where the dramatic style of St Peter's is transposed to a domestic scale suitable to an opulent fantasy of detail. After inserting servants' quarters in a mezzanine above the second story (Pl. 43b), Michelangelo had to raise the upper windows and Order correspondingly higher than those below, which justified the abandonment of the arch motif in favour of a trabeated system, as on the façade window. The restricted height and width of the pilaster Order were counterbalanced by the grouping of three pilasters and a consequent multiplication of vertical accents. The cornice (Pl. 46a) is more radical in design than that on the exterior; its elements are bizarre variations on classical themes, and the miniscule ornament dissolves into a pattern of highlights and shadows when seen from below. The fantastic window frames are manifestoes of an anti-classical spirit surely calculated to shock the academicians. Their lateral frames extend below the sills as if they were hanging from the lions' heads like bell-cords; and the pediments, with their extraordinary recessed tympana, are detached from their supports and lose their structural rationale. Again, Michelangelo's consciousness of the purely conventional character of the classical aedicula prompted him to satirize the convention. Ironically, his leaps of fancy were to become conventions for early Baroque architects.

It is not merely a talent for invention that distinguishes Michelangelo's design from Sangallo's, but an ability to make every surface and detail essential to the vitality of the total effect. The upper story is without those mechanically executed neutral areas such as the arch spandrels that appear in Sangallo's elevations. Moreover, Sangallo lacked the sensitivity to texture that Vasari noticed in Michelangelo's portion of the court and used to illustrate the virtues of Travertine as a building material.[4] Although Travertine was used by both architects, Michelangelo evoked from it a warmer and more rugged texture, while achieving, as Vasari noted, the sharp precision typical of marble carving.

Michelangelo's later Florentine projects were distinguished by a dynamic treatment of spatial sequences that impelled the observer along predetermined axes. This kinetic factor is absent from the Farnese palace as envisaged by Sangallo and as completed in the later sixteenth century; but it was an essential element of Michelangelo's original project. Evidence for his rejected scheme is preserved in engravings of 1549 and 1560 (Pls. 41 and 43b), and in the closing paragraph of Vasari's account of the palace (VII, p. 224):

In that year [1545–1546] there was found in the Antonine [Caracalla] Baths a marble seven *braccia* square [over 4 m.] on which the ancients had carved Hercules on a hill holding the bull by the horns, with another figure aiding him and around the hill various shepherds, nymphs and other animals . . . and Michelangelo advised that it be transported into the second [garden] court and restored so that it might spout water, which pleased everyone. For this purpose the work has been in the process of restoration by the Farnese family until now [1568]. Michelangelo then directed that a bridge should be built in line (with the fountain), crossing the Tiber River so that one might go from the palace into Trastevere, where there was another Farnese garden and palace [adjacent to the Villa Farnesina], with the intention that from a position at the main portal of the palace toward the Campo di Fiori one might see at a glance the court, the fountain, the via Giulia, the bridge, and the beauties of the other garden terminating at the other portal giving onto the Strada di Trastevere.

This grandiose concept would have transformed the introspective palace block into a great open vista embracing architecture, sculpture, greenery and water; the static quality of the court would have become dynamic by the introduction of a dramatic axis of vision and communication.

4. Vasari, I, p. 123.

The engraving of 1560 (Pl. 43b) illustrates the architectural components of the new design, but the engraver, who probably knew only
Michelangelo's loggia model of 1549, was unaware of the total plan,
and installed behind the palace a fictitious panorama with ruins after the
fashion of northern landscape painters. Even without the monumental
fountain, and the Tiber bridge and gardens, the engraving conveys an
impression of flow that would have drawn visitors through the court
toward distant goals. From ground level the open loggia of the second
story gives a glimpse of the sky and lessens the great weight of the building, but its chief purpose was to provide a *belvedere* on the *piano nobile* for
the delight of the inhabitants. Though there are only three open bays on
the court side, there are five toward the rear, so that the distant vista might
be had from any point along the second-story galleries around the court.

The grandeur and uniqueness of Michelangelo's plan must have been
appreciated, but abandoned for practical reasons; by reducing the rear
of the court to the depth of one bay, it sacrificed an important portion
of the private living quarters apparently indispensable to the accommodation of the Farnese family.

Michelangelo cannot have intended to reduce the entire rear wing to
the depth indicated in Pl. 43b: this would have destroyed the apartments
started by Sangallo in the right rear corner (Fig. 10) and would have disrupted the symmetry of the side façades by eliminating the four bays
nearest the river. It is likely that to the right and left of the rear loggias
the palace was to extend back to the line of Sangallo's garden front. The
resulting ⊔-shaped rear façade with open loggias at the base revived the
favoured form for the suburban villa of the Roman Renaissance. A distinguished and particularly relevant example was the Villa Farnesina,
which stood directly across the river near the goal of Michelangelo's perspective. The aptness of the decision to complement the sombre urban
façade with a more pastoral one facing the garden must have delighted
Michelangelo's contemporaries.

The façade engraving of 1549 (Pl. 41) illustrates a project for the piazza
in front of the Palace which is too ingenious to be explained away as a

convention of the engraver.[5] It is improbable that Michelangelo would have developed an embracing scheme for the garden area behind the palace without organizing the urban setting in front of it. The planning of an ample piazza within the crowded medieval quarter was essential if the façade was to gain its full effectiveness, and the problem must have been discussed just at the moment when the façade was completed and the engraving was published. The pavement of the piazza as represented in the engraving is subdivided by bands into squares of a kind dear to the perspective painters of the early Renaissance (Pl. 34a). Each square corresponds to the width of one bay of the façade, so that an observer in the piazza would find underfoot a measure of the scale of the palace, thus giving to the façade design a third dimension (significantly, the piazza pavement extends along the streets on either side of the palace). Assuming that Michelangelo's piazza was roughly of the same form as the existing one, its principal entrance would have been directly opposite the portal along a short and narrow street connecting it to the medieval market place – called the Campo de' Fiori. For an observer entering the piazza along this street the bands in the pavement leading to the façade would act as orthogonals in a perspective construction, the vanishing point of which would lie beneath the central arch at the rear of the court; the engraver accordingly took special care to demonstrate that the central subdivision of the piazza continued the perspective of the entrance vestibule. By this device the first distant glimpse of the façade would carry with it an invitation to follow the pre-ordained path through the palace to the goal beyond the Tiber.

So, in spite of its apparent perfection, the Farnese Palace must be added to the long list of Michelangelo's unfinished works; though the portions that he completed are vigorous and effective, the unexecuted planning scheme is a more imposing mark of his genius, a giant stride – fully realized in the Campidoglio and Porta Pia – toward an extension of the confines of architecture beyond the limits of the static and self-sufficient structure.

5. Wolfgang Lotz brought this to my attention.

CHAPTER VIII

The Basilica of St Peter

ALMOST every major architect in sixteenth-century Rome had a hand in designing the Basilica of St Peter; each in succession changed his predecessor's scheme, yet the final product is a cohesive whole, formed more by the genius of the Italian Renaissance than by the imagination of any individual. The evolution of the Basilica shows the degree to which Michelangelo's image of buildings as organisms pervaded the architecture of his time. Although Bramante's successors were inspired by the originality and majesty of his design, each felt free to feed the organism new ideas and to cast off obsolete ones (Fig. 11). The oscillation between central and longitudinal plans apparent even in Bramante's drawings continued throughout the century and was halted only with the construction of the nave one hundred years after the foundation. Consistency was assured by the huge scale of the structure; architects were compelled to accept and to accumulate the portions built by their predecessors, and once Bramante had raised the crossing piers, no subsequent innovation could be wholly independent.

Medieval monuments the size of which necessitated comparably long periods of construction were much less cohesive in style. The large French cathedrals grew by the accretion of successive units, each of which reveals the fashion of its time; at Paris and Laon, the bays at the end of the nave differ from the rest, and at Chartres the two façade towers are entirely dissimilar. Even in the Renaissance, great châteaux such as Blois, Fontainebleau and the Louvre became museums of architectural history in which each wing or court was built as a pure example of the style of its period.

This extreme differentiation is the manifestation of a peculiarly French logic, but it is found in Italy to a lesser degree. At the Ducal

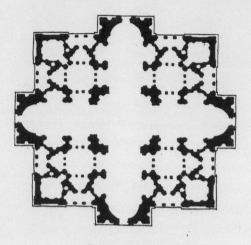

a. Bramante, 1506.

b. Bramante-Peruzzi, before 1513

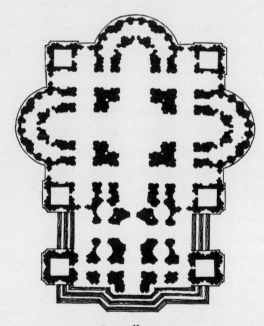

c. Sangallo, 1539.

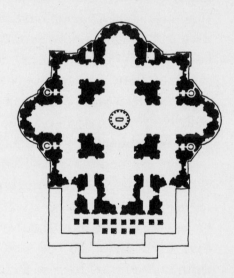

d. Michelangelo, 1546–1564.

Fig. 11. Plans for St Peter's

Palaces in Venice and Urbino, Gothic portions were retained and completed in their original form, while new construction was initiated in Renaissance style. The Certosa of Pavia remained consistent until, in the 1490's, a façade of an entirely different design was added to complete the church; and at the Cathedral of Florence, Brunelleschi retained the basic scheme of the fourteenth-century dome project, but added a lantern and aediculas inspired by ancient architecture. As long as Renaissance architects were forced to continue medieval structures, inconsistencies were inevitable. Only buildings started in the Quattrocento could be entirely harmonious in style, but they posed another problem so vexing that, whenever their construction extended over a long period, they often remained, like the palaces and churches of Brunelleschi and Alberti, unfinished. The mathematical principles of Quattrocento design established an interdependence among elements in the plan and elevation that encouraged consistency but discouraged flexibility. The design of a structure begun in accordance with a modular system of proportions could not be changed much, and the architects who succeeded Brunelleschi at San Lorenzo (Fig. 3) and at Santo Spirito had to adhere anonymously to his style. This became more difficult as time passed and as the style became old-fashioned, so that when Michelangelo was called to design the New Sacristy and façade of San Lorenzo he could not avoid innovations that differed radically in character from Brunelleschi's forms.

The style of the early sixteenth century was less restricting to the extent that it was less geometrical; moreover, a new attitude was encouraged by professional and technological changes. While most Florentine Quattrocento buildings were small in scale and could be designed and supervised by one architect, the grandiose schemes of the following century turned the *fabbrica* into a community in which elder architects were partners and younger ones students. Because Raphael, Peruzzi, and Sangallo had worked with Bramante at St Peter's and the Vatican Palace, and because Sangallo assisted Raphael at the Villa Madama, there was no break in continuity when the masters died. Patrons awarded commissions on the basis of competitions and sometimes – as in the project for the San Lorenzo façade – attempted to enforce collaboration. By the mid-century it was possible for Julius III to assign the relatively modest programme for the Villa Giulia to a team of three architects: Vignola, Ammanati and Vasari, with Michelangelo as a consultant. In architecture as in the political structure of the Renaissance state, size promoted collaboration, centralization and continuity, and kept designers as well as princes from disrupting the orderly evolution of the institutions they directed.

Structural factors, above all, secured the organic growth of St Peter's. Bramante, in visualizing the Basilica as an expansion of spatial volumes and masses about a vast central area, made the crossing the heart of a cellular structure (Fig. 11a). Every element in his design depended for its stability upon the four central piers, and the dome, in turn, depended on the buttressing powers of the four arms. So the construction had to proceed uniformly outward from the core toward the periphery. This radial evolution differed radically from the chain-like process demanded by the bay-system of Gothic structures, in which spatial frames, each depending on neighbouring frames for stability, had to be raised in sequences beginning at the apse, at the façade, or any terminal point in the plan.

Though the Gothic system survived into the Renaissance, the autonomy of the single bay often gave way to what might be called a box system, in which cubic or cylindrical volumes were applied to a core; even the central-plan buildings of the Quattrocento give the impression of having been built up by the addition of autonomous units. The uniqueness of Bramante's St Peter's project – visible in the plan (Fig. 11a) to a greater degree than in the less radical elevation (Pl. 51a) – was in the interdependence of the core and its arms. A study of the malleable wall masses of ancient Roman architecture must have helped Bramante to break down the confines of the Quattrocento box, but it was the Byzantines, not the Romans, who had found techniques for integrating domed and longitudinal volumes.

Consciously or not, Bramante revived the structural principles of Hagia Sofia in Constantinople, where all spaces had been generated outward from a domed core. Surviving drawings from Bramante's workshop indicate that the four crossing piers were raised before the final form of the arms had been determined, and for decades after his death each of his successors in turn was free to clothe his skeleton in a new skin. Sixteenth-century views of the Basilica (Pls. 52a-b, 53a) show how its radial evolution gave Michelangelo a maximum of freedom in designing the exterior façades.

The interior volumes, however, were firmly fixed at the time of Sangallo's death in 1546: one arm had been completed entirely, another partially, so that the remaining arms could not be changed; the vaults that form aisles around the crossing, between the outer buttressing piers and the crossing piers, had been built, too. Even when Michelangelo got leave to lop off the outer rings of the hemicycles that terminated all but the façade arms, he was constrained to keep the inner ring, and could reform only its exterior plan (Fig. 12). The limitations here were greater even than those imposed on the design of the Medici Chapel: the interior could be influenced only by the design of the central dome, the four domed areas at the corners, and the hemispherical vaulting at the ends of the arms. Michelangelo was left in undisputed command solely of the lighting, since these restrictions did not limit the formation of the exterior surfaces. But after his death in 1564, most of his plans for the interior were altered: della Porta redesigned the central dome and those of the four corner chapels, so that all we can see of Michelangelo on the interior of St Peter's is the main drum and the vaulting of the terminal hemicycles; but the original character of both is entirely changed by an overlay of seventeenth-century ornament and veneers.

The extent to which Michelangelo was able to impose his personal style upon St Peter's without essentially altering the interior is astonishing. We can see in comparing his plan to Sangallo's (Figs. 11, 12) that a few strokes of the pen were sufficient to change a complex and confused form into a simple and cohesively organized unit. Sangallo, in taking from Bramante the scheme of a major cross echoed in four lesser crosses at the corners, had expanded the latter to constitute isolated pockets of

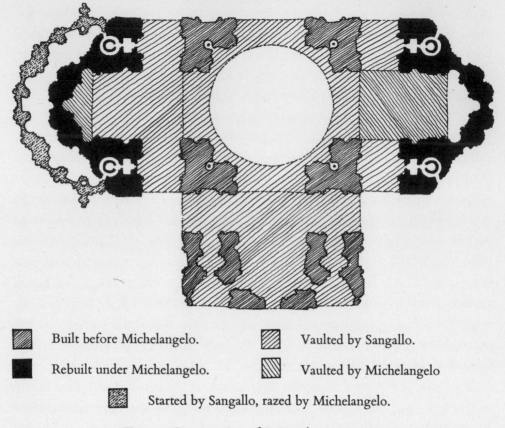

Built before Michelangelo.   Vaulted by Sangallo.

Rebuilt under Michelangelo.   Vaulted by Michelangelo

Started by Sangallo, razed by Michelangelo.

Fig. 12. Construction of St Peter's, 1506–1564.

space no longer knit into the fabric of the crossing; similarly, his semi-circular ambulatories became independent corridors – superfluous successions of volumes and Orders which forced him into absurd devices for lighting the main arms. (Pl. 51c, far right). Michelangelo, by merely walling off the entrances to each of Sangallo's disconnected spaces, made one church out of many; he surpassed the clarity that he admired in Bramante's plan in substituting for the concept of major and minor crosses a more unified one of an integrated cross-and-square, so that all circulation within the Basilica should bring the visitor back to its core. The solution was strikingly simple, and far more economical than any proposed before: it even seems obvious, once it is familiar; but in a generation distinguished for great architects, it took one trained as a sculptor to discover a form that would express the organic unity of the structure.

Unity was Michelangelo's contribution to St Peter's; he transformed the interior into a continuum of space, the exterior into a cohesive body. In the exterior massing he was restricted less by earlier construction, since his predecessors had not arrived at the outer periphery. Here again, the problem was to find a form which would integrate two autonomous motifs in the plan – the cross and the square – and again it was solved with the simplest and most economical means (Fig. 11). With a minimum of construction the secondary buttressing piers were transformed to serve entirely new practical and expressive functions. Inside, the passages which Sangallo had cut through the piers were ingeniously converted into stairwells; outside, the diagonal faces of the piers bound the hemicycles of the cross to the angles of the square in such a way that the two shapes were fused without losing their distinctness. The solution was technically impeccable; it changed the form of the piers without affecting their structural function and it efficiently solved the problem of lighting the stairwells. Aesthetically, it was an inspired breach of classical dogma. In plan, the piers were formed essentially as mirror-images of the crossing-piers. But unlike the crossing-piers, their diagonal outer faces do not form a forty-five degree angle; they were drawn on the principle that a straight line is the shortest distance between two points, without regard for the angle of incidence, and in violation of Renaissance laws of geometry and proportion. Michelangelo interpreted these diagonals as building elements – as muscles, not the limits of a regular polygon. Simple as the form seems to a modern eye, it represents – even more than the oval and trapezoid of the Campidoglio – a bold and difficult revolt against the immemorial sovereignty of rational geometric figures in architecture.

Comparison with Sangallo's plan reveals the skill with which Michelangelo resolved the continuing conflict between the centralized and longitudinal schemes (Fig. 11). Sangallo had artificially appended a nave and façade onto one arm, forming, in effect, another church. Michel-angelo differentiated the façade arm just enough to give the Basilica a major axis without prejudicing the centrality of the interior. The Pantheon-like columnar porch emphasized the entrance axis, yet per-mitted the pilaster system of the side and rear elevations to continue across the façade without interruption. Moreover, the pediment carried over the forward row of columns was low enough to leave an unimpeded view of the dome from the piazza (a virtue lacking both in Sangallo's and in Maderno's designs); its triangular form would have directed the eye toward the dome, while its proportions and forward projection would have announced the scale and significance of the nave beyond.

The façade was to be a screen before the undulating mass of the Basilica; it is astonishing how much Michelangelo managed to alter Bramante's formulation of the character of this mass (Pls. 50, 51a, 60). Bramante saw the exterior as a society of distinct geometrical forms bound together by proportion, Michelangelo as a single body so cohe-sively organized that the differing functions and structural features of the interior plan barely can be discerned. The structural technique – a revival of the heavy, plastic wall-masses of Roman and Byzantine archi-tecture – permitted Michelangelo to treat the body of the Basilica as a sculptural block, and left him free in the choice of surface articulation; the exterior Orders were to be exclusively expressive. Perhaps this is why the colossal pilasters and the strips behind them were distinguished so clearly from the wall surfaces (Pls. 63, 64): they carry a projecting segment of the entablature so that the whole decorative apparatus appears as a detachable overlay (at the Capitol, where similar pilasters have an essential structural function, they support an unbroken entablature). Fenestration was the sole limiting factor: it dictated a tripartite division of the hemicycle elevations and inspired the rhythmical sequence of broad and narrow bays separated by pilasters. The dynamic vertical accents of the pilasters, reinforced by the strips behind them, by the projections in the entablatures, and by the multiplication of shadows that results from compressing two pilasters into one that bends around each angle, entirely overwhelms the discontinuous horizontals of the window and niche frames. The dominance of verticals makes the Basilica appear to grow upward rather than to weigh ponderously on the ground; it suggests an aspiration comparable only to the effects of Gothic architecture, and anticipates a climax in the equally Gothic buttresses and ribs of the dome.

Turning again to Bramante's elevation (Pl. 51a) we find an entirely opposing effect; horizontals dominate in spite of high campanili, and the weight of the structure is expressed by the accumulation of masses toward the earth, beginning with the low ribless dome and its stepped base, which seems to settle into the drum. Bramante, who developed the plan from the crossing outward, must have designed the elevation from the dome downward. For him, the great central volume was the cause of the design; for Michelangelo it was the result. Such a distinction is warranted by the peculiar chronology of Michelangelo's studies for the construction; the design was not wholly fixed at the start, but grew as the builders advanced upwards from the foundations. At the beginning, only the lower portions were determined definitively: probably the model of 1546/1547 had a bare attic, and no façade, roof or domes. When the existing attic was built in 1557, it was left without an exterior facing, with the intention of adjusting its design to future decisions on the dome. In the same year the drum was begun, before the construction of a dome model in 1558–1561 (Pl. 57b). Between 1561 and Michelangelo's death in 1564, the dome was again revised, the attic was designed, and the façade project, which was dependent on the definition of the attic, was tentatively sketched in plan. This does not mean that Michelangelo ignored the dome until the end: his earliest studies for it (Pls. 54, 55a) pre-date the model of the lower portions. But these studies constantly evolved as Michelangelo watched the walls rise and saw the effects of his vigorous verticals in full scale. We can imagine that the definitive design of 1546 for the paired colossal pilasters was accompanied by a decision to use external ribs on the dome and paired columns on the buttresses. If Michelangelo ever considered retaining Bramante's smooth, stepped hemisphere, he would have abandoned the thought before generating a dynamic upward thrust in the lower part of the building. But only the ribs and buttresses survived to the end; the design of the drum and the lantern changed, and above all, the profile of the dome, which developed from the elevated curve of Plate 54 to the hemisphere of Plates 60 and 61.

The progressive lowering of the dome is a key to the understanding of Michelangelo's purpose, yet modern critics were at first reluctant to accept it as a fact. A progression from the spherical dome of the engravings (Pls. 60 and 61) to the raised profile of Pl. 54 (now recognized as an early study) to the dome executed by della Porta (Pl. 63) seemed natural; moreover, it is admirably suited to the popular Wölfflinian theory of a somehow preordained and systematic evolution from classic Renaissance to dynamic Baroque forms. The irrelevance of these presuppositions is sufficiently proven by the elevated profile proposed by the most "classic" of early Cinquecento architects, Antonio Sangallo (Pl. 51c) and by the low dome of Michelangelo's San Giovanni de' Fiorentini (Pls. 70b, 71a-b), which is contemporary to the St Peter's dome model.

Shortly after determining the insistent verticals of his elevation, Michelangelo wrote to Florence for measurements of the Cathedral lantern. The Florentine cupola had exerted a strong influence upon him from the start; he took from it the double-shell construction, the raised profile and octagonal lantern of Pl. 54, the rib construction and the drum *oculi* of Pl. 55a. The Cathedral cupola was the only available prototype of scale comparable to St Peter's, and its medieval rib construction gave a secure and sufficiently calculable means of controlling great loads. The Gothic profile was congenial to the vertical thrust of the colossal Order, which could not have been resolved in a sunken or smooth dome of Bramante's type. Bramante's dome (Pl. 51a), with its solid mass of masonry, and without external buttressing, would have been excessively difficult – perhaps impossible – to build over such a span. In his last work, the Torre Borgia cupola of 1513 (Pl. 51b), Bramante embraced the structural and expressive potentialities of the Gothic rib: this design probably suggested to Michelangelo the advantages of increasing the eight ribs of the Florentine dome to sixteen, as a means of avoiding an over-emphasis on planes.

Bramante's dramatic Torre Borgia lantern had the effect of resolving the forces of the converging ribs; Michelangelo also found the lantern to be the key to his design: before and after writing to Florence in 1547 he was preoccupied with its form and proportion more than with the dome profile (Pls. 54 – with five lantern-elevations and two plans – 55a-b); on completion of the dome model in 1561 he was still uncertain of the lantern scheme, and later even Vasari was confused about the final design. Since the accents of the paired colossal pilasters on the body of the Basilica were to be channelled into the paired drum columns and from there into the dome ribs, the lantern became the climax and resolution of the dynamics of the entire composition. The letter and the drawings show that Michelangelo cared less about the dome profile than about the ratio in height between the dome and the lantern; his choice was between an elevated dome with a low lantern and a hemispherical dome with a high lantern.

The final solution recorded by Dupérac (Pls. 60, 61) shows the lantern raised on a high podium to compensate for the lowering of the dome, so that the overall height of the Basilica would not have been much less than in the early designs. Moreover the diminution in the width of the dome ribs toward the top would have preserved by perspective illusion the original effect of the elevated profile. The hemispherical profile represents not so much a rejection of Gothic in favour of classic prototypes as an internal crisis in Michelangelo's style. In the space of twelve-to-fourteen years between the design of the lower order and the construction of the dome model, he had turned from the active tensions of the Campidoglio project and the frescoes of the Cappella Paolina to the subjective gravity of San Giovanni dei Fiorentini and the late Passion drawings. The state of mind that produced the reserve and calm horizontality of the San Giovanni model (1559–1560) cannot have been wholly congenial to the uninhibited verticality of the initial St Peter's designs (1546): the hemispherical dome (1558–1561) approaches the mood of San

Giovanni without denying the forces generated in the body of the Basi-lica; the steps in the ribs and the rings of dormer windows reinforce the new sedative element. We know from Dosio's drawings that Michel-angelo thought at one point of combining the low dome and low lantern, but he must have found through experiments on the model that this would over-emphasize the shift in style; the early spirit had to be resolved in the lantern.

After completing the dome model, Michelangelo in his last years turned to the design of the attic, where he achieved the same balance of force and repose. He may have made no decisive designs before this time since the model was built without an attic facing (Pls. 58a, 59a), but the construction of the apertures implies that he had intended to give the window frames a vertical axis. In the revised design, the apertures were covered by horizontal frames which help to inhibit the vertical surge. The new accent was to have been reinforced by a continuous balustrade (Pl. 58b).

The restraint of vertical forces in the final project did not result in the kind of tensions found at the Campidoglio, but in equilibrium gained without loss of vigour. The co-existence of static and dynamic forms – a product of the profound introspection of Michelangelo's late years – was too subtle to be understood by contemporaries. In executing the existing dome, della Porta could not rise to the challenge of Michel-angelo's testament; in his details he greatly reduced its rigour by eliminat-ing the distinctions between horizontal-circumferential accents and vertical-radial ones. His rich decoration obscured and softened the clarity of Michelangelo's transitions, and disconnected the bones of the struc-ture. By thinning the ribs and their supports, and eliminating their perspective diminution, by elevating the dome profiles and lowering the lantern, della Porta summoned the more familiar image of the Florentine dome. But the aspiring effect of della Porta's dome would have been more powerfully achieved in Michelangelo's final solution, where the climax at the lantern is amplified by the contrasting calm of the dome. We cannot tell how Michelangelo's minor domes would have influenced the final solution: though he probably planned them, he apparently left no designs; those on the engravings seem to be by Vignola, while the existing ones were built from della Porta's design.

Michelangelo's dome fused the forms of antiquity and the Middle Ages in a way incomprehensible to della Porta, who had to return to the more consistent solution of the early studies, and to many modern critics, who failed to see the logic behind the evolution of the design. But for all its deficiencies, della Porta's dome preserved the essential potency of the original concept, and gave the architects of the Baroque one of their most compelling sources of inspiration.

While Michelangelo absorbed certain medieval forms into the predominantly Roman character of Bramante's Basilica, the final design was so thoroughly transformed by the individuality of his own style that it no longer symbolized its traditional roots. It was a statement so unique and so powerful that it became itself a symbol for future centuries. The form of the dome was to become the receptacle for the expression of civic as well as religious ideals; even in Protestant countries where its association with the centre of Catholicism might have discouraged emulation, the functions of local and national government are carried on under the cover of replicas of Michelangelo's dome.

Twenty-five years after Michelangelo's death, his design for St Peter's as emended by della Porta was represented on a fresco in the Vatican library (Pl. 58b). The Basilica appears in the centre of a huge square surrounded by porticoes designed in the style of Serlio, the construction of which would have required the removal of the Vatican Palace. None of the architects of St Peter's could have hoped to demolish the palace, but the fresco represents more than a painter's fantasy; it demonstrates a great sensitivity to the spirit of the design. The artist returned to a fifteenth-century formula typified in Perugino's *Delivery of the Keys* in the Sistine Chapel, in which a monumental central-plan structure appears in the centre and to the rear of a vast piazza with a pavement marked off into squares. Perugino and his latter-day heirs illustrate the principles of Leone Battista Alberti, who demanded that the principal "temple" of the city should be centralized in plan, that it should be isolated in the centre of an ample square, and that it should be raised on a podium to elevate it from worldly things. Alberti would have approved of Michelangelo's pedimented entrance-porch which, in fact, he had used himself in his Mantuan churches.

In all of the centralized projects for St Peter's the impact of the form would have been severely compromised by the congestion of the surroundings. The observer would have been frustrated by the fact that while the form of the Basilica invited him to circulate freely around it, the buildings on either side and the slope of the Vatican hill barred the way. Circulation was invited much more by Michelangelo's design (Pl. 50) than by Bramante's, where block-like forms established finite, self-sufficient planes. Michelangelo, constrained by the portions already built to retain the ideals of the Quattrocento, but unwilling to compromise the kinetic force of his own style, brought into focus the paradox between the early Renaissance aesthetic of stability and centrality and the late Renaissance aesthetic – in the foundation of which he played a dominant role – of movement, axis, and climax. No wholly successful solution to this paradox was possible; one alternative is represented in the fresco; another – prompted by the symbolism and liturgy as well as by the taste of the Counter-Reformation – in the existing Basilica, where centrality was destroyed and the effect of the dome obscured by the extension of the nave.

CHAPTER IX

San Giovanni de' Fiorentini
The Sforza Chapel

WHEN Michelangelo prepared preliminary sketches for San Giovanni de' Fiorentini in 1559 to show to the commissioners of the Florentine colony in Rome, he returned to the central-plan proposal that his predecessor Sangallo had considered and later abandoned (Pl. 66a). But the plans have nothing else in common. Sangallo had reverted to a fifteenth-century concept: a domed circular central area with radiating chapels and entrances, its simple uniformity broken only by an unintegrated façade and by a choir somewhat larger than the chapels but disguised to appear the same size. For the Quattrocento, a major aim in central planning had been to retain the regularity of a simple geometric figure; where that figure was a circle or a polygon, the favoured method was to construct all major lines radially from the central point, so the observer would be drawn to the centre from which he was intended to contemplate with equanimity the stabilizing uniformity of his surroundings.[1]

At first glance, Michelangelo's studies for San Giovanni appear to be motivated by this geometric spirit too. In his first drawing (Pl. 66b) a square intersects a circle and the central altar is an octagon; in the second (Pl. 67) the octagon dominates, while in the final study (Pl. 68) the circle reappears with a square central altar podium and oval chapels. But the fact that none of these figures is consistent throughout the series indicates that Michelangelo felt no commitment to a particular geometrical shape.

1. On the Renaissance central-plan tradition and its philosophical overtones, see, R. Wittkower, *Architectural Principles in the Age of Humanism*, London, 1949, pp. 1–28.

Furthermore, the purity of each figure is violated in some way by another. The consistent spirit throughout the series is rather a fascination with *axes*; in all the studies they are sketched first and the building takes shape around them. There are two patterns of cross axes, one a + which accents the entrances and is assigned to circulation, the other a × which accents the chapels and is assigned to liturgy. In the first plan, the former dominates; in the second, including the auxiliary sketches, the latter, while in the last drawing they are equalized.

An understanding of the contrast between a plan generated from axes and one formed from regular geometric shapes is of basic importance in evaluating Michelangelo's aim. One principle implies directed movement; the other, stability. Furthermore, if the axial principle is complicated by the superposition of two pairs of cross-axes, dynamic tensions are established; the suggested movements are in conflict.

While it would be possible to emphasize axes without abandoning a truly radial construction, Michelangelo persistently sought to avoid focusing on a central point. He was so little concerned with the radial concept of his predecessors (Pl. 66a) that in his first drawing (Pl. 66b), those lines (from the circle of columns to the circular wall) that should be radial are not, while the choice of an octagonal altar tabernacle of *unequal* sides makes a consistent radial construction impossible. In the second study (Pl. 67) nothing is constructed from the centre; the pier-system is emphatically anti-radial. The same is true of the last drawing (Pl. 68) though the heavily-inked altar podium obscures the fact that the principal structural lines cross away from the centre to form a perfect octagon about it. In establishing a focus in an area *about* the centre rather than upon a point *at* the centre, Michelangelo again displays his ability to think in three-dimensional terms. His axes are not lines, but channels of space that converge in an area rather than at a point; and this is the area chosen for the altar in all but one of the studies. Michelangelo's decision to distinguish the circulation + from the chapel × conforms with his requirement (p. 1. above) that "when a plan has diverse parts, all those that are of one kind and quality must be adorned in the same way and in the same style . . . But when the plan is entirely changed in form, it is . . . necessary to entirely change the adornments, and likewise their corresponding portions". The two crosses offered the opportunity Michelangelo always sought to create a tension between equal and opposing forces. But evidence of a gradual relaxation of tension can be found in the revisions required to transform the drawings into a sound and usable structure. A more restrained, less physical solution emerges that reflects the religious intensity of the artist's late years.

Michelangelo's last drawing (Pl. 68), unlike the earlier two (Pls. 66b, 67), reveals his awareness of the problem of supporting a dome; heavy masses gather to resist thrust. But the inner circle of paired columns is mystifying; the columns are far too fragile to support a drum or even the groin vault planned behind them, though a pair of sketches is preserved that toys with the problem.[2] But to thicken them sufficiently would have overcrowded the central area, already too small for convenience. Accordingly, the first step in preparing a definitive design was to draw the columns back against the buttressing piers, changing them in the process to pure decoration, and allowing the piers to carry all the weight. The plan copied by Vannocci (Pl. 69b) is a record of this initial sacrifice to statics; it results in a diminution of axial tension, but the central altar, which in two of the earlier drawings is spiritually the generator of that tension, is still retained. In the succeeding stage the central altar is abandoned, too. The removal of the altar to the chapel opposite the entrance had already been proposed in the second of the preparatory drawings (Pl. 67); but there the diagonal axes were so vigorously emphasized that it was almost hidden: the focus remained in the central area. This illustrates the major problem of the centralized church in the Renaissance: while architects wanted a central altar for the sake of formal consistency, the clergy demanded that it be placed on the periphery where it would stand free of the congregation and be simpler to service. Michelangelo discovered that in acceding to liturgical tradition it was not enough merely to move the altar; he had to give the entrance-to-altar

2. Casa Buonarroti, No. 36A; D. 80; F. 223.

axis special emphasis, which further compromised the theme of an unresolved conflict of axes.

The first model (Pl. 70b) seems to be an initial response to the changed conditions: the entrance portico is elaborated and the side entrances are suppressed, so that the effect of centrality is sacrificed. The Calcagni plan for the engraved model (Pl. 69a) must be later, because it represents a subtler solution, restoring the centrality of the drawings without requiring a central altar. Now the axial emphasis is on the +, for the × axes of the chapels are subdued by narrowing the chapel entrances (the classicist Regnard overlooked this in engraving the plan). The solution is liturgically defensible and even suggests concern for symbolizing the Cross.

In the final model (Pl. 71a), the resolution of conflict in the central area is accompanied by a new emphasis on the axial theme in the peripheral entrance ways and chapels. The former are expanded – for no functional reason – to become ample rectangular vestibules which have their own axes, counter to those of the principal +, while the chapels are now elliptical so that they, too, have counter-axes. In Calcagni's drawing (Pl. 69a) the focus of the small chapel-altars is not at the centre; instead, each pair of flanking altars is oriented toward the two foci from which the ellipse is constructed. In this astonishingly un-Renaissance solution, the chapel plan fully anticipates Bernini's scheme for San Andrea al Quirinale, an archetypal Baroque church.[3]

The many alterations in plan between the last of the preparatory sketches (Pl. 68) and the model did not compromise the emphatically sculptural quality of the initial conception. In the sketch, Michelangelo thought of the exterior as a great cubic block the four faces of which were defined by the four rectilinear porticoes, while the chapels were carved out of the corners. It is a unique quality of Michelangelo's sculpture that a sense of the outer surfaces of the original block is preserved in the finished work, because he cut back from the foremost plane in a sequence

3. Wolfgang Lotz (Die ovalen Kirchenräume des Cinquecento, *Römische Jhb.*, VII, 1955, pp. 20 ff., Fig. 5) has found a prototype for the chapel design in a study for San Giovanni by Baldassare Peruzzi.

of planes rather than working continually around the block. The method produced a certain frontality in all of his sculptures, and the same effect is achieved in San Giovanni where, for the first time in the Renaissance, we find a circular plan that is entirely successful on the exterior. Earlier architects were caught in a dilemma: if their exteriors were circular, it was impossible to sufficiently differentiate their entrance façades; if they designed a monumental entrance façade, the effect of circularity was lost. Here the problem is solved, because for a great sculptor there is no necessary conflict between plane and modelling.

It is characteristic of Michelangelo's sculptural approach that in the evolution from sketch to model the major changes were made on the interior, while the exterior remained nearly the same. The exterior massing, light effects and rhythms could be studied in the rough clay model, as in a terra-cotta sketch for statuary; but the interior design involved the exclusively architectural problem of enclosed space. Michelangelo visualized the interior entirely in terms of modelling (Pl. 68). The sole plane surface in his plan is in the chapel opposite the entrance, because only there is the plan of the exterior cube revealed. A reflection of the generating cube is preserved, however, in the central altar podium, which is not modelled because it has no structural function.

As the plan developed, the dynamic modelling was subdued (Pl. 69a): niches were reduced in size or eliminated, to be replaced by planes in the vestibules and passage ways. The changes primarily affected the periphery; the central area retained much of its plasticity. To the extent that the reduced modelling represented Michelangelo's intentions and not the academic hands of Calcagni and the engravers, it can be seen as consistent with the reduced conflict of axes and with the restful understatement of the exterior. Even in the short period of gestation between the sketches and the model, Michelangelo's style appears to have departed from the dramatic tension and aspiration of his earlier work.

For the first time, Michelangelo proposes to allow the great mass-forms to speak for themselves rather than placing emphasis on articulating members. On the exterior there are no lantern-colonettes or volutes, no dome ribs, no buttressing or even membering on the drum (Pl. 71). Inside, there is not even a cornice to separate dome from drum; outside, the pilaster order is raised on a high podium to lighten it. The minimizing of vertical and horizontal incidents reinforces the unity of the design, as is especially notable in the exterior entablature and attic of the lower story: uninterrupted by projections of any sort, they bind together the powerful rectilinear and curvilinear bodies of the porticoes and chapels. But more remarkable is the unity achieved by eliminating any conflict of effect between the façades and the dome: the latter remains in full view, uninhibited by any of the habitual Renaissance façade solutions – pediments, balconies, projecting cornices. The engravings accentuate the horizontals of the exterior and the verticals of the interior, but Michelangelo must have sought an equilibrium throughout: the inner shell of the dome is a grid (Pls. 70b, 71) that keeps the directional forces balanced; within the grid – in the final model (Pl. 71a) – the rising accents of small vertical ovals are stabilized by large circles in alternating fields.

We have seen that changes in the dome and attic of St Peter's made during Michelangelo's last years were also calculated to increase equilibrium; but there the powerful verticals of the lower portions designed in the 1540's had already set in motion dynamic forces that could no longer be restrained. At San Giovanni, Michelangelo was free to express a mood which he could no longer impose on St Peter's; for the first time he affirmed the crushing weight of masonry construction. The aspiration of the ribs and lantern of St Peter's dome is quite absent from the smooth semisphere of San Giovanni, its springing hidden in the final solution by spreading steps to emphasize a settling quality. But the most evocative feature of the design is the gradual increase in plasticity from dome to base on both the interior and exterior, which subtly stresses the accumulation of weight and forces towards the ground. What is achieved in massing is reinforced by illumination, for the light gains intensity toward the base: the small lantern apertures would have spread a diffused light on the dome, but the large drum windows with their angled embrasures are channels through which the brightest light would constantly be focused on the floor of the central area.[4] On the periphery, each chapel is amply lit by three relatively low windows, to attract attention along the axes rather than upwards. Nothing in Michelangelo's previous architecture prepares for what might be called the resignation of this late project. It is surely another manifestation of the profound religious experience of his last years, an architectural version of the Pietàs and Passion drawings of the 1550's, where again the forms sink gravely earthwards.

The San Giovanni model was a preamble to the more radical solution for the Sforza Chapel in Santa Maria Maggiore. Michelangelo left the execution of the chapel and the design of details to assistants, so that the crude elevations of the structure today tend to overshadow the extraordinary inventiveness of the plan (Fig. 13). This plan is the most subtle variation on the centralized type; its length and width are equal, as in a Greek cross, but the square of the crossing has been moved from a central position toward the entrance. In part, this solution was a response to lighting problems: as the chapel was an appendage to an existing church, no light could be had from the entrance and little from the side. The altar-chapel was the most promising source of illumination, and Michelangelo decided – after initial experiments with a more centralized scheme (Pl. 72c) – to extend it at the expense of the entranceway. This would have been unnecessary had the chapel been provided with a dome and lantern (probably a dome was intended in Pl. 72c), but Michelangelo decided to give the chapel an unprecedented covering in the form of a slightly deflated version of the balloon vault used by Brunelleschi at the Foundling Hospital in Florence and elsewhere. The engravings (Pl. 72a, b) show how the vault section echoes the segmental plan of the chapels: both must have been – even more than the ovals of San Giovanni – an affront to Renaissance taste, which demanded the "completeness" of

4. For this and other insights into the projects for San Giovanni and the Porta Pia I am indebted to Elizabeth MacDougall.

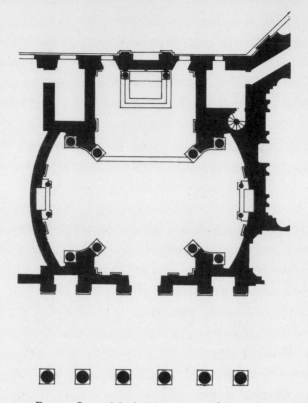

Fig. 13. Rome, Santa Maria Maggiore, Sforza Chapel. Plan.

hemicycles and hemispheres. These curves imply a state of becoming rather than of being; their form is essentially unstable in masonry constructions.

The conflict of axes that Michelangelo had planned for San Giovanni is absent from the chapel scheme, for there is but one entrance, and this necessarily makes the altar-axis primary. An early plan study (Pl. 72c) minimized the longitudinal axis in proposing three nearly equal chapels flanking the crossing: it is wholly consistent with the last of the San Giovanni plans, an echo of the design for the three entrance porticoes in Pls. 68 and 69b. We recognize in this preliminary study the calming classicism noticeable at San Giovanni, but it is gone again in the final project (Fig. 13), as if Michelangelo could sustain only momentarily a state of repose.

A slight change in the placement of the four central columns dramatically shifted them from a passive to an active role; now they seem to jut aggressively into the central space, forming the beginnings of an $\times$ made not of voids, as at San Giovanni, but of masses (Pl. 73a, c). Perhaps this free use of the Order was suggested by the decision not to employ a dome.

The plan as a whole, with its equal but differentiated arms and its dynamic forms was to become one of the most influential of Michelangelo's inventions. Architects of the following generations learned from it how to combine the virtues of a longitudinal and centralized plan, and were fascinated by Michelangelo's demonstration that the side chapels could be dramatized without prejudicing the dominance of the altar chapel. The influence on Borromini's planning is especially noticeable (San Carlo alle Quattro Fontane; Sant' Agnese in Piazza Navona).

If the unprecedented character of the design for San Giovanni can be related to the religious intensity of Michelangelo's late years, then the church cannot be understood as a typical Renaissance centralized structure inspired by antique models. At the height of the Counter-Reformation the humanists' arguments for the central plan, stressing the perfection of the circle, square and polygon, were considered irreligious, and would not have appealed to either Michelangelo or his patrons if Christian tradition had not offered equally convincing justification.

The central plan was suitable at San Giovanni, as at St Peter's, because it was the form chosen in Early Christian times to memorialize martyrs. This helps to explain why Michelangelo in his first plan turned to two martyria: the ancient Santo Stefano Rotondo, where the circular colonnade is also interrupted by cross axes, and the modern project of Bramante for the *Tempietto* precinct of San Pietro in Montorio, where, as we know from Serlio, the famous central shrine – like the altar tabernacle of Michelangelo's drawings – was to have been surrounded by a colonnade with an ambulatory behind which chapels were set in the corners of a square. But a more subtle symbolism is implied in the octagonal altar base with its tabernacle supported on columns (Pl. 66b), the prototype for which may be found only in baptisteries; the octagonal central font and colonnade of the Lateran Baptistery was apparently Michelangelo's altar model;[5] the wide entrance-vestibule with niched sides appears to come from the same source. The connection is confirmed by the first model (Pl. 70b) in which the vestibule becomes an open portico with two free-standing columns, a virtual replica of the Baptistery as it appears in sixteenth-century drawings. A shift in symbolism from the martyrion to the Baptistery tradition would be inconceivable in any church other than one consecrated to St John the Baptist; and even here it might have escaped detection and was ultimately abandoned. In the second plan (Pl. 67), the baptismal symbolism passes from a central tabernacle to the octagonal form of the building itself. Michelangelo may have presented this plan to the Florentine colony as a version of the Baptistery at home; the two have in common an octagonal form visible from the exterior, a free central space, and three entrances, the principal one in Florence – Ghiberti's "Gates of Paradise" – being opposite a high altar.

The symbolism of the octagon disappears in the mature schemes, but the Early Christian portico type (familiar also from Santa Costanza in Rome, San Vitale in Ravenna and elsewhere) is preserved, and the treatment of contending axes begins to reflect Roman prototypes as the modelled masses of the wall suggest Roman construction. The opposition of $+$ and $\times$ axes is a frequent manifestation of the Roman fascination with conflicting choices of direction: it appears in the domed areas of the Domus Aurea, the Flavian Palace on the Palatine, in the Piazza d'Oro of Hadrian's Villa in Tivoli, and in nearly all the Baths.

Axial planning became Michelangelo's guiding principle because of its suggestion of movement and because it could be used to symbolize the Cross and baptismal font. The fact that it was tested first in an Early Christian, and finally in a Roman context demonstrates that Michelangelo used tradition as a means of reinforcing his individualized form

5. Tolnay believes that in this drawing Michelangelo actually may have projected a font rather than an altar.

and not as an end in itself. This conclusion is borne out by his claim that in this design he had surpassed both the Romans and the Greeks.[6] Vasari said that this was a rare boast for such a modest man; we may add that it was an impossible one for a truly Renaissance man, and marks the end of an era.

There is an almost neo-classic repose, simplicity, and unity in the San Giovanni design. It is as if Michelangelo, having foreseen seventeenth-century architecture at St Peter's, was now ready to face the problems of the eighteenth century. Had this church been built under his supervision, the future history of architecture would have been quite different.

6. Vasari, VII, p. 263.

CHAPTER X

The Porta Pia

PIUS IV PONT. MAX. PORTAM PIAM SUBLATA NOMENTANA EXTRUXIT VIAM PIAM AEQUATA ALTA SEMITA DUXIT, the inscription on a tablet in the pediment of the Porta Pia, records the construction of both the gate and the avenue running through it (Pls. 74 and 76a). Twenty years later the project was described by Ferrucci:[1] "Be it known that Pius IV, in 1561 or 1562, wishing to leave a handsome street, which along with the city gate should bear his name, opened, or rather re-modelled and levelled the beautiful *strada* Pia, where earlier there had been an old street,[2] curving and irregular, signs of which still appear where [the tops of] certain gates of villas or gardens . . . now serve as benches or railings on account of the unevenness of the site as it used to be. The Pope had in mind to begin this street at the portal of the Palazzo San Marco[3] because he was accustomed to go there every summer; from there it was to curve up to the Quirinal hill and continue through the Porta Pia to the bridge on the Nomentana. This was begun, but since the portion from San Marco to the Quirinal was not much used, and indeed was not open in those days, due to the difficulties of the ascent which was very steep and uneven, not much progress was made. In addition, certain individuals were greatly incensed on account of the considerable damage which their homes and property suffered from this street. Therefore he began the street from the Cavalli di Tiridate,[4] making it long, wide, and level all the way to the Porta Pia, which is more than a mile; and from the gate he continued on with a straight, but in some places uneven road for some distance beyond the gate, levelling certain portions and continuing to the church of Sant' Agnese. Because this street was in a most agreeable site and enjoyed the most perfect and salubrious air of all the parts of the city of Rome, it is full of the most beautiful gardens and pleasure spots of the most distinguished citizens . . ."

1. In A. Fulvius, *L'antichità di Roma*, Venice, 1588, fol. 23.
2. Called "L'alta Semita": see the inscription above.
3. *I.e*, the Palazzo Venezia. For an earlier project to link this palace with the Quirinal hill, see the Catalogue, pp. 294 f.
4. Statues of the Dioscures as horse-trainers stood in a clearing at the peak of the Quirinal hill (see Pl. 76a).

The Porta Pia, erected on the inner face of an ancient fortified gate enclosure just north of the original Porta Nomentana (Pl. 81a), differed in function and form from any city gate of the Renaissance or earlier times. Though set into a defensive system, it was an indefensible, thin brick screen barely strong enough to sustain its own weight (cf. the plan, Pl. 75) – a record of the moment when the Romans abandoned hope of using their ancient walls as an effective defence against modern artillery. Furthermore it faced inward, toward Rome, evading for the first time a tradition which from prehistoric times had turned gates toward the highway and countryside as an introduction to the city behind. Michelangelo's gate belongs more to the street than to the walls; it was pure urban scenography – a masonry memento of the temporary arches erected in the Renaissance to celebrate the arrival of princes, though without their triumphal connotations. The street, too, was more theatrical than utilitarian, since it crossed one of the least populated and congested quarters of Rome, where no important buildings were raised before the end of the century.

The scheme as a whole calls to mind the most popular Renaissance convention for stage scenery, borrowed from Vitruvius' account of the ancient theatre: a broad and regular city street, shown in perspective, which terminates in a monumental arch (Pl. 80c).[5] Tragic drama demanded settings of palatial, severely classical architecture, while comedy permitted more common and varied structures. There is something of both in Michelangelo's gate: the nobility of the monumental tradition, and a fantasy and variety more commonly associated with villa design. Pls. 76a and 81a show the original Via Pia, bordered by the walls of villas rather than by Palace façades – walls punctuated at intervals by new gates which succeeded so well in simulating Michelangelo's ingenuity that they were attributed to him as long as they survived (Pl. 80b).

5. S. Serlio, *Il secondo libro di prospettiva* (*Tutte l'opere d'Architettura*), Venice, 1584, fols. 48–51; cf. R. Krautheimer, "The Tragic and Comic Scene of the Renaissance", *Gazette des Beaux-Arts*, ser. 6, XXXIII, 1948, pp. 327 ff. Only the tragic scene has a gate, as Tolnay reminded me.

Whether theatrical conventions were consciously adopted or simply absorbed from the atmosphere is of no account. In either case it is not the specific devices but the conception of the city street as an integral work of art that establishes Pius' programme as one of the great innovations in urban design. For half a century before, the Popes had been levelling, straightening and broadening Roman streets (e.g. Julius II's Via Giulia, Pl. 70a), but their aim was primarily utilitarian, and aesthetic only to the extent that order was preferable to chaos. The Via Pia was much more than an ennobled traffic artery: it was a kind of extended enclosure, terminated at one end by an imposing gate façade and at the other by the colossal statues of the Dioscures, and closed on the sides by walls embellished with architectural incidents designed to fit the scheme (Pls. 76a, 81a).[6] Italians had always been alive to the aesthetic factor in urban vistas; the novelty here was in the homogeneity of the conception. The Via Pia is to earlier streets what the Campidoglio was to earlier *piazze*, in that the designer exercised absolute control over the environment while his predecessors had only managed to improve existing conditions.

In all these respects Michelangelo's design anticipated the urbanistic programme of Sixtus V and Domenico Fontana (1585–1590), which is generally designated as the source of Baroque city planning.[7] The Sistine plan is characterized by long street perspectives terminated by obelisks which, like the narrow attic of the Porta Pia – where Pius IV also wanted to place an obelisk – give the pedestrians a measure of distance, a goal that rises above the buildings along the street and is silhouetted against the sky. The use of ancient sculptures as a focus of major streets and squares is another feature of the plan. Sixtus V must have thought of his programme as a continuation of Pius', because his network of streets crosses and continues the avenues of his precursor. He particularly emphasized the point at which the Via Sistina-Felice, from Santa Maria

6. The spirit of the design is vividly captured in two views of the Via Pia by the seventeenth-century Fleming Lieven Cruyl, who pointedly exaggerated the width of the street (Egger, *Römische Veduten*, II, Vienna, 1932, Pls. 69, 70).

7. L. von Pastor, *Sisto V, creatore della nuova Roma*, Rome, 1922; S. Giedion, *Space-Time and Architecture*, 3rd ed, Cambridge (Mass.), 1954, pp. 41–106.

Maggiore to the Pincio, crossed the Via Pia; there Fontana embellished the intersection by inserting fountains at the four corners (hence the name of Borromini's San Carlo alle Quattro Fontane). And farther along the Via Pia, he placed the monumental fountain at the outlet of a new aqueduct, the Aqua Felice (Pl. 76a).

If the basic components of Baroque urban design were inherited by Sixtus V from Pius IV, then credit for the new vision goes to Michelangelo rather than to Domenico Fontana, whose desiccated architecture has always made him seem poorly cast in the role of father of modern town planning.

Drawings for the Porta Pia show that Michelangelo was almost exclusively interested in the central portal. He thought of the gate façade as a neutral field, an extension of the medieval walls where a few sculptural ornaments might be placed. The role of the gate as street scenery made the portal and attic the heart of the design, since they were all that could be seen from a distance. The centre is therefore isolated by a dominance of travertine over brick and by dramatic contrasts of light and shadow which are minimized on the sides by the use of flat bands and cartouches with shallow recessions. The absence of definitive drawings for the attic would surprise anyone unfamiliar with Michelangelo's habit of designing from the ground up; he drew the attic of St Peter's only after the construction of the Order below (Pl. 59a). But the general effect of an attic was not overlooked in the process of sketching portals: in each of the drawings known to be for the Porta Pia, preliminary construction lines extend the vertical lines of the portal frame beyond its pediment to indicate the placement and dimensions of the upper story. Probably Michelangelo never arrived at a definitive attic solution; the spiritless attic of the engraving (Pl. 75) must have been invented by someone else.

The surviving drawings do not indicate that Michelangelo designed more than the portal and the central cartouches (Pl. 79a). Other details, except perhaps the spheres perched on the crenellations and the round platters with pendant bands, could have been added by assistants. The size and placement of the cartouches imply that Michelangelo determined the overall proportions of the gate, and a vague similarity in composition to the Palazzo dei Senatori reinforces this impression.

The misty technique of the portal sketches (Pls. 77b, 78a, b), while partly due to Michelangelo's advanced age and to the collaboration of assistants, was obviously calculated, and reveals something about the effects intended for the building. They are perceptual rather than conceptual, in that overall impressions are more important than the objective forms of the members that produce them. While certain basic patterns and rhythms consistently appear in the studies, the specific architectural motifs that make them possible remain in flux: volutes may become a pediment (Pls. 77b and 78b) only to mature into a pediment-volute; or a bull's horn may be transformed into a garland (Pls. 74 and 78a). Capitals, bases and mouldings are mere blurs of light and shadow fused by an ambient atmosphere, as in the contemporary painting of Titian, where patterns of light and colour overcome the individuality of figures. In his latest years Michelangelo had turned from a sculptural to a painterly approach to architecture, perhaps stimulated by the fact that the scenographic, two-dimensional Porta Pia was more like a canvas than a statue. The unifying impressionistic vision, in de-emphasizing single elements, abandons the effects of tension which in Michelangelo's early work were created through conflict of strongly individualized members. We are no longer expected to read the members as metaphors of human limbs; they have become a variegated pattern of optical effects organized by internal rhythms. Thus, there is a freedom, even a looseness, in the executed portal which is unique in Michelangelo's architecture, and which explains his extraordinary achievement in imparting to a massive and grandiose structure an air of festivity, almost of gaiety.

The portal has the most complex architectural detail of the era and an extraordinary variety of curves and angles. Its multiplicity of forms is the result of accumulating rather than selecting the ideas generated so rapidly in the preparatory drawings, so that each sheet contains several superimposed designs. No structural or theoretical principles guided the sequence of drawings – only an inspired, almost unconscious search for visual impressions. A last-moment shift from columnar to pilaster supports is symptomatic of the painterly approach to design; here Michelangelo suddenly wanted vertical shadows rather than masses, even if it made no sense in terms of tradition and the weight of the superstructure. He succeeded because the vitality of the fluting fully compensated for the loss of body.

In the actual building the impression of the drawings could not be fully sustained; the chisel was bound to sharpen the atmospheric softness. But close inspection shows the extent to which the portal rejects the linearity and sharpness of Michelangelo's earlier work; the drafting of the jambs and arch gives an impression of cushion-like blocks; the mouldings have been stripped of the multiple channels and protrusions of antiquity to become simple plane or curved surfaces. The impact of such subtleties is lost to the modern eye, but their significance for the Renaissance is amusingly revealed in a sketch from the portal made by Giovannantonio Dosio, who automatically drew intricate mouldings into the pediment, and later had to add the note "tutto questo non ci va".[8]

The Porta Pia was an innovation in city-gate design which had neither forerunners nor imitators. Historically, its most notable feature is that it is not Roman. Everything we know of sixteenth-century civic architecture would lead us to expect that the first major Renaissance city gate built in Rome would imitate, or at least obviously refer to the surviving ancient gates – such as the Porta Maggiore – or triumphal arches. The pride and symbolic meanings that accumulated about city gates in antiquity and the Middle Ages should have conspired to place them among the architectural forms least susceptible to innovation, and the rarity of modern gates in the Renaissance is probably due to the sacrosanct character of those surviving from earlier times. In the twilight of humanism, Roman forms could have been avoided only by intention;

8. Uffizi, *Arch.* 2148, see E. MacDougall 1960, Fig. 13, p. 103.

Michelangelo and his patron must have favoured a language that would give Counter-Reformation monuments a vocabulary of their own.

Accordingly, the Porta Pia recalls the medieval, rather than the ancient walls of Rome, with its crenellations, which Michelangelo used to support Medici *palle*. Antique elements could not be avoided entirely in the portal, but their conventions were totally ignored: if the Order of the portal is classified as Tuscan because its "capitals" are composed of gigantic *guttae* (the wedge-shaped pegs) transplanted from the Doric/Tuscan entablature, then Roman *decorum* would not permit the pilasters to have Ionic fluting. The fantastic miscegenation makes the canonical Corinthian Order of the attic in Pl. 75 particularly suspect, and suggests that the nineteenth-century restorer came closer than the Renaissance engraver to Michelangelo's spirit. But the odd pilasters were not concocted specifically for the Porta Pia; they appear in slightly different form in the vestibule tabernacles of the Laurentian library (Pl. 24), and in the portals of the Palazzo dei Conservatori (Pl. 35a). In casting off ancient formulae, Michelangelo adhered to conventions he had established himself; even the greatest genius needs schemata. It is surprising how many motifs he recalled from sketches of thirty-five years before. The Library drawings include portals in which a segmental pediment is set into a triangular one, and in which inscription tablets with projecting upper mouldings project forward at the centre of the pediment. In studies for the central cartouches of the Porta, a motif from the ceiling of the reading room reappears nearly unchanged. (Compare Pls. 19a and 79a). Only Michelangelo could have succeeded in using the same vocabulary in both a small interior and a huge civic monument; the choice is another proof of his indifference to ancient gate traditions.

The flat arch is the only motif that remained unchanged throughout the series of preparatory drawings; possibly an element of conscious anti-Romanism guided experiments in new arch forms which are the insignia of Michelangelo's late style (the Farnese galleries; the Sforza Chapel; the plan of San Giovanni dei Fiorentini; the arches of the Ponte Santa Trinita). At the Porta Pia, however, the combination of motifs is inspired by a structural logic as well as by a search for new forms: the flat arch would not sustain its stresses without a semicircular relieving arch in the wall above it, and the tympanum is a visible expression of the inner workings.

There are so few surviving Renaissance city gates that it is tempting to over-emphasize the eccentric character of the Porta Pia. In old engravings and in illustrations to theoretical works we find that a certain fantasy was *de rigueur* in sixteenth-century gate design that would not have been admissible in other civic structures. Together with villas and garden architecture, gates were classified in the genre called Rustic, partly for the reason that the grandest of all ancient Roman city gates was the rusticated Porta Maggiore. The popularity of the Rustic genre is attested by Serlio's *Libro estraordinario* of 1551, containing "thirty gates in mixed Rustic style (*opera*) with divers orders; and twenty in delicate style of divers kinds . . .". The Rustic genre not only favoured roughly finished masonry but encouraged unorthodox motifs, combinations of Orders and materials. Serlio, in the Preface to his book, explained the fashion on the grounds first, that the public liked new things, and secondly, that the taste for inscriptions, arms, symbols, sculptural relief and statuary could be better accommodated by cautiously breaking the rules: "But", he added, "if you architects steeped in the doctrine of Vitruvius (to which I grant the highest praise and from which I do not intend to depart much) hold that I have gone astray with so many ornaments, so many panels, so many cartouches, volutes and other superfluities, I beg that you consider the country where I am [the book was published in Lyons] and that you supply what I have missed: and stay sound". This cautious variation of traditional rules is illustrated in Serlio's plates, where the ancient Orders, though overlaid with roughly dressed masonry and mannerist ornament, remain basically Vitruvian. Sanmichele was equally orthodox in his famous Rustic gates of Verona. Serlio's model gates have several motifs used in the Porta Pia; in No. XXX, for example (Pl. 80a), a three-bay, three-story façade is crowned by a central pedimented attic and there are obelisks at the corners; even a segmental arch appears. But the differences are more revealing than the similarities; the parts of the Porta Pia designed by Michelangelo abandon all conventions whether of ancient, or of modern rusticated Orders.

Rustic can be characterized as a genre rather than an Order because there is more in it than a certain vocabulary of ornament. Associated with the countryside rather than with the city, it may be thought of as an architectural equivalent to the pastoral genre in literature, connoting what we would call today a romantic or primitive rather than a classical spirit. It was this distinction that imparted to villa and gate design its licence to fantasy and invention; perhaps the whispered suggestion of rustication which Michelangelo executed for the first time in the jambs and arch of the Porta Pia was intended as an application for that licence.

CHAPTER XI

Santa Maria degli Angeli

IN 1561 the ruins of the huge Baths of Diocletian (Pls. 81a, 81b) were consecrated by Pius IV as the church and monastery of Santa Maria degli Angeli, and the reconstruction of the well-preserved structures at the centre of the building complex was begun under Michelangelo's direction. Ancient Roman buildings had been remodelled often into churches in Early Christian times (the Pantheon, as Santa Maria Rotonda; the tomb of Constantia as Santa Costanza; the temple of Antoninus and Faustina as SS. Cosmas and Damian, *etc.*), but the tradition died out in the later Middle Ages. It is symptomatic of the Renaissance failure to resolve the conflict between an intellectual adoration of the pagan past and a spiritual adherence to Christianity that this tradition could not be revived until the Counter-Reformation had confirmed the primacy of the Church.

The transformation of the Baths was promoted by a pious Sicilian priest, Antonio del Duca, who, inspired by a vision of the angels, pestered the papacy for twenty years to gain his end. Rebuffed by Paul III and only temporarily encouraged by Julius III, he finally won enthusiastic support from Pius IV, who envisaged the church as the crowning ornament of the Via Pia, the new avenue he had started alongside the Baths under Michelangelo's direction. Today almost nothing can be seen of Michelangelo's church: the remodelling carried on throughout the eighteenth century altered the plan and covered every accessible surface with late Baroque ornament (Pl. 83b). Only the plain stuccoed vaults of the main hall remain to recall the original attempt to form a church with the minimum of change in the ancient remains (Pl. 81b). Because Michelangelo left the elevations untouched except for the addition of plain partition walls, two entrance portals, and window mullions, his design can be reconstructed by a study of the plan alone (Fig. 14).

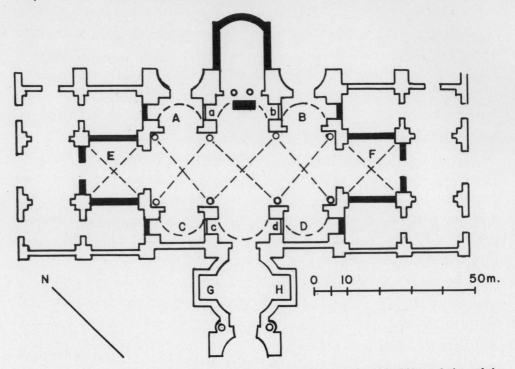

Fig. 14. Rome, Santa Maria degli Angeli. Plan, showing (in black) Michelangelo's
additions to the existing structure of the Baths of Diocletian
(after Siebenhüner)

Discussion of the plan has focused on the unprecedented use of the
great hall of the Baths. It has been read as an over-sized transept, antici-
pating the Baroque emphasis on the cross-axis (Borromini's Sant' Agnese,
Bernini's Sant' Andrea al Quirinale) and conversely, as a radial central-
plan with no crossing – only a single central space with attached vestibules on three sides, a major chapel on the fourth, and without anything
that might be called a nave.[1] Modern interpretations of Santa Maria degli
Angeli have been clouded by unwillingness to admit that Michelangelo
could be moved by anything except a will to form. Without denigrating
the aptness of Michelangelo's solution, we may see in it more common
sense than inspiration; any competent architect might have hit upon it.

1. H. Siebenhüner, "Santa Maria degli Angeli in Rom", *Münchner Jhb.*, VI, 1955, pp. 194 f.

Given the problem of converting the Baths with a minimum of new construction, two equally practical solutions were available. The more obvious and conventional, in a liturgical sense, was that of Antonio del Duca, who wanted to use the great hall as a long nave; the entrance would have had to be at the northwest (Fig. 14, E), where there was access to the Via Pia; consequently the altar found its place in the anteroom at the opposite, southeast end. Michelangelo chose the only alternative axis, at a right angle to del Duca's, placing the entrance at the rotonda on the long side (Fig. 14, G/H) and the altar across the hall, where there had been a broad passage to the exterior frigidarium. The decision not only produced a more interesting relationship of spaces, but had several liturgical advantages as well, the most important of which was its response to the needs of the Carthusian monastery, emphasized by Vasari.[2] When del Duca's plan was temporarily adopted in 1550, the church had not yet been granted to the Carthusians. After the grant, the plan became impractical because it offered the monks, whose rule was the most hermitic of any Renaissance Order, no seclusion from the lay congregation. Michelangelo's alternative isolated the chancel from the main hall with its public altars, giving it a maximum of privacy. In Plates 81b and 83, where we look into a deep chancel with the altar in an apse at the end, Michelangelo's design had already been changed. Earlier views (Pl. 82a) show the altar in front of the chancel and, behind it, two columns preserved from the ancient Baths (Fig. 14). By preserving the columnar screen, Michelangelo gave the brothers an isolated choir required by the traditions of monastic architecture. The choir was probably opened to view after 1565, when Pius IV violated his contract with the Carthusians by declaring Santa Maria degli Angeli a titular church.

The setting of the cloister (Pl. 81a) and the need to connect it directly with the chancel was a second determinant. Only one area of the Baths was sufficiently unencumbered by ruins to erect a cloister without costly demolitions: the site of the frigidarium, a huge pool originally open to the sky on the northeast of the main hall. So economic and liturgical

2. VII, p. 261: "con tante belle considerazioni per comodità de' frati Certosini".

demands conspired to place the altar on the northeast, or, to accept the inaccuracy of the contemporary chronicler Catalani, on the east, in conformity with traditional orientation.

In satisfying the Renaissance predilection for symmetry, Michelangelo's choice was aesthetically more conventional than del Duca's. If the great hall had been used as a nave, the plan would have been grossly unbalanced by the large rotonda on one side. In making the rotonda into the main vestibule, every part of the church became symmetrical about the entrance-to-altar axis. Michelangelo's orientation had appealed to Renaissance taste long before it was suggested by the needs of the Carthusians: around 1515 and 1520 Giuliano da Sangallo and Baldassare Peruzzi both anticipated it in perspective drawings which show the main altar in its present position.[3] Finally, it followed the principal axis of the ancient Baths, as may be seen from the layout of the ruins surrounding the church, especially the great exedra (Pl. 81a).

While Peruzzi intended to close the ends of the main hall (Fig. 14 E, F) with semicircular apses, Michelangelo left them open and made the adjoining rectangular chambers into entrance vestibules. Then he used the door-to-door measurement to fix the distance from the main (southwest) entrance to the end of the new apse. This simple solution, involving a minimum of new construction, produced a Greek cross plan which, on account of the great difference in the scale and form of the arms, is difficult to experience visually. A Greek cross with vestibules on three sides and an altar on the fourth was the underlying scheme of the final plan for San Giovanni de' Fiorentini (Pl. 68), drawn only two years before, so that Michelangelo had a ready-made iconographic exemplar to impose upon the Baths.

Years before, del Duca had taken the cross-axis of the Baths, together with the cruciform brick-stamps of Diocletian's kilns, as proof that the original builders had been Christians. Members of the intelligentsia were

3. Uffizi, *Arch.* 131, 161, identified with S. M. Angeli by Tolnay 1930, p. 21; cf. Siebenhüner 1955, Figs. 17, 18. The Bianchini engraving (our p. 83b) was discovered and published by Tolnay 1930, Fig. 10.

not so naïve: their description of the ruins "magnificentissimae illae Caesaris Diocletiani thermae toto orbe celebres" has suggested to modern critics[4] that the programme for the church, which left the ancient remains virtually unchanged, was evidence of the pervasive humanistic passion for the pagan past. But the fact that the first Renaissance conversion of a major monument into a church should have been achieved only at the height of the Counter-Reformation warns against a simple humanist-antiquarian interpretation. The taste that formed St Peter's on the model of Roman Baths was far different from that which half a century later reversed the process to turn a Bath into a titular church. Counter-Reformation society respected ancient monuments in so far as they might be made to contribute to the glory of the church; and the more "magnificent" the monument, the greater the contribution.

Though humanist patrons had pilfered from the ruins every portable stone and column, their respect for the ancients was so great that they dared not openly invite comparison by turning antique buildings to Christian uses. So the Christianization of the Baths was not inspired or even supported by humanists; it was the achievement of a simple Sicilian visionary who despised the ancients and wanted only to honour the Virgin and the Angels. This dream was fulfilled not only by the construction of the church, but by the motto inscribed in the apse: "Quod fuit Idolum, nunc Templum est Virginis – Auctor est Pius ipse Pater, Daemones aufugite". In the same spirit, the anti-humanist Pope Sixtus V (1585–1590), who zealously destroyed some of Rome's greatest remains, spent incredible sums to re-erect antique obelisks before the major churches in order to top them with crosses and thereby to symbolize the triumph of Christianity over the pagan past.

Michelangelo, as we know him in his profoundly religious late poetry and drawings, was equally far removed from the humanist position. The sense of liberation from the weight of the past that had prompted his claim to have surpassed ancient architecture in the design of San Giovanni now made it possible for him to mould it in his own image. Admittedly,

4. Particularly Siebenhüner, *op. cit.*, pp. 201 f.

he did as little moulding as possible, and left the ancient remains almost as he found them (Pl. 81a, 81b); but this does not necessarily indicate a reverence for the past. Though his design could be explained by economic restrictions alone, it must have been intended to conform to the spirit of Pius' inscription. The Virgin's victory was surely more impressive in the days when the austere halls of Her antagonists were left untouched. After eighteenth-century reconstructions had covered all but the vaults and columns of the original building (Pl. 82b), the thermal atmosphere evaporated, carrying away the whole drama of Her struggle with the demons.

CHAPTER XII

Conclusion

CERTAIN common traits may be found in reviewing the whole of Michelangelo's work which help us to characterize his architectural style.[1] Among these are what I call a "relief" style, dominant in designs before the Laurentian library, and a "kinetic" style – suggesting movement along axes – dominant in the library and in subsequent buildings. I shall also examine the transition from the two-dimensionality of the earlier buildings to the volumetric character of the later ones, promoted by a series of bold experiments in the expressive potentialities of structure, and finally, Michelangelo's vocabulary of motifs, which remained the most consistent feature of his architectural style.

Relief played a major role in Michelangelo's sculpture: in the early years, bas-relief in the familiar sense, and later, as a feature of full-round statuary – such as the *Pietà* in Florence – which remained frontal and restricted in depth. The same may be said of the architecture: early projects (the chapel front at Castel Sant' Angelo, Pl. 2a; the San Lorenzo façade and reliquary tribune, Pls. 5b, 14c; the Medici chapel, Pl. 7a) were reliefs to be applied to plane surfaces, and a late design such as the Porta Pia returned to the same principle.

Bas-relief is to be seen from one position, preferably at a fixed distance on its central axis; it discourages the observer from movement because nothing happens on its sides or back; in this respect it is like painting. Before 1500, architects borrowed from painting both its static and its planar character; after 1500 a new taste for the definition of masses in space prompted the building-out from and digging-into surfaces. The relief style marks a transition from the panel-painter's to the sculptor's

1. There are two brief but excellent essays on Michelangelo's architecture as a whole: D. Frey, *Michelangelo Buonarroti architetto*, Rome, 1923; C. de Tolnay, "Michelangelo architetto", *Il Cinquecento*, Florence, 1955.

approach to architecture; it also represents an adjustment by architects interested in a complete conquest of the third dimension (e.g. Bramante at St Peter's, Pl. 51a) to the conditions of congested urban settings, where typically only one – two-dimensional – façade is exposed to view. In Bramante's and Raphael's palace façades the wall plane disappeared behind a dense armature of sculptural elements – columns, balconies, roughly-rusticated blocks – which invited a rich interplay of lights and shadows. The Medici palace windows (Pl. 6c) prove Michelangelo's awareness of these experiments; the upper parts are surprisingly close to those of Raphael's Antonio da Brescia house in Rome. But other early designs were not so aggressively anti-Quattrocento: they rather followed Giuliano da Sangallo (Pls. 3a and 3d) in preserving some of the linear, two-dimensional quality of the Florentine past. That quality was peculiarly suited to programmes requiring monumental sculpture (the San Lorenzo façade and the Medici chapel, Pls. 5a, 7a), where the architecture had to be a frame for figural compositions; had the building itself been as sculptural as Bramante's it would have overshadowed the figures. For a Florentine artist of this period, the preservation of Quattrocento values, by evoking recollections of the days of leadership and liberty, must have been an act of patriotism, and Michelangelo's Florentine buildings, like contemporary paintings of Pontormo and Andrea del Sarto, could preserve local traditions without being either conservative or provincial.

When Michelangelo turned to architecture at about forty, he was deeply involved in work on the tomb of Julius II, and it was a short step from this sculptural composition of architectural scale to architectural commissions dominated by sculpture. He found a bond between the two arts in the material itself: the white-to-ivory marble of Carrara adopted for architectural as well as for sculptural elements in the chapels of Leo X (Pl. 2a) and the Medici (Pl. 7a), and in the San Lorenzo façade (Pl. 5b), invites the linear, crisp effects which Michelangelo sought as a younger man, and which are emphasized by the tools and techniques of his earlier drawings (Pl. 5a) by contrast to the effects of later drawings (Pl. 79b) which suggest less exacting, more malleable travertine and brick. The years wasted in the quarries fruitlessly extracting the blocks for San Lorenzo must have discouraged Michelangelo from the further architectural use of marble, but he continued to get comparable properties from traditional Tuscan materials: hardness and precision from grey pietra serena; whiteness from stucco (Pls. 7a, 17).

The façade and chapel at San Lorenzo are the last projects in which Michelangelo attempted to combine architecture and sculpture; chances are that the façade would not have met its author's expectations; the rather delicate architectural trellis would have been overwhelmed by the force of the reliefs and statues it was destined to support. Later Michelangelo preferred to treat buildings themselves as if they were sculptures rather than merely a framework for sculptural compositions. Why is it that the Renaissance, which cultivated both architecture and sculpture with such distinction, produced no monuments in which the two arts are joined as successfully as in the Parthenon and Chartres Cathedral? Probably because the Renaissance emphasis on individuality destroyed the gift of anonymity which in primitive, and occasionally in sophisticated societies promotes the collaboration of large teams of gifted artisans without sacrifice of quality. Michelangelo, an archetype of the new image of the individual, had to dominate every step from quarrying, to architectural design, to carving, yet he was still enough of a medieval artisan to want to do so by working with his own hands. A century later Bernini was to fuse the other arts with monumental architecture without loss of individuality by organizing a specialized labour force trained to function as an extension of his own hands.

The relief style of the early designs was a solution to commissions which emphasized architectural ornament rather than the design of buildings. For the Laurentian library new principles were needed; problems of statics and of utility elicited from Michelangelo a hitherto dormant genius for structural design and for the composition of enclosed spaces.

In the library, for the first time in the Renaissance, the wall ceased to be the dominant structural and aesthetic element; piers and columns supporting a framework of roof trusses formed the basic system, and a thin wall merely sustained and strengthened it (Fig. 5). By this means attention was deflected from wall surfaces, which hide the force and direction of stresses, to the armature which, like the musculation in the body, discloses stresses. Technically the system was more Gothic than antique; but where the Gothic architect sought by progressively dematerializing his structure to remove awareness of load, Michelangelo used supports to accentuate it, so that the observer should experience the conflict of forces acting in the structure. A medieval device thus achieved a characteristically Renaissance goal, by urging the observer to identify with the building physically. The library experiment was continued in the design of the Campidoglio (Pl. 35), where the frame became dominant, leaving the wall to function only as a curtain to screen interior spaces. The frame-system of the library interior and the palace exterior emphasized individual bays to a degree unknown in Renaissance architecture, and permitted construction by the addition of autonomous, boxlike units; the effect is of unprecedented cohesiveness and strength.

But Michelangelo's purpose in accentuating structural members was not invariably to specify the forces at work in a building; he might exaggerate or repress apparent stresses to evoke a certain mood. So the design of the Conservators' palace does not merely reveal the structural system – it exaggerates the apparent weight of the cornice and minimizes the apparent strength of the pilaster-piers to intensify the conflict between supporting and supported elements.

This demonstration of the manipulation of structure for expressive ends was a preamble to the design of St Peter's, where powerful tensions are suggested in the body of the Basilica which are quite unrelated to the actual structure (Pl. 63). A surface network of dynamic horizontals and verticals in apparent conflict covers a dense masonry mass which really just sinks down. The colossal Order supports nothing – it merely draws attention to the drum and dome, where actual structural forces could again be revealed and exaggerated by the treatment of ribs and buttresses. The dome, where stressed supports alternate with lighter, unstressed planes, is a hemispherical counterpart of Michelangelo's earlier bay-designs, and the drum is essentially an inversion of the wall-system in the library vestibule: the columns now project while the tabernacle/window frames with their alternating pediments recede (compare Pls. 17 and 63). Michelangelo turned to Brunelleschi's Florentine dome for inspiration because across the 130-year gap the two designers were bound by a common sensitivity to the interdependence of form and structure. In the intervening years architects had learned from Roman antiquity to hide the skeleton and muscles of buildings under a rich Vitruvian vocabulary and stuccoed, painted or veneered surfaces.

It is hard to understand why the contemporary projects for San Giovanni de' Fiorentini (Pls. 70b, 71) are so different; there the design arose from a predisposition to certain principles of space and mass composition rather than from any structural considerations. The dome gives no clue to technique: its exterior, apparently monolithic, returns to the antique type, while the exterior Order is minimized to the same degree that that of St Peter's is magnified. The exterior of San Giovanni was to communicate through the interplay of simple masses alone, the interior chiefly through volumetric spaces. So the project preserved neither the relief character of the first buildings nor the anatomical character of the intervening years; it is a sculptor's architecture in a new sense, close in concept to the statue carved from a block. But prophecies of the new style may be discovered at St Peter's: while structure was still applied as ornament in the manner of relief architecture around the body of the Basilica, it was more convincingly integrated with the wall than ever before, and the fact that it was applied no longer to a two-dimensional surface but to an undulating mass encourages us to see it, as we do the San Giovanni project, in terms of body rather than planes. More important is that the evolution of the St Peter's dome from an elevated curve inspired by Florence Cathedral to the classical hemisphere in Michelangelo's last solution (Pls. 60, 61) prepared the way for the low, Pantheon-like dome of San Giovanni. Nevertheless, the San Giovanni project emphasizes a factor of unpredictability in Michelangelo's work which makes it especially difficult to define the style of his architecture as a whole or a consistent "development" in style. The design shows a fresh respect for antique sources used with unprecedented sobriety and reserve in tune with the Counter-Reformation. Still, it is almost coeval with the antithetical Porta Pia, which achieves a festival brilliance by fantastic distortions of antique sources. Finally, after discovering that Michelangelo made the church of Santa Maria degli Angeli merely by raising a few partitions in the Baths of Diocletian (Fig. 14), we may wonder whether this was due to respect for the ancient monument or to a new spirit of Christian asceticism.

Michelangelo's later architecture, like his painting and sculpture, might be called "kinetic"; it incites an emotional response through its capacity to move the observer physically as well as emotionally. One is drawn around, into, through his buildings not only by the composition of spaces but by that "organic" design of masses that makes a wall or a stairway seem to be in motion. The kinetic spirit, repressed by the limitations of Michelangelo's earliest commissions – none of which required even the making of a plan – first emerged in the Laurentian library, where spaces as well as surfaces might be controlled (Fig. 5, Pl. 16). These spaces were arranged in a sequence – square, high vestibule; long, narrow reading room; triangular study (Pl. 18b) – each unit of which was distinct, even in the technique of covering, and yet integrated into the whole as the head, body, and limbs of a statue. The stairway, which seems to flow downward from the reading room into the vestibule (Pl. 18a) shows how the integration is aided by masses as well as by voids. In place of the typical Renaissance symmetry in all directions about a central point, Michelangelo proposed a symmetry on either side of the central axis along which a visitor had to proceed. For the first time in Renaissance architecture, movement was "built in", since the design of the interior unfolded only as one advanced along a predetermined path. The substitution of an axis for a point as the focus of architectural planning was a necessary preamble to the substitution of dynamic for static design.

Both the biological metaphor and the invocation of movement emerge extravagantly in the fortification drawings of 1528 (Pls. 26–28a). The bastions are devouring sea monsters calculated to frighten the enemy

by their form as well as by their function. Here again, although space is
envisaged for the movement more of missiles than of men, the design
is generated axially; but where the library provided movement in two
directions along one axis, the bastions provide it in one direction –
outward – along many.

This concept of axes exploding outward from a central core was
inverted in the plan of the Capitoline Hill, where paths from all directions in the surrounding space converge upon the piazza and from there
are diverted toward the interior of the Senators' palace (Pls. 36b, 37).
Instead of implying an aggressive expansion of forms, the Campidoglio
plan is enclosed and somewhat introverted, suggesting a room more than
a building complex. As in the Laurentian library, the full impact of the
design is reserved for the observer *inside*, for once within the space he
finds his freedom of action and of experience guided into the channels
prepared by the architect. As in the library, these channels are complex
and calculated to involve the observer psychologically: just as an ascent
of the vestibule stairway seems a struggle against a descending cascade,
so the crossing of the Capitoline piazza seems challenged by the expanding rays of the central oval.

Michelangelo's desire to control the observer even in the out-of-doors
is illustrated in the design of single buildings as well as in large planning
projects. The engraving of the Farnese palace (Pl. 41) preserves a proposal for integrating the piazza and the façade by means of the pavement
pattern, and for drawing the observer into and through the palace, the
garden, and across the Tiber, with the result that the stable, cubic mass
of Sangallo would have been transformed into another axial, dynamic
composition. Even at St Peter's (Pl. 50), where the environment could
not be changed, every attempt was made in forming the building to urge
the observer into constant, circulatory motion. It is impossible to believe
that Michelangelo planned to build the piazza illustrated in Pl. 58b, since
it would have supplanted the Vatican palace, but he must have had ideas
for a square before the Basilica that would have drawn the visitor inward.
The sense of protective enclosure, of gathering-in, that one gets from

the piazza as ultimately designed by Bernini owes much to the planning concepts of Michelangelo.

The indoor quality that passes from the library to the Campidoglio explains the strange flatness which gives the Porta Pia an effect of temporary ceremonial architecture (Pl. 74). The gate is to be seen as the end of the long, corridor-like Via Pia – an ornamental screen marking the transition from a controlled urban space into the open countryside where architecture no longer commands the environment (Pl. 76a). The Via Pia itself is an application of the axial principle of the Laurentian library to the problems of town planning. Without the benefit of this principle Renaissance urbanism might never have progressed beyond the design of squares.

Seen in this context, Michelangelo's preoccupation with axes in the San Giovanni projects (Pls. 66b–68) becomes understandable. The drawings resemble those for the fortifications of Florence in that the boldly modelled masses appear to throb with life and the axes of movement – now widened to accommodate a congregation – seem to push outward in a similar way. Even in a centralized building, with its inevitable focus on a point at the centre, Michelangelo found ways of prompting the visitor into action. The same is true of the Sforza chapel; within restricted cubic confines he formed a dominant longitudinal axis, though the transverse axis is equal in length and more compelling in design. This principle is expanded to monumental scale in Santa Maria degli Angeli, where means were found to focus attention on the altar in spite of a colossal transverse vessel. Baroque church and chapel designers were profoundly affected by Michelangelo's success in emphasizing the altar without sacrificing the unity of the centralized scheme.

In architectural as well as in literary expression, vocabulary is a major component of style, and nowhere is the cohesiveness of Michelangelo's work more clearly revealed than in the ornamental motifs that he used consistently throughout his life. Half-human, half-animal masks give a frieze (Medici chapel, Pl. 8; Farnese palace, Pl. 46a) that zoomorphic character found in some of the plans. A related antique motif is the ceremonial bucranium holding swags and banderoles which appears on the sarcophagi of the Medici chapel, the ceiling of the Laurentian library (Pl. 19a) and in the window pediments of St Peter's and the Farnese palace (Pls. 46a, 59a). One of Michelangelo's favourite devices was a bracket in the form of a volute; from its earliest appearance on the Julius tomb he used it as an expressive rather than a structural element, attracted by the curvilinear and swelling profiles so uniquely suited to his purposes. It plays an important role in all the early commissions (particularly the library vestibule, Pl. 17), and a variation appears as a transition from the lantern to the cone of St Peter's (Pl. 63); at the Porta Pia it is frivolously used to form mock-crenellations (Pl. 74).

Michelangelo's door and window frames may be classed in two categories: the conservative, in which a simple frame is topped by a triangular or segmental pediment stoutly supported on blocky brackets (San Lorenzo façade, Pl. 5b; Medici palace windows, Pl. 6c; library exterior, Pl. 15; windows at the Campidoglio and St Peter's, Pls. 35, 64; and the destroyed portals of Santa Maria degli Angeli, Pl. 82b); and the fantastic, in which the component elements either play their normal role in an unexpected way, or are borrowed from some foreign source (tabernacles at the Medici chapel and the library, Pls. 9, 24; inner portals of the Conservators' palace, Pl. 38a; Farnese windows, Pl. 46a; dormers of St Peter's dome, Pl. 60; the Porta Pia, Pl. 74). An example of the unexpected is the pilaster narrowed toward the base, as in the library tabernacles and Campidoglio portals; the same design shows the commonest form of borrowing: the transposition of *guttae* (pegs) from the Doric entablature to the base or crown of an effaced capital. Other motifs that appear more than once in buildings and drawings are the colossal Order (Pls. 3b, 37, 63) and the recessed column (Pls. 13b, 17, 38a).

Michelangelo's lifelong predilection for certain formal configurations contributed also to the unity of his work; for example, the symmetrical juxtaposition of diagonal accents in plan and elevation. Often the diagonals form quasi-triangular shapes and serve to focus attention on the apex of a composition, as do the sarcophagi and figures of the Medici chapel (Pl. 8), which at the same time accentuate the effigies and bind

together the strong vertical elements in the architecture. In the fortification drawings (Pls. 26–28) the expressive potential of diagonal forms
is at its height; they demonstrate how vigorous movement may be
communicated by the mere inclination of lines. Perhaps this is because
diagonal strokes seem to echo more convincingly than horizontals or
verticals the spontaneous motion of the draughtsman's hand. Elements
of these Florentine schemes are combined at the Campidoglio (Pl. 37),
where the symmetrical diagonal appears both in elevation – the Senator's
stairway, a repetition of the Medici chapel scheme – and in plan (Pl. 36b);
at the Cortile del Belvedere the double-ramped stairway was used again to
focus attention at the centre of the composition (Pl. 65c). By using diagonal
wall-masses to fuse together the arms of the cross, Michelangelo was able
to give St Peter's a unity that earlier designs lacked (Fig. 11), and the
diagonal again is basic to the plans of San Giovanni axes of the chapels
(Pls. 67, 68) and of the Sforza chapel (Fig. 13, axes of the projecting
columns).

Michelangelo's taste for oval forms was equally persistent. The free-
standing project for the tomb of Julius II was to have had an oval interior
chamber – so far as I know, the first space of its kind proposed in the
Renaissance – and the form appears again in the wooden ceiling of the
Laurentian library (Pl. 19a) and in the central steps of the vestibule
(Pl. 18a). The oval becomes dominant in the Campidoglio plan (Pl. 36b)
and reappears in the chapels of San Giovanni (Pl. 69a) and, in incomplete
form, those of the Sforza chapel (Pl. 72). Oval ornamental frames appear
in versions of the interior design of the domes of St Peter's and San
Giovanni (Pl. 71). But the figure does its most valuable service in suggesting an unprecedented approach to the design of arches and vaults.
Michelangelo designed for the corridors of the Farnese palace and later for
the Sforza chapel vaults half-oval in section (Pls. 43, 72) to bring about
the first major innovation in the form of coverings since Brunelleschi.[2]

2. These experiments were prepared in studies for the vaults of the Laurentian library, particularly Pl. 21, which is an innovation not only in form but in its illumination through windows in
the sides and crown of the vault. The vaulting of the triangular room planned for the library
(Pl. 18b) would have been equally unconventional.

One of the earliest and most effective fruits of this contribution was the Ponte Sta Trinita in Florence.

The diagonal and the oval are dynamic transformations of two of the basic forms of classic composition, the upright and the circle.

Michelangelo's architectural vocabulary is one indication of a casual attitude toward antiquity antithetical to Renaissance Humanism. While his contemporaries spoke of emulating and rivalling ancient Rome, he took from it only what suited his taste, rarely adopting a motif without giving it a new form or a new meaning. Yet he invariably retained essential features from ancient models in order to force the observer to recollect the source while enjoying the innovations. By the time Michelangelo turned to architecture, the Renaissance of antiquity was no longer an issue for every artist; it had been achieved, and one might borrow classical forms as readily from some building of the century 1420–1520 as from the ruins. Michelangelo learned from ancient Rome rather its syntax than its vocabulary: ways of using shadow and texture, a sense of scale, and the like. Otherwise he was not more inclined to pagan than to Christian antiquity; in his architecture as in his sculpture, Early Christian and later medieval elements gained equality with the Roman. This was a result of the acceptance of the Renaissance as an accomplished fact; once no medieval institutions survived to challenge the supremacy of Renaissance culture – once, that is, the Middle Ages had become ancient, too – the past could be surveyed dispassionately, as a continuum.[3] The shift from an exclusive to an inclusive historical ethic – from a Renaissance to a "modern" view of the past – immensely increased the storehouse of tradition to which artists might look for inspiration.

Because Michelangelo emerged so late as an architect, his contemporaries belonged, paradoxically, to an earlier generation: two major

3. In the 1460's the Florentine sculptor-architect Filarete still called Gothic architecture "moderna" and the Renaissance style "modo antico". See the fascinating study of Renaissance attitudes toward ancient and Medieval art and literature by E. Panofsky, *Renaissance and Renascences in Western Art* (The Gottesman Lectures, Uppsala University, VI), Stockholm, 1960.

architects of the Classic age – Bramante and Raphael – had died at the start of Michelangelo's building career; a third, Peruzzi, had already developed a mature style. In the period 1520–1550 several able younger men carried individualized versions of Bramante's style to the north (Sanmichele, Giulio Romano, Jacopo Sansovino), so that Michelangelo was challenged in central Italy only by Antonio da Sangallo the Younger. None of these was touched by Michelangelo's style, which began to exert its influence only after mid-century, when Michelangelo was the sole survivor of the group. Faint signs of his impact may be found first in the later portions of Serlio's treatise and in the early work of Palladio (Palazzo Chiericati, Vicenza, of 1550, which reflects the Conservators' palace). During the '50's and '60's still younger architects formed into two distinct camps of Michelangelo adherents. The Tuscans (Ammanati, Dosio, Vasari, Buontalenti) seemed to learn only from Michelangelo's Florentine buildings; the Romans (Guidetti, del Duca, and especially della Porta) only from those in Rome. The Tuscan branch flourished in the third quarter of the century (e.g. Vasari's Uffizi palace, a free transposition of the library reading room to the outdoors) but quickly settled down to the simple domesticity of the typical seventeenth-century villa; it was the Roman works that were destined to guide the future – particularly the Campidoglio and St Peter's, which for centuries influenced the planning of squares and the design of domes. Della Porta deserves a share of the credit, since he finished these buildings effectively by modifying the original designs to suit a less sophisticated and more imitable fashion. Porta showed Roman architects of the seventeenth century how Michelangelism could profit from the master without losing originality. From Rome the style spread in an expanding circle to encompass the western world, penetrating more deeply, however, in Catholic countries than in England and North America, where taste veered toward the more cerebral architecture of Palladio. Yet if Michelangelo had not reluctantly become an architect, the domes of St Paul's in London and of the Washington Capitol could not have been the same, and the Capitol surely would have had another name.

THE PLATES

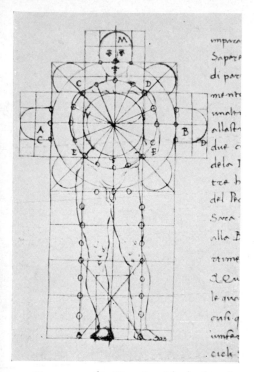

1a. Francesco di Giorgio. Ideal church plan.

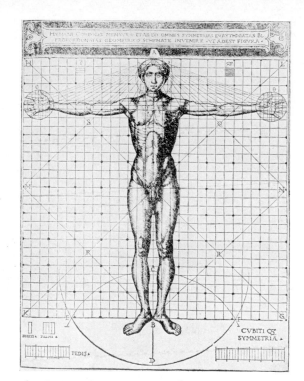

1b. C. Cesariano. Vitruvian figure, 1521.

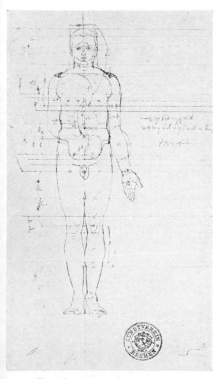

1c. Albrecht Dürer Proportion study.

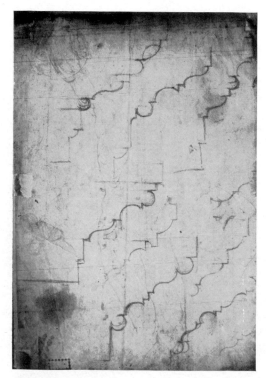

1d. Profile studies.

2b. G. B. Sangallo. Castel Sant' Angelo. Chapel exterior, after Michelangelo.

2a. Castel Sant' Angelo. Chapel of Leo X. Exterior (1514).

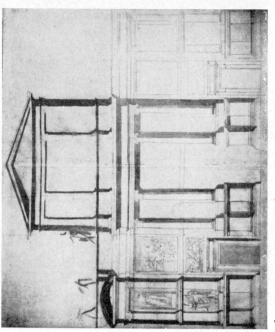

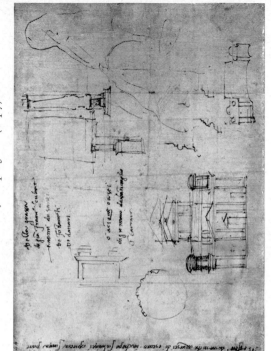

3b. San Lorenzo. Façade project. (copy)

3d. San Lorenzo. Façade proiect.

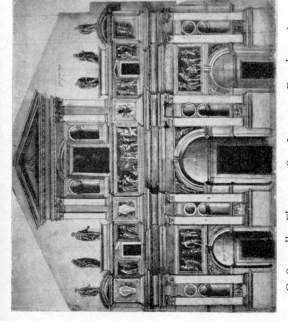

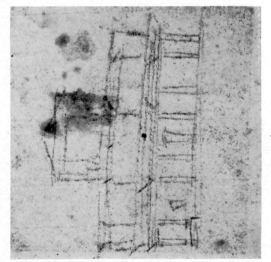

3a. G. Sangallo. Florence. San Lorenzo. Façade project.

3c. San Lorenzo. Façade project.

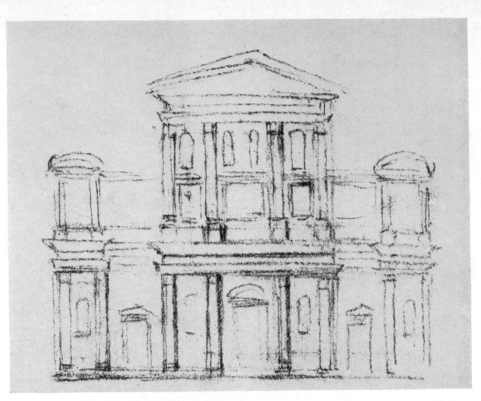

4a. San Lorenzo. Façade project.

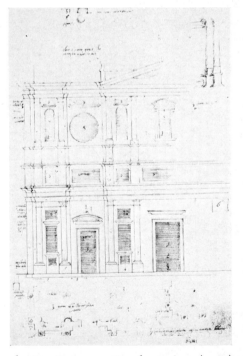

4b. San Lorenzo. Façade project (copy).

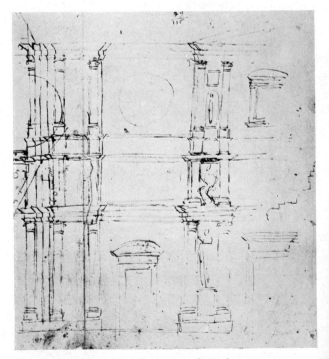

4c. San Lorenzo. Façade project (copy).

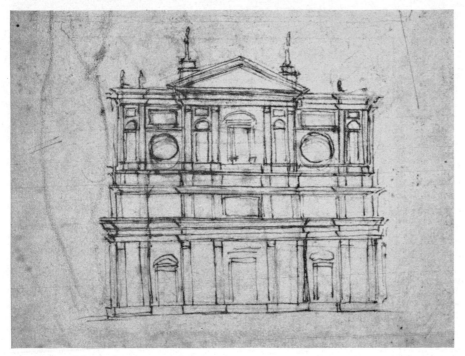

5a. San Lorenzo. Façade project.

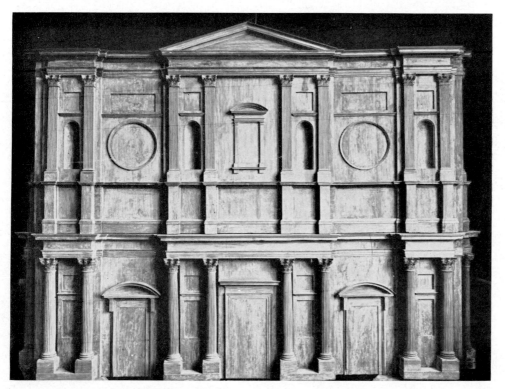

5b. San Lorenzo. Façade. Wooden model.

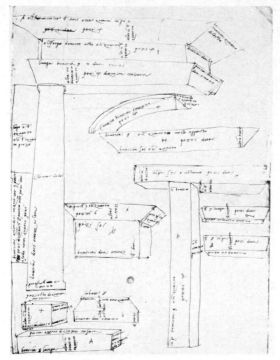

6a. San Lorenzo. Blocks quarried for the façade.

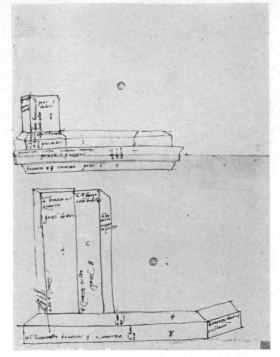

6b. San Lorenzo. Blocks quarried for the façade.

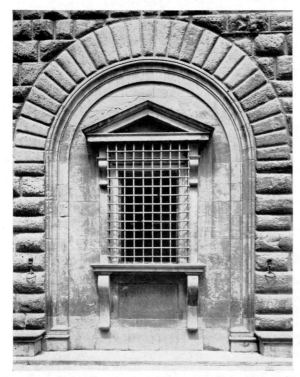

6c. Medici Palace. Ground-floor window (*ca.*1517).

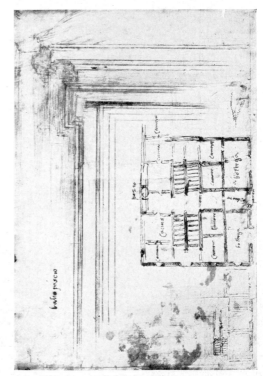

6d. "Altopascio" house. Plan project.

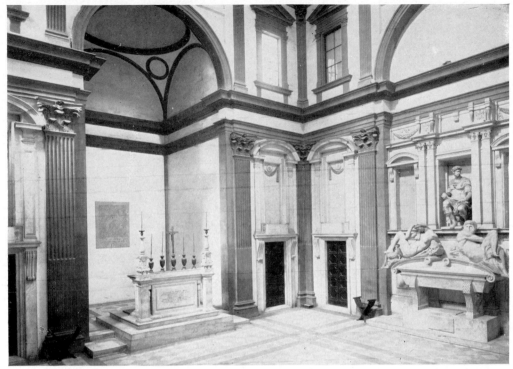

7a. Medici Chapel. Interior, towards altar.

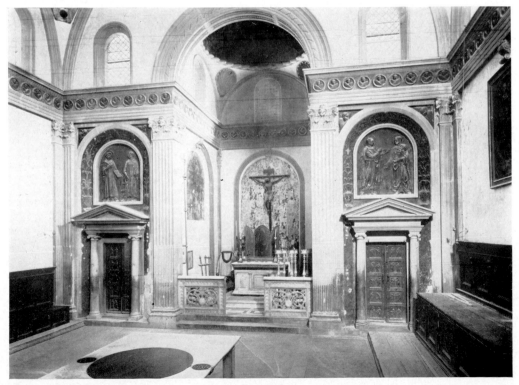

7b. San Lorenzo. The Old Sacristy (1421–1429).

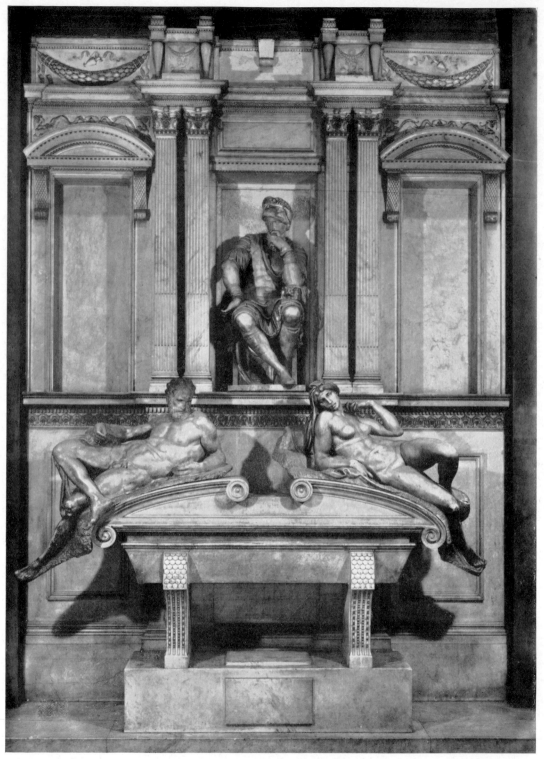

8. Medici Chapel. Tomb of Giuliano de' Medici.

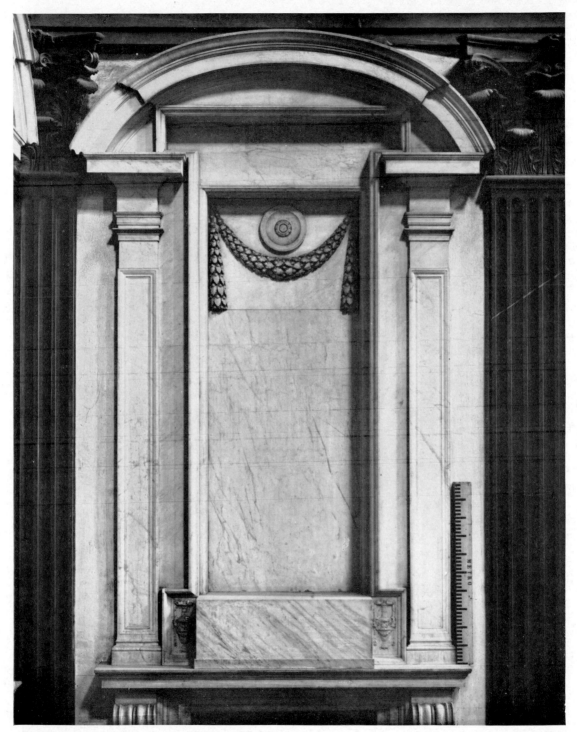

9. Medici Chapel. Tabernacle over entrance door.

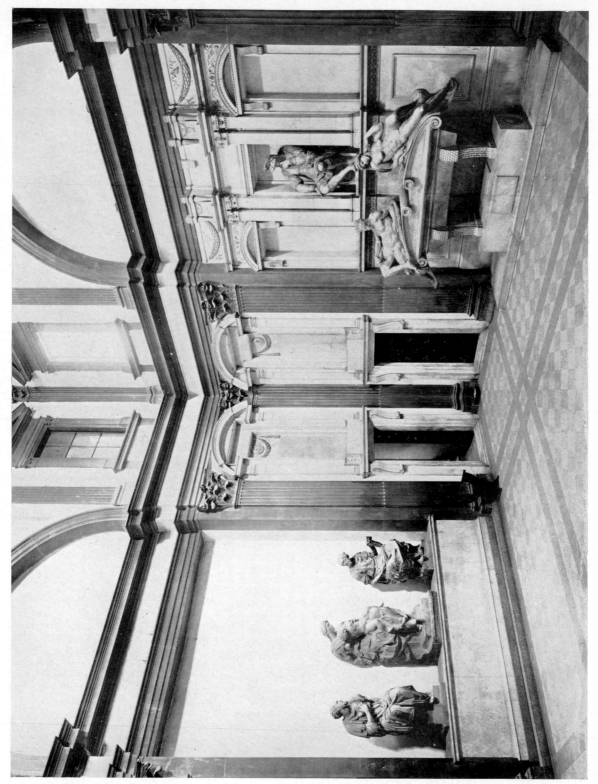

10. Medici Chapel. Interior, toward entrance.

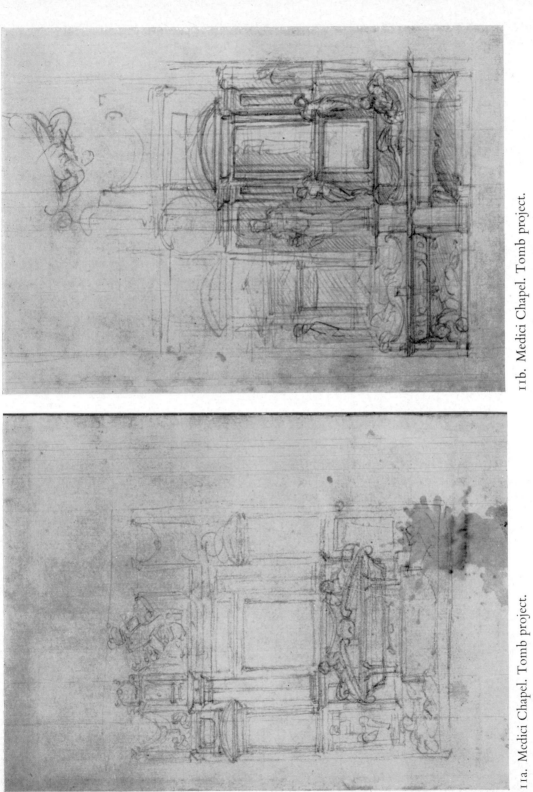

11b. Medici Chapel. Tomb project.

11a. Medici Chapel. Tomb project.

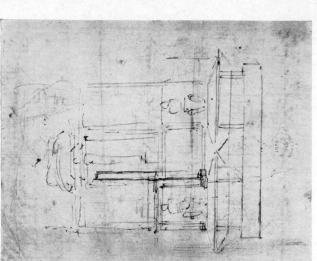

12c. Medici Chapel. Tomb project.

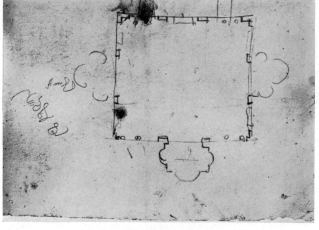

12b. Medici Chapel. Plan project.

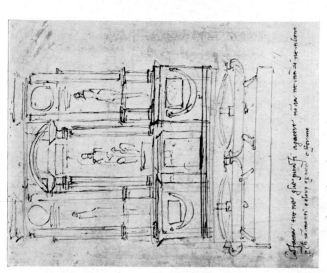

12a. Medici Chapel. Tomb project.

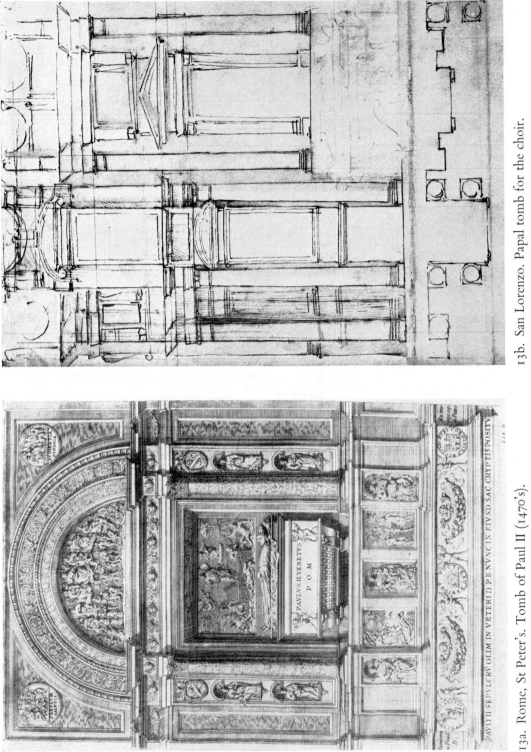

13a. Rome, St Peter's. Tomb of Paul II (1470's).

13b. San Lorenzo. Papal tomb for the choir.

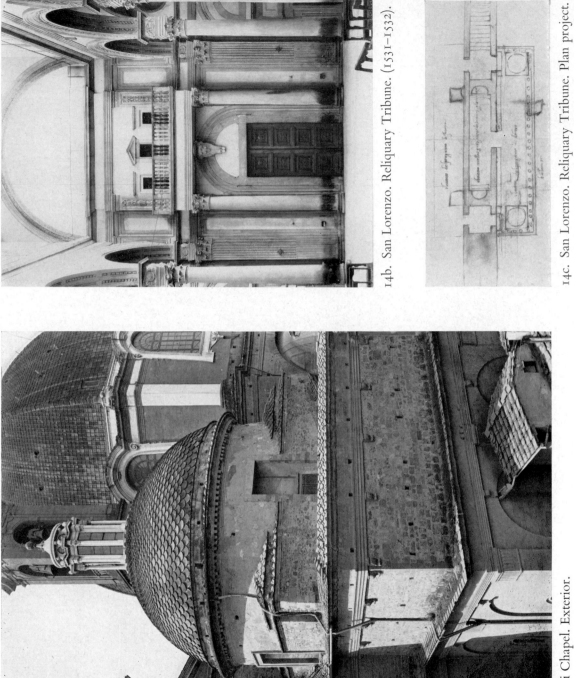

14b. San Lorenzo. Reliquary Tribune. (1531–1532).

14c. San Lorenzo. Reliquary Tribune. Plan project.

14a. Medici Chapel. Exterior.

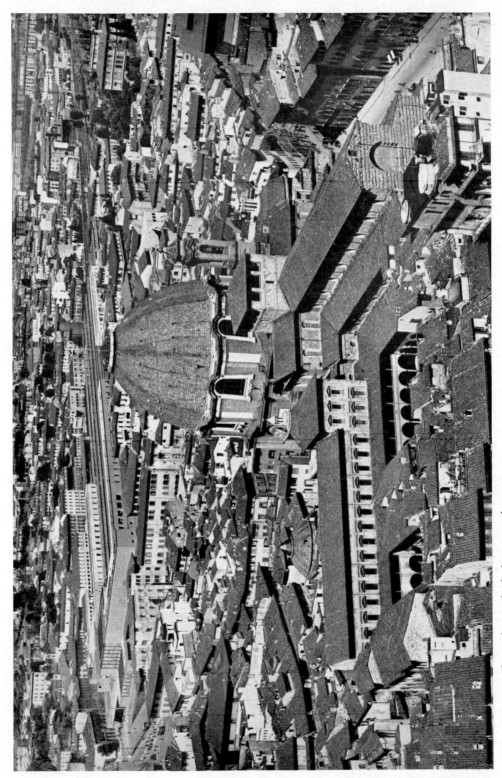

15. San Lorenzo, from the Cathedral campanile.

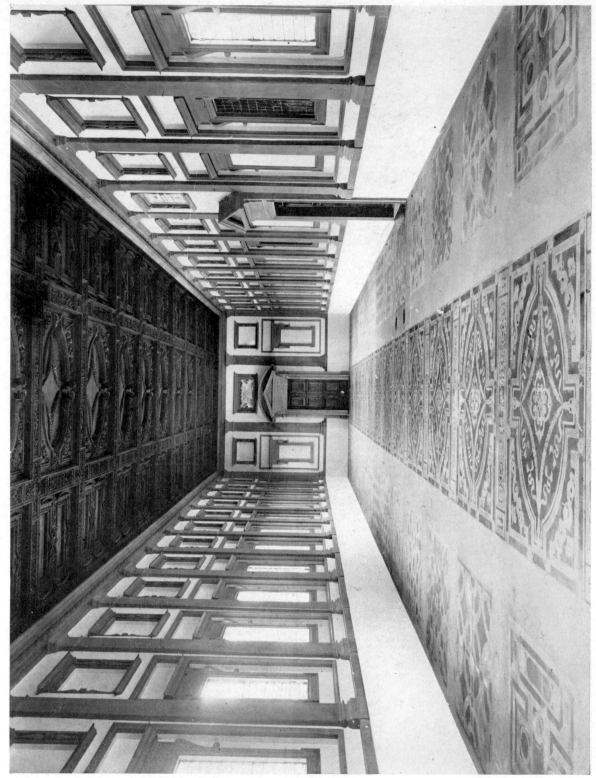

16. Laurentian Library. Interior of the reading-room.

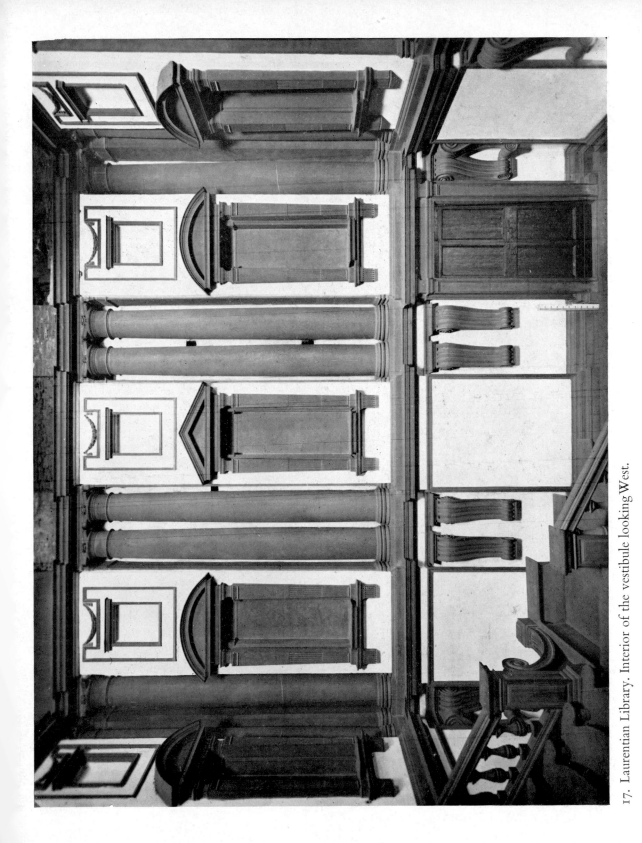

17. Laurentian Library. Interior of the vestibule looking West.

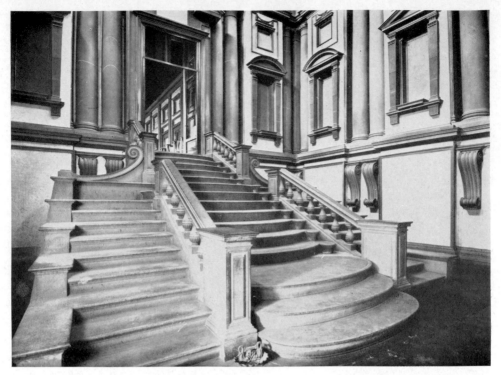

18a. Laurentian Library. Vestibule stairway.

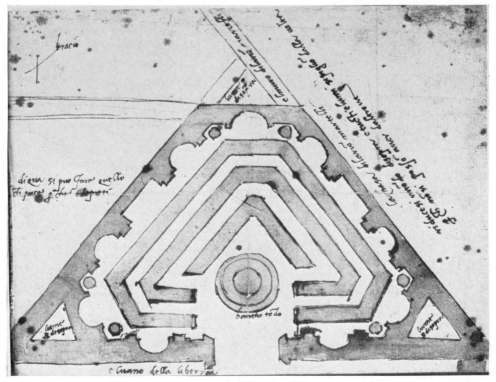

18b. Laurentian Library. Project for a rare book study.

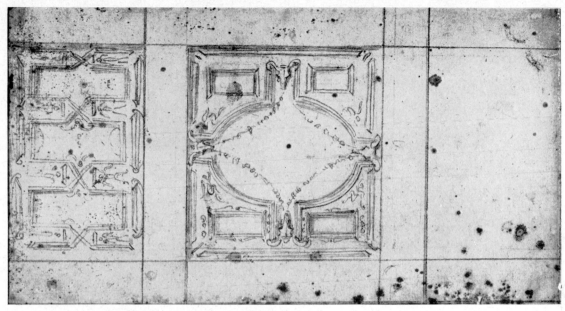

19a. Laurentian Library. Reading-room. Ceiling study.

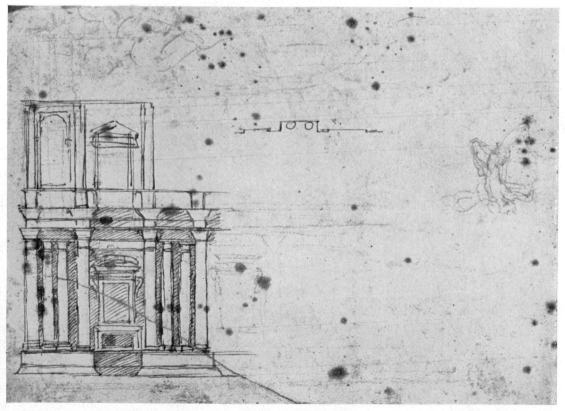

19b. Laurentian Library. Reading-room. Interior elevation study.

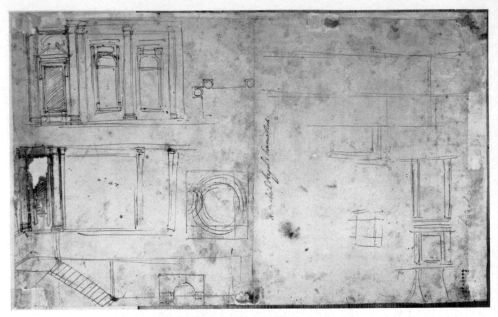

20a. Laurentian Library. Vestibule. Interior elevation study.

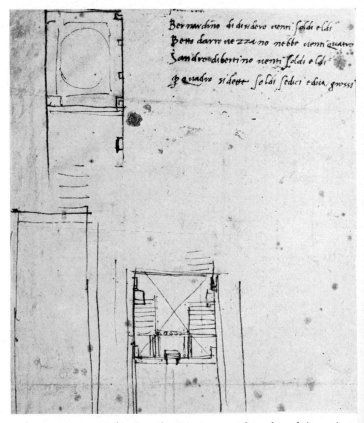

20b. Laurentian Library. Plan project, with a chapel (? top).

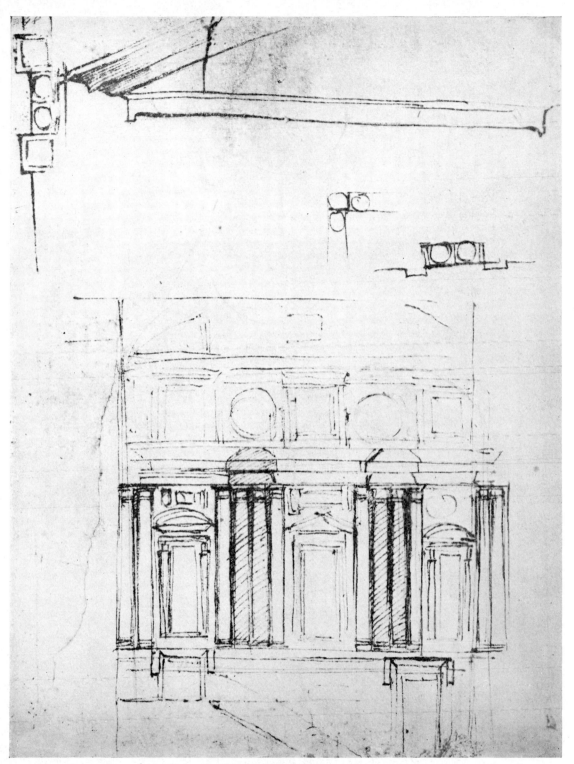

21. Laurentian Library. Vestibule. Study for the West elevation.

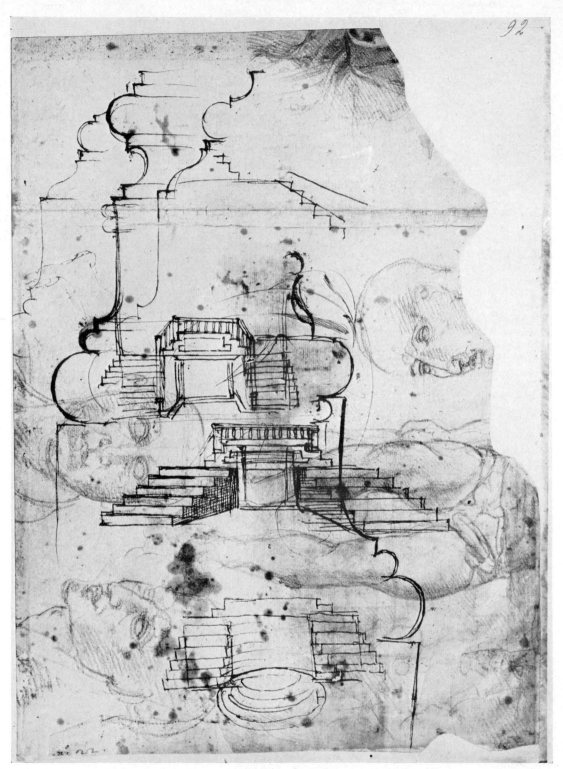

22. Laurentian Library. Vestibule. Studies for the stairway and column profiles.

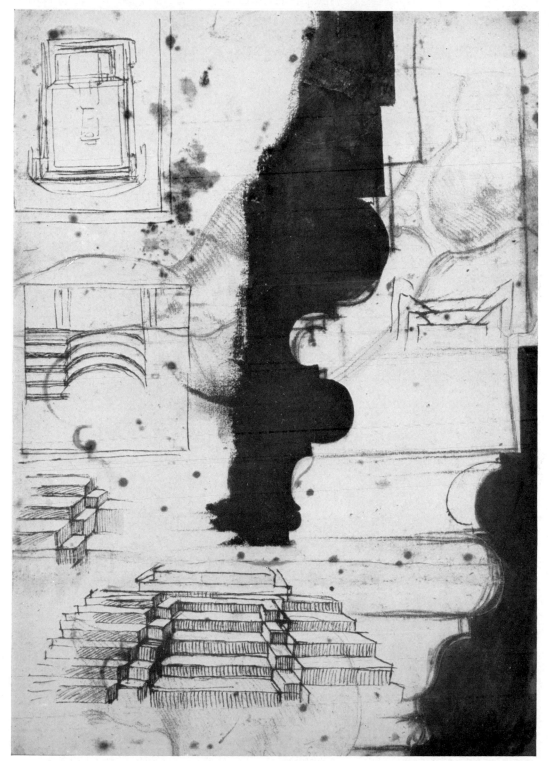

23. Laurentian Library. Vestibule. Studies for the stairway and column profiles.

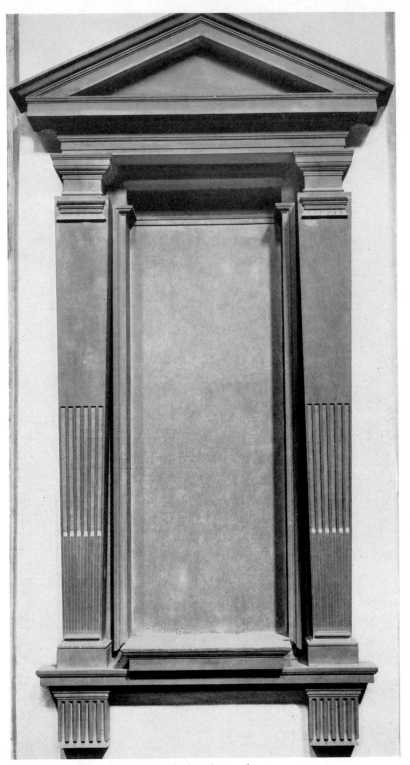

24. Laurentian Library. Vestibule tabernacle.

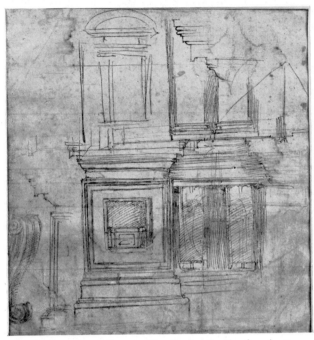

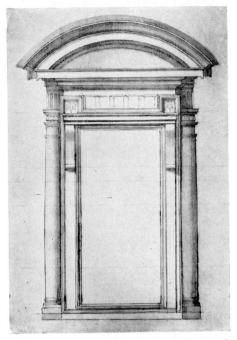

25a. Laurentian Library. Vestibule. Study for the interior elevation and section.

25b. Laurentian Library. Vestibule. Study for the reading-room portal.

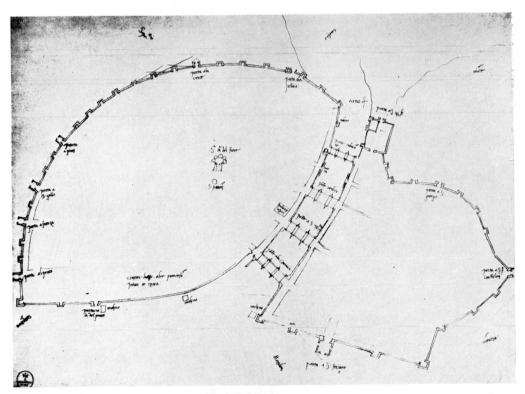

25c. Peruzzi. Plan of Florence's medieval fortifications.

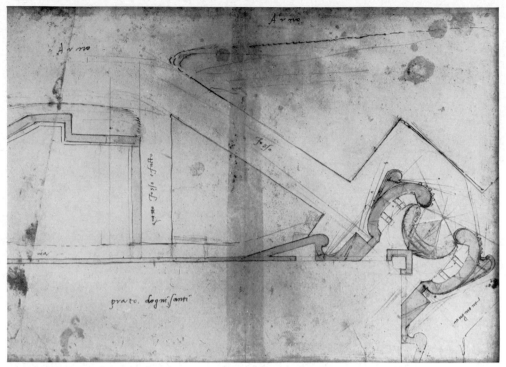

26a. Preliminary project for the Prato d'Ognissanti.

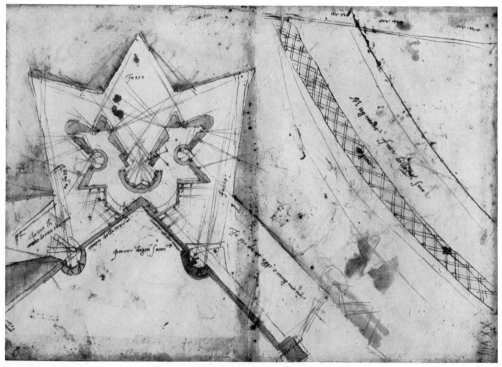

26b. Developed project for the Prato d'Ognissanti.

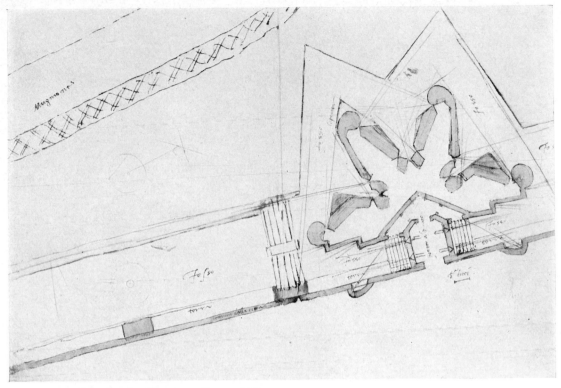

27a. Project for gate fortifications. Porta al Prato.

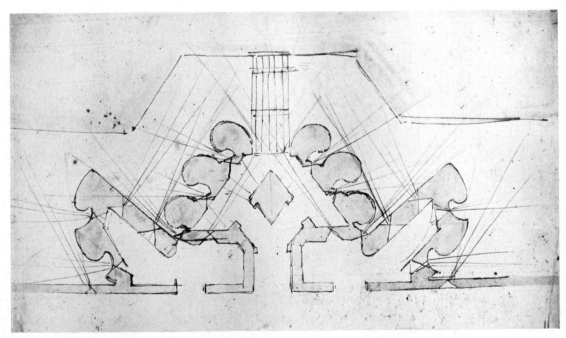

27b. Project for gate fortifications. Unidentified.

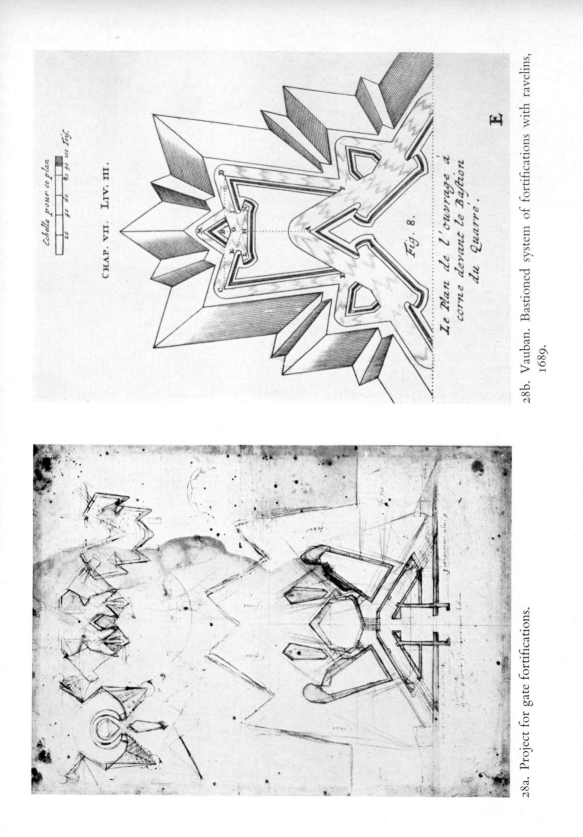

Echelle pour ce plan

CHAP. VII. LIV. III.

Fig. 8.

Le Plan de l'ouvrage à
corne devant le Bastion
du Quarré.

E

28b. Vauban. Bastioned system of fortifications with ravelins,
1689.

28a. Project for gate fortifications.

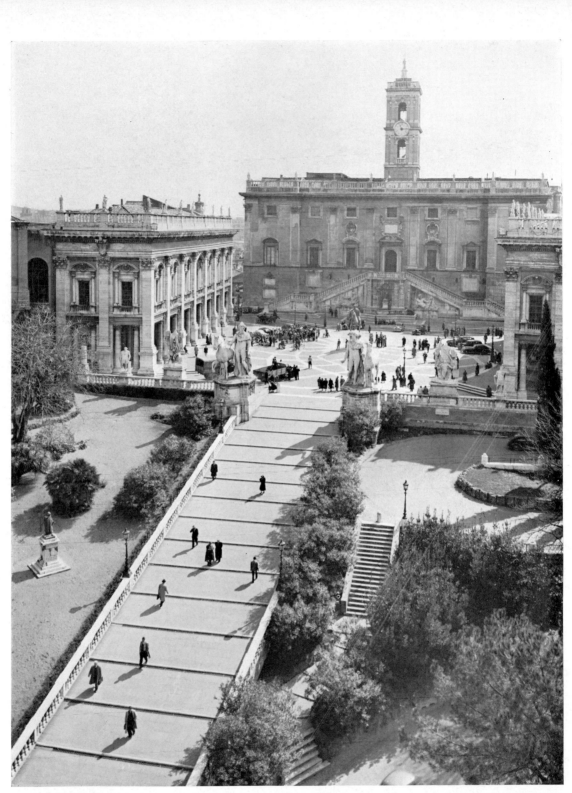

29. Capitoline Hill. View.

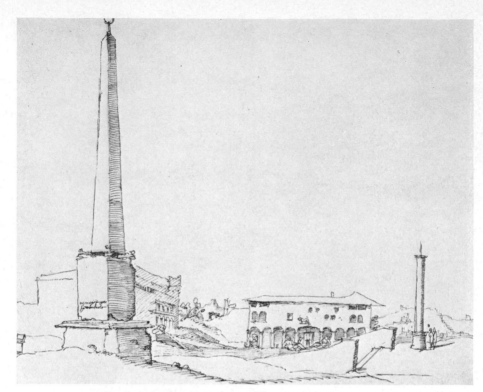

30a. Marten van Heemskerk. Capitoline Hill. View, *ca.* 1535–1536.

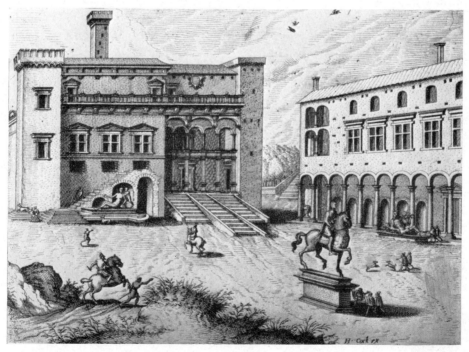

30b. H. Cock. Capitoline Hill. View, *ca.* 1547.

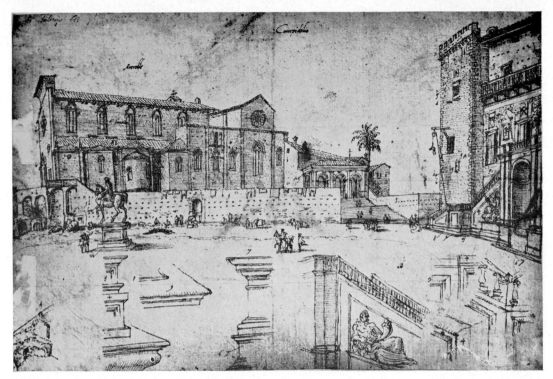

31a. Anonymous. Capitoline Hill. View, *ca.* 1554–1560.

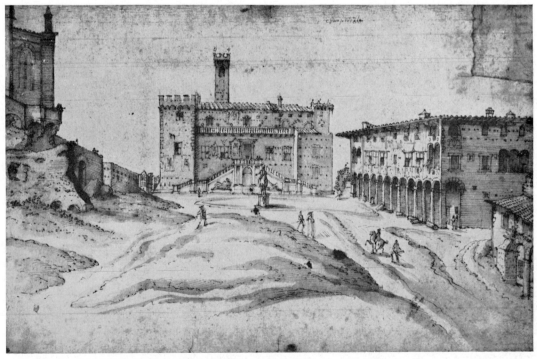

31b. Anonymous. Capitoline Hill. View, *ca.* 1554–1560.

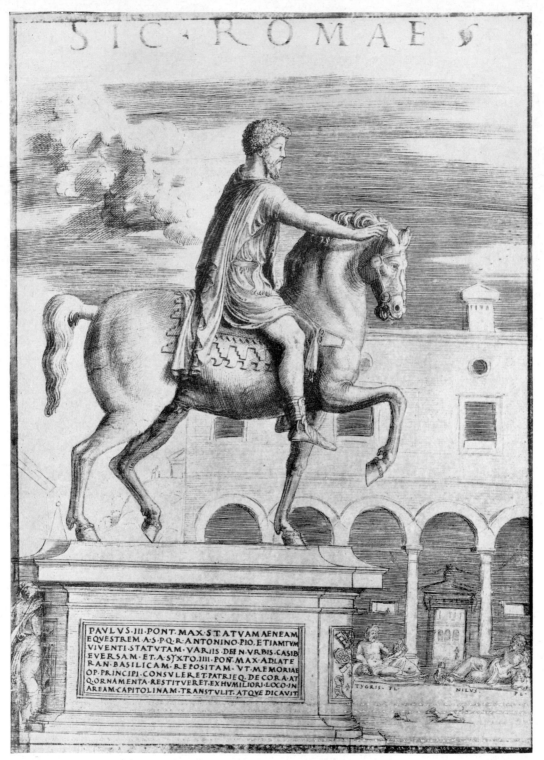

SIC·ROMAE

PAVLVS·III·PONT·MAX·STATVAM·AENEAM
EQVESTREM·A·S·P·Q·R·ANTONINO·PIO·ETIAMTVM
VIVENTI·STATVTAM·VARIIS·DEIN·VRBIS·CASIB
EVERSAM·ET·A·SYXTO·IIII·PON·MAX·AD·LATE
RAN·BASILICAM·REPOSITAM·VT·MEMORIAE
OP·PRINCIPI·CONSVLERET·PATRIEQ·DECORA·AT
Q·ORNAMENTA·RESTITVERET·EX·HVMILIORI·LOCO·IN
AREAM·CAPITOLINAM·TRANSTVLIT·ATQVE·DICAVIT

TYGRIS·FL·   NILVS·FL·

32. Francisco d'Ollanda. Statue of Marcus Aurelius, 1538–1539.

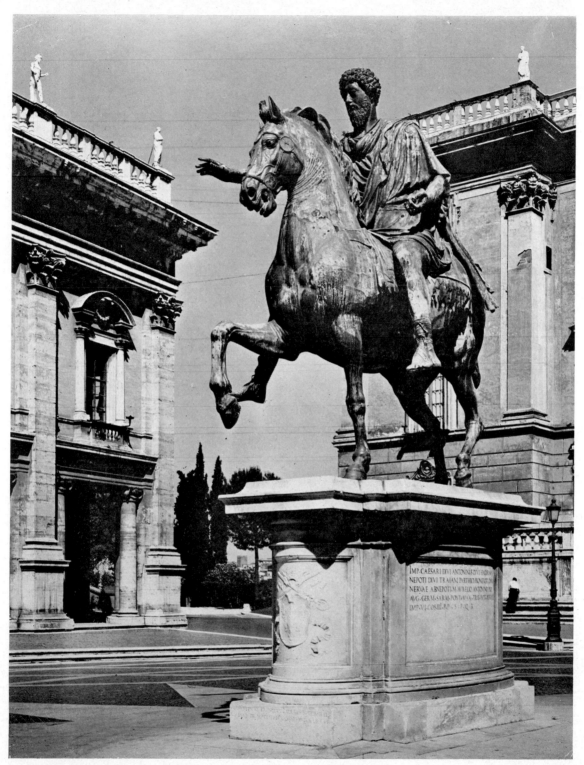

33. Capitoline Hill. Statue of Marcus Aurelius on Michelangelo's base.

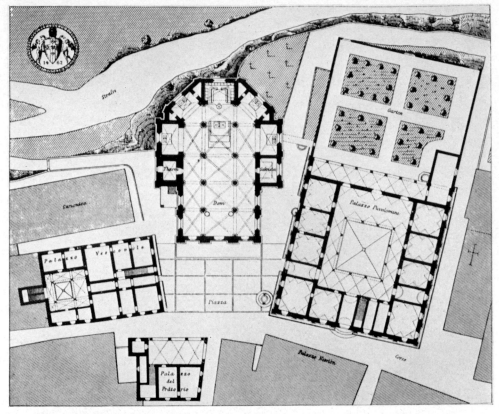

34a. Pienza. Cathedral square. Plan.

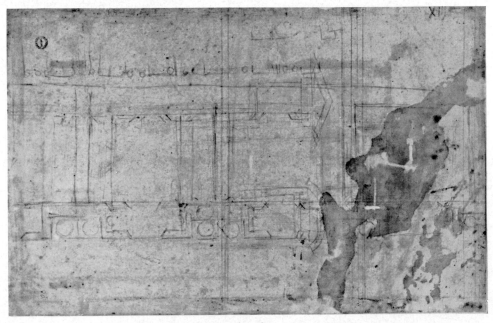

34b. Capitoline Hill? Plan and elevation sketches.

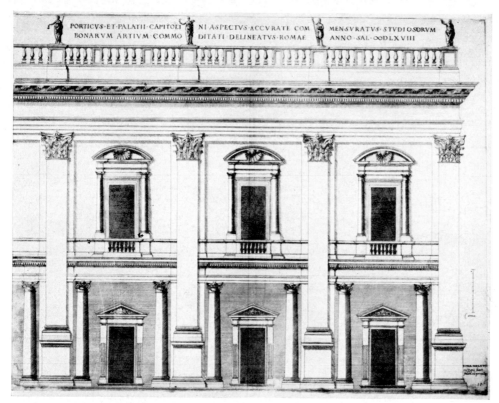

35a. Palazzo de' Conservatori, 1568.

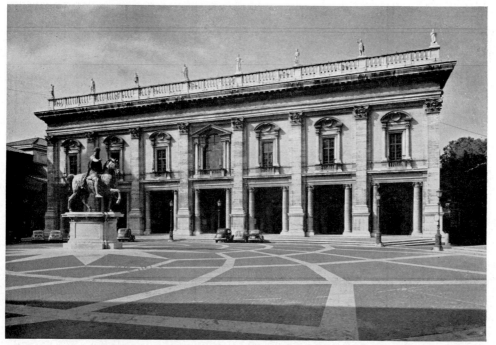

35b. Palazzo de' Conservatori. View.

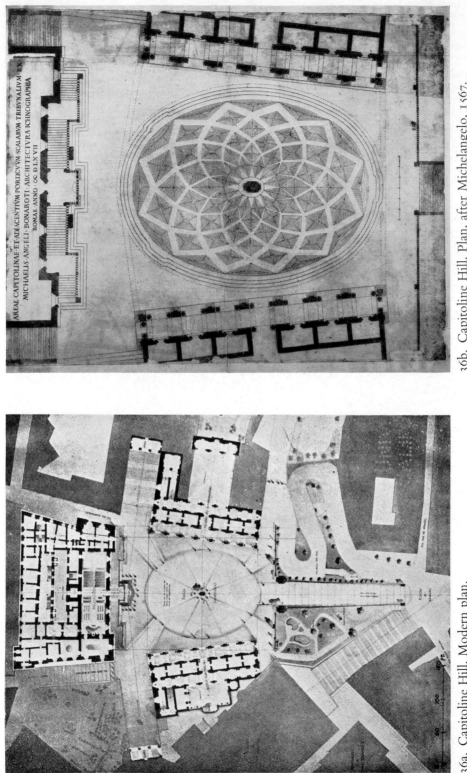

AREAE CAPITOLINAE: ET ADIACENTIVM PORTICVVM SCALARVM TRIBVNALIVM· EX
MICHAELIS·ANGELI·BONAROTI·ARCHITECTVRA ICHNOGRAPHIA
ROMAE ANNO· ꝏ· D LX VII

36b. Capitoline Hill. Plan, after Michelangelo, 1567.

36a. Capitoline Hill. Modern plan.

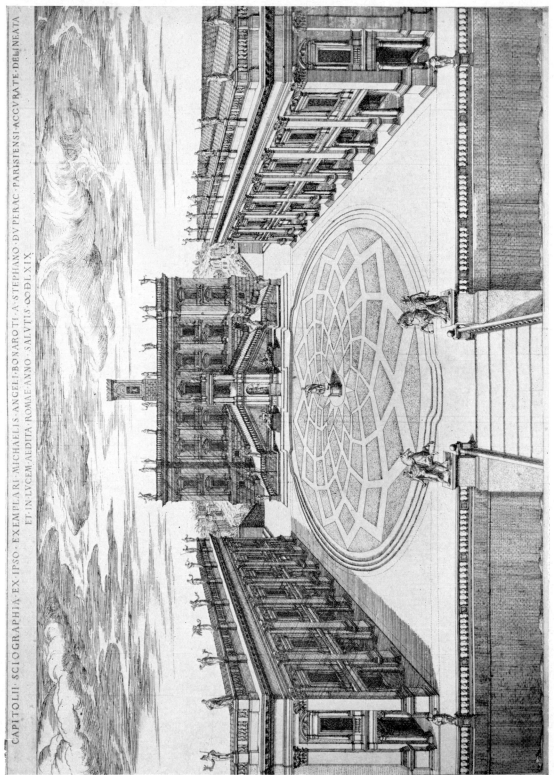

CAPITOLII · SCIOGRAPHIA · EX · IPSO · EXEMPLARI · MICHAELIS · ANGELI · BONAROTI · A · STEPHANO · DV PERAC · PARISIENSI · ACCVRATE · DELINEATA ET · IN · LVCEM · AEDITA · ROMAE · ANNO · SALVTIS · ⅭⅮⅬⅩⅠⅩ

37. Capitoline Hill. Perspective, after Michelangelo. 1569.

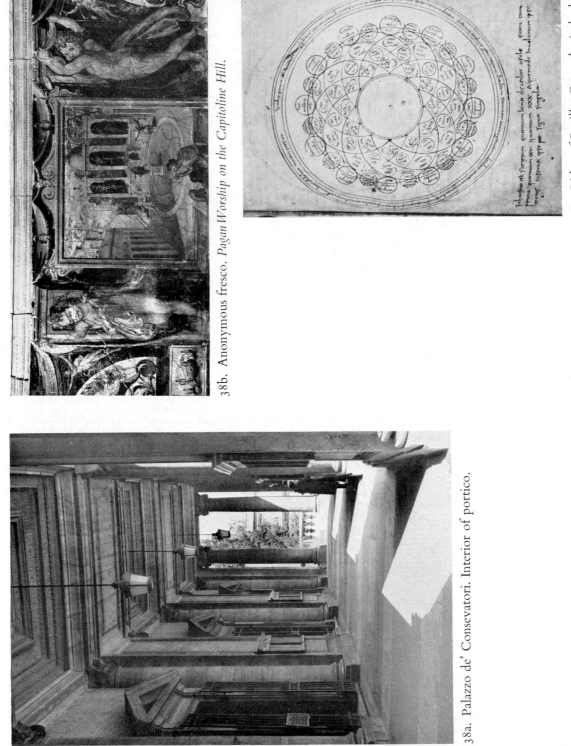

38b. Anonymous fresco. *Pagan Worship on the Capitoline Hill.*

38c. Isidor of Seville. Cosmological schema.

38a. Palazzo de' Consevatori. Interior of portico.

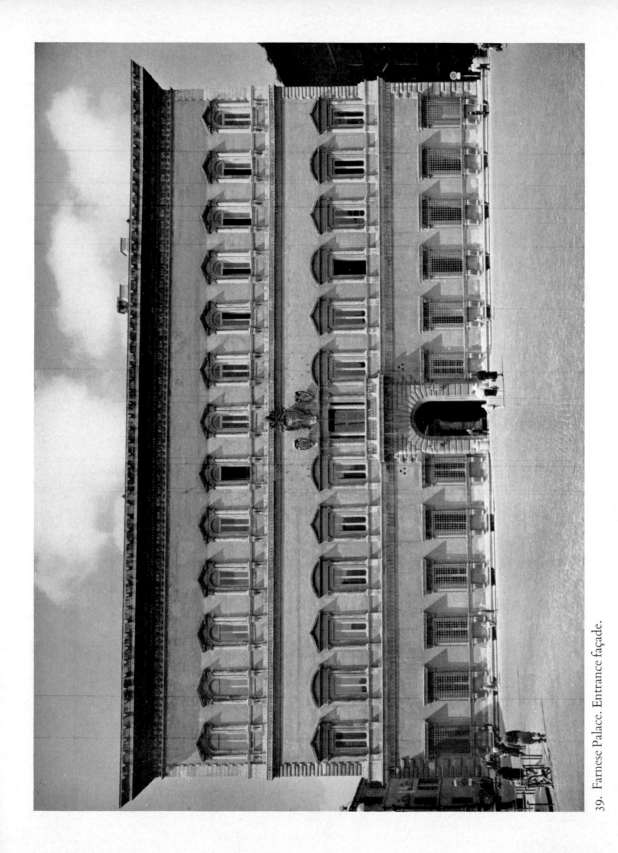

39. Farnese Palace. Entrance façade.

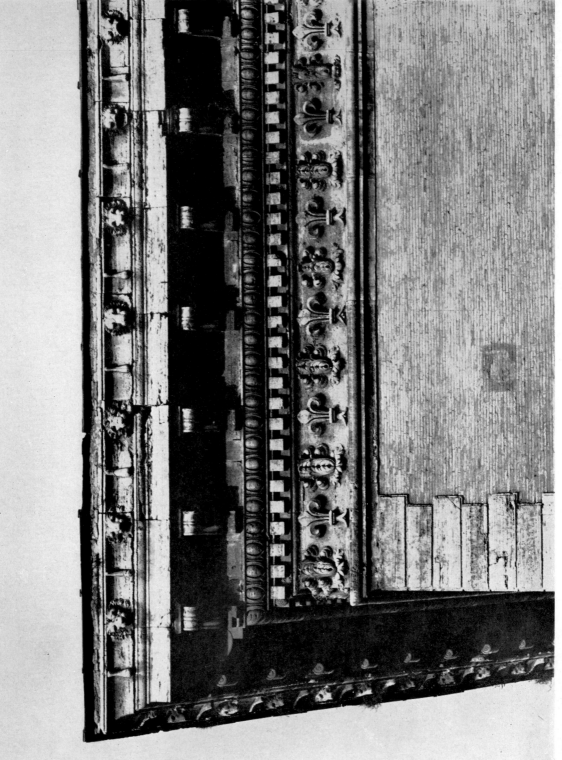

40. Farnese Palace. Cornice.

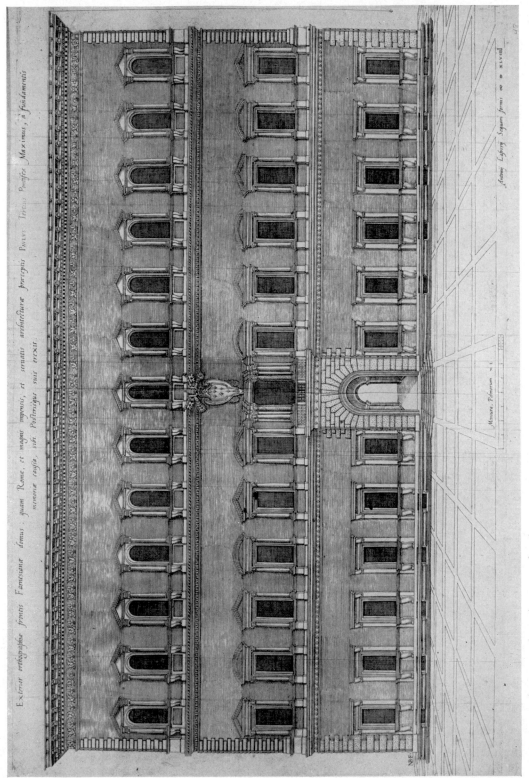

Exterior orthographia frontis Farnesianae domus, quam Romae, et magno impensis, et servatis architecturae praeceptis Paulus Tertius Pontifex Maximus, a fundamentis memoriae causa, sibi Posterisque suis erexit.

Mensura Palmorum X.

Antony Lafrerÿ Sequani formis ∞ ɔ xxviij

41. Farnese Palace. Façade and project for the square, 1549.

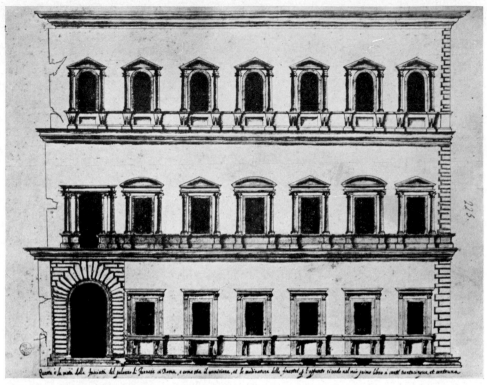

42a. Farnese Palace. Elevation in 1549.

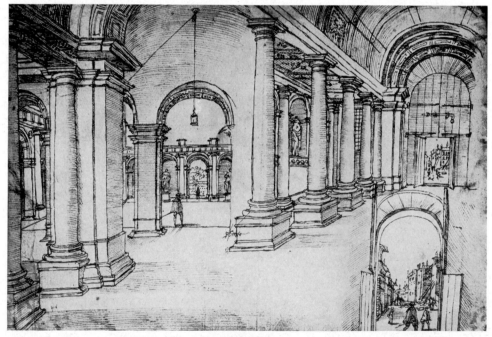

42b. Anonymous. Farnese Palace. View of the court, *ca.* 1554–1560.

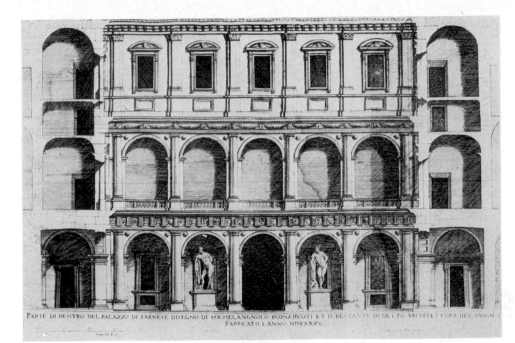

43a. Farnese Palace. Court, before remodelling, 1655?

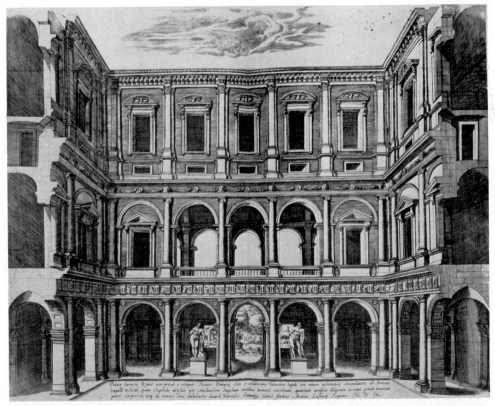

43b. Farnese Palace. Project of the rear wing, after Michelangelo, 1560.

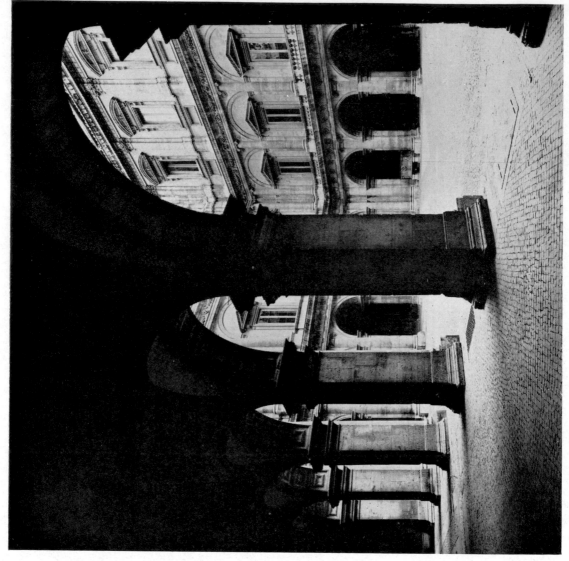

44. Farnese Palace. Court.

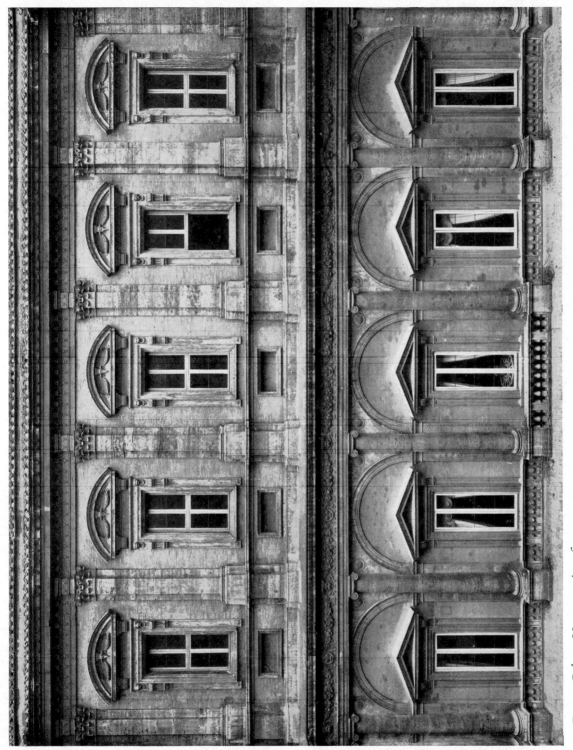

45. Farnese Palace. Upper stories of court.

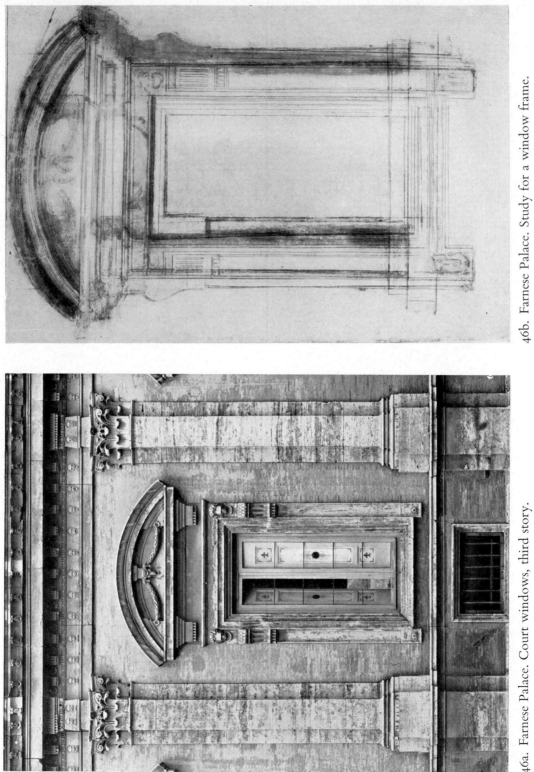

46b. Farnese Palace. Study for a window frame.

46a. Farnese Palace. Court windows, third story.

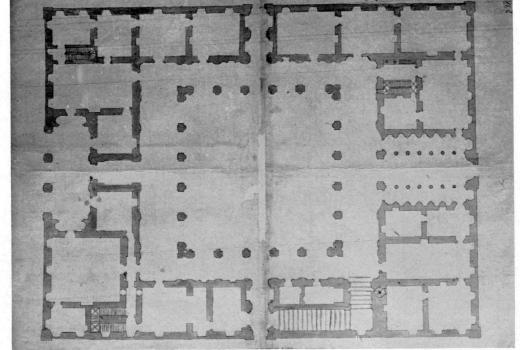

47b. After Sangallo and Michelangelo. Farnese Palace. Plan, 1549.

47a. A. Sangallo. Farnese Palace. Plan project.

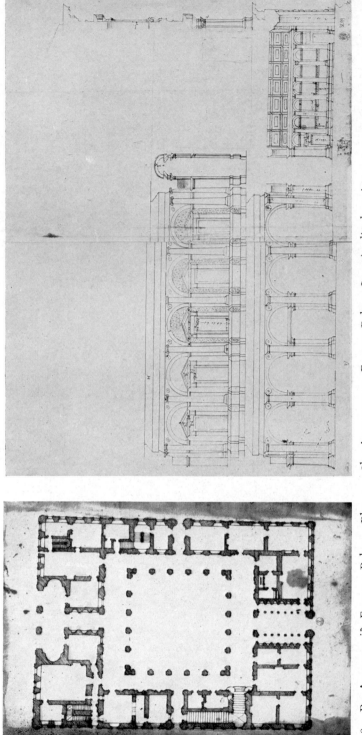

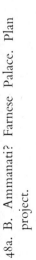

48b. Anonymous. Farnese Palace. Longitudinal section, *ca.* 1558–1568.

48a. B. Ammanati? Farnese Palace. Plan project.

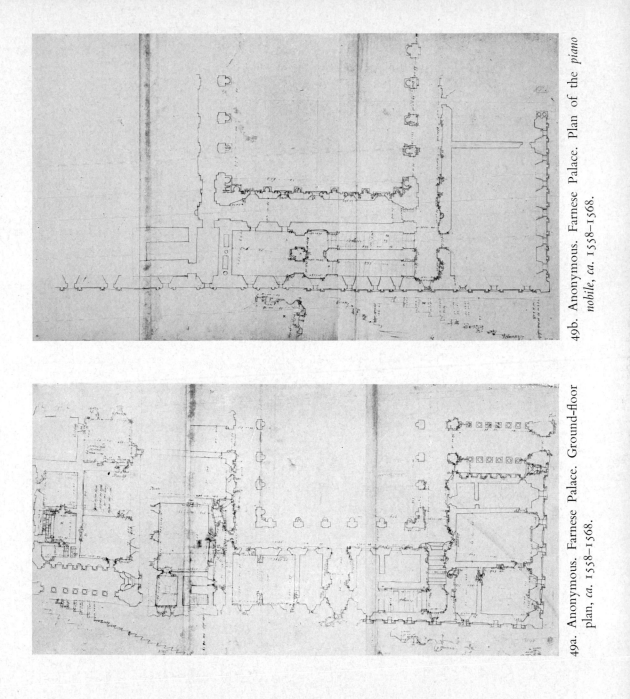

49b. Anonymous. Farnese Palace. Plan of the *piano nobile, ca.* 1558–1568.

49a. Anonymous. Farnese Palace. Ground-floor plan, *ca.* 1558–1568.

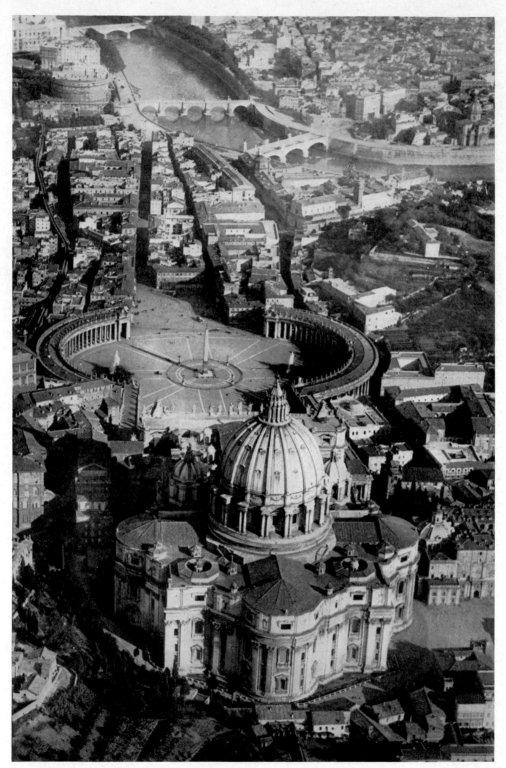

50. St Peter's. Air view.

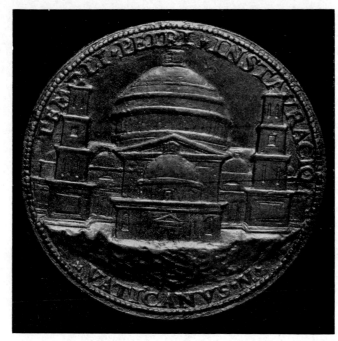

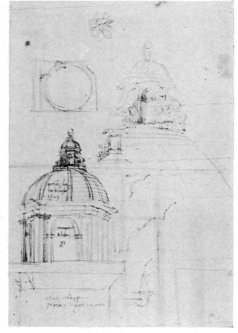

51a. Bramante. Project for St Peter's, 1506.

51b. Bramante. Vatican, Torre Borgia cupola, 1513.

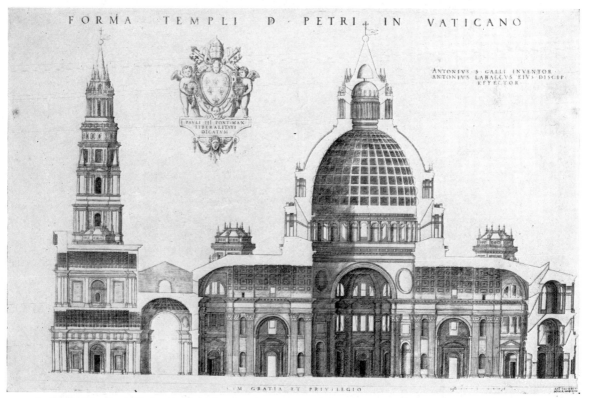

51c. A. Sangallo. Project for St Peter's, 1545.

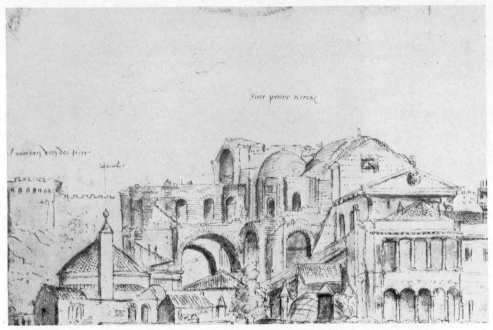

52a. Anonymous. St Peter's. View in 1544.

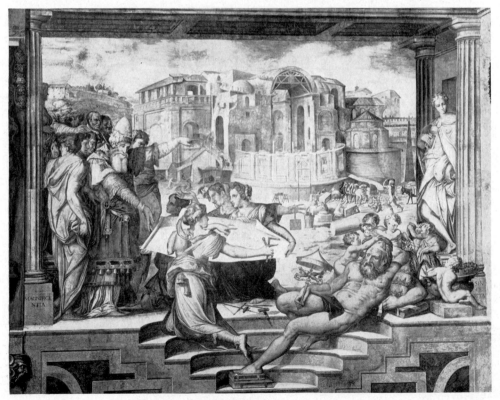

52b. G. Vasari. St Peter's. View in 1546.

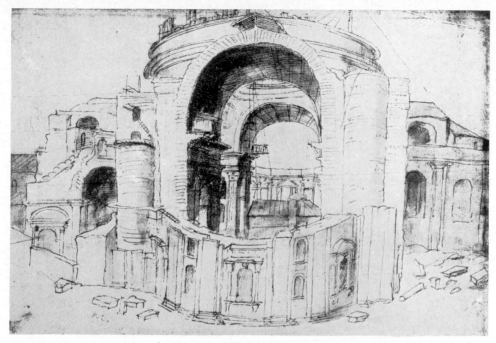

53a. Anonymous. St Peter's. View, *ca.* 1554–1555.

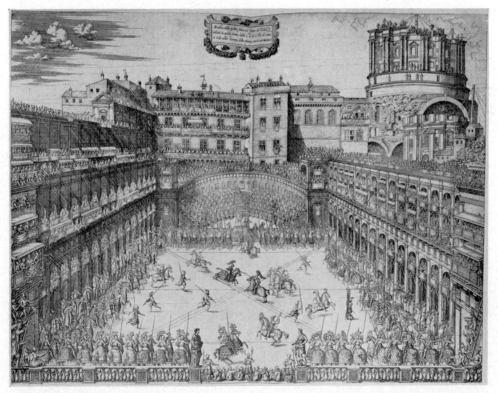

53b. Master H. C. B. St Peter's. View in 1565.

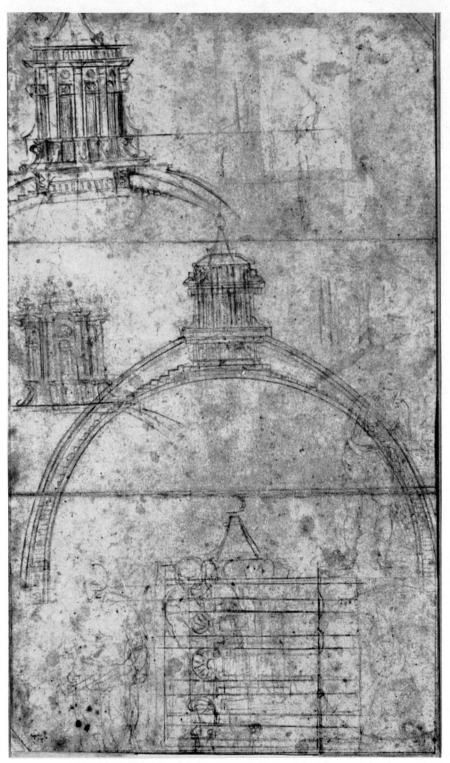

54. St Peter's. Projects for the dome and lantern.

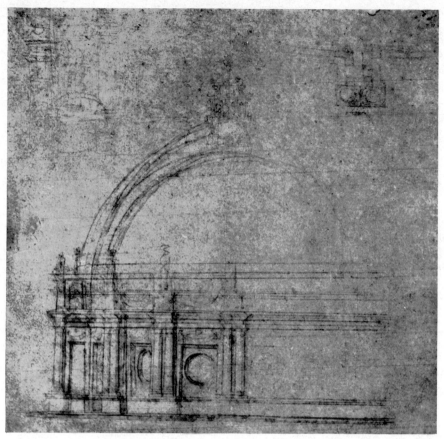

55a. St Peter's. Study of the dome.

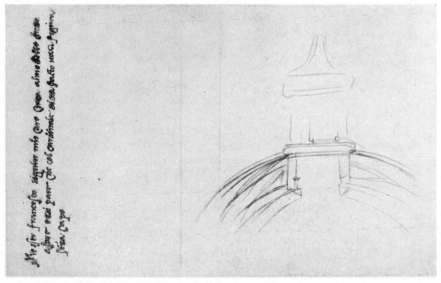

55b. St Peter's. Sketch for the main lantern.

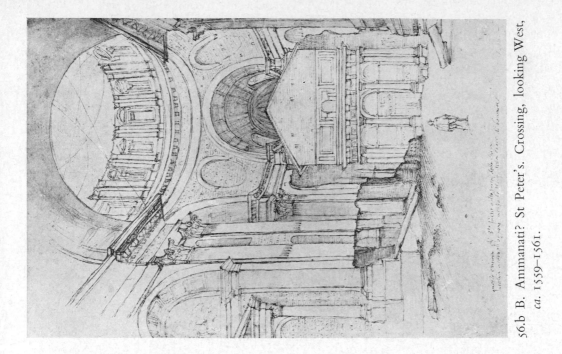

56.b B. Ammanati? St Peter's. Crossing, looking West,
ca. 1559–1561.

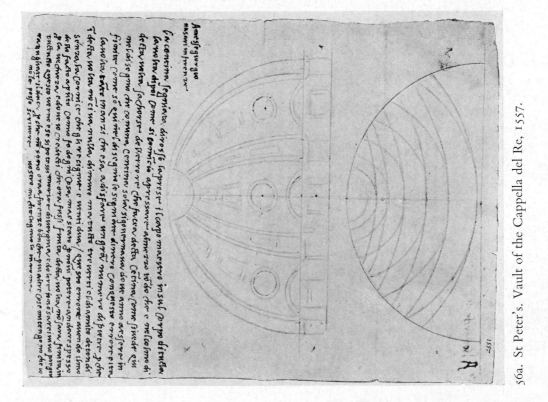

56a. St Peter's. Vault of the Cappella del Re, 1557.

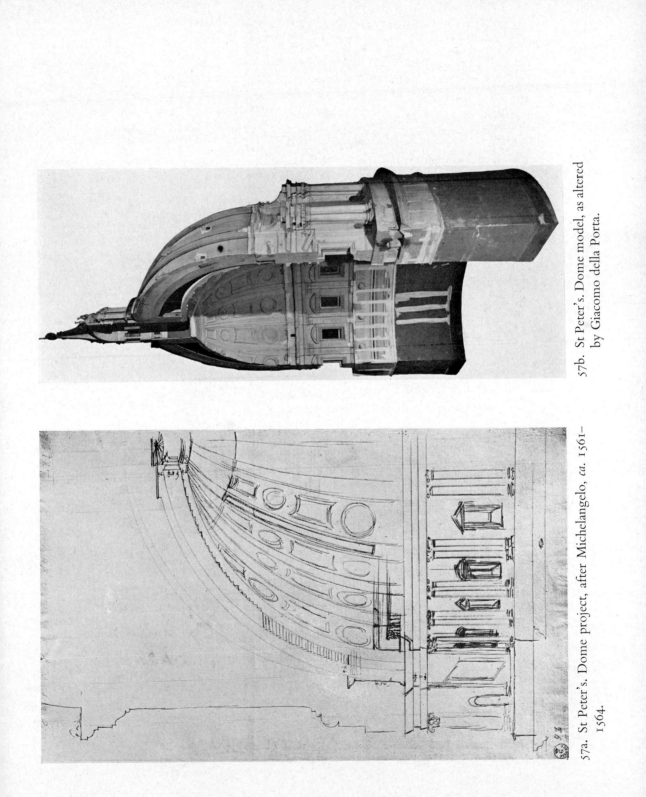

57b. St Peter's. Dome model, as altered by Giacomo della Porta.

57a. St Peter's. Dome project, after Michelangelo, *ca.* 1561–1564.

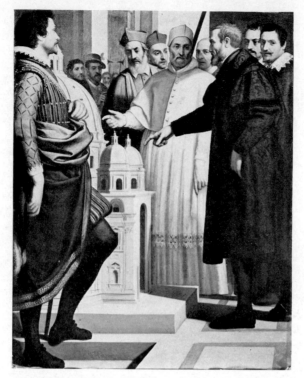

58a, D. Passignani. *Michelangelo presenting his model
to a Pope*, 1620.

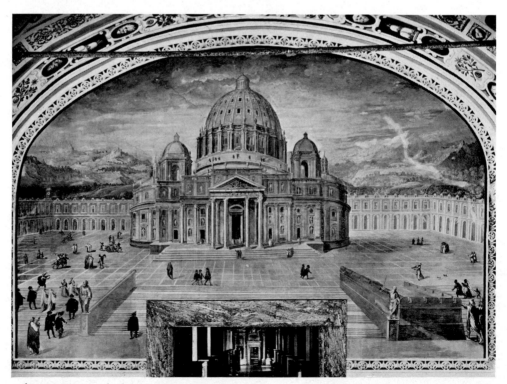

58b P. Nogari. Ideal view of St Peter's, *ca.* 1587.

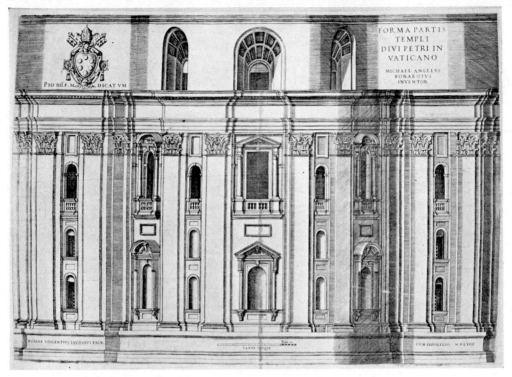

59a. St Peter's. Exterior elevation, 1564.

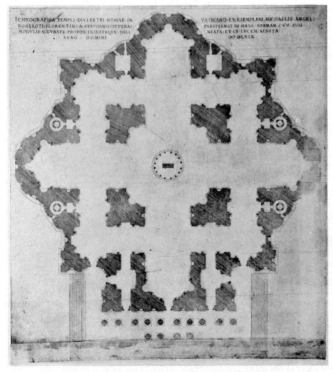

59b. St Peter's. Plan, after Michelangelo, 1569.

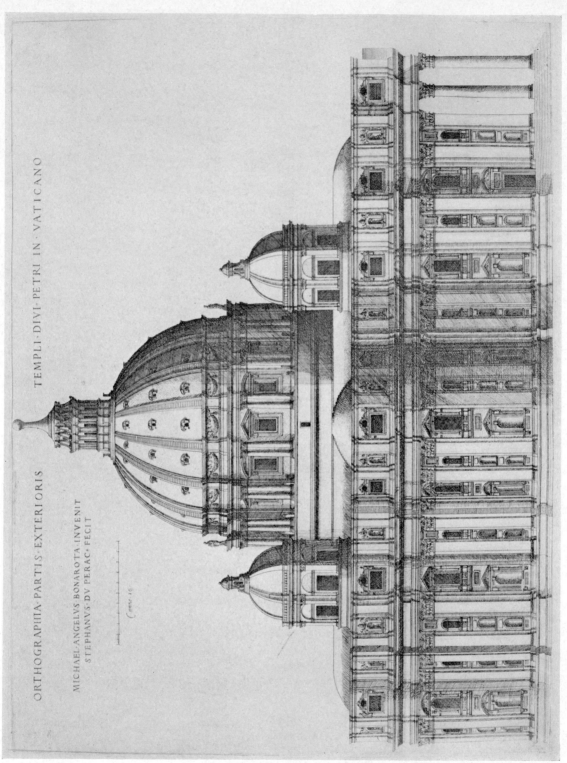

ORTHOGRAPHIA·PARTIS·EXTERIORIS   TEMPLI·DIVI·PETRI·IN·VATICANO

MICHAEL·ANGELVS·BONAROTA·INVENIT
STEPHANVS·DV·PERAC·FECIT

60. St Peter's. South elevation, based on Michelangelo, 1569?

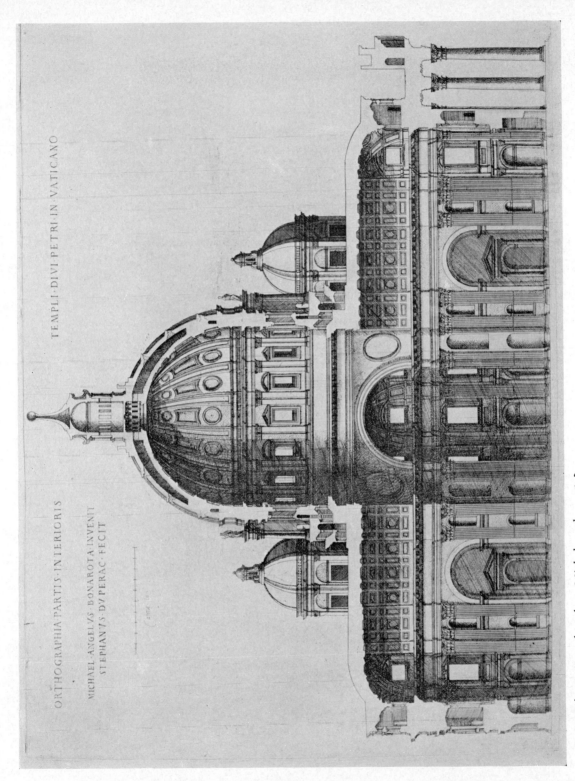

ORTHOGRAPHIA PARTIS·INTERIORIS

TEMPLI·DIVI·PETRI·IN·VATICANO

MICHAEL·ANGELVS·BONAROTA·INVENIT
STEPHANVS·DV·PERAC·FECIT

61. St Peter's. Section, based on Michelangelo, 1569?

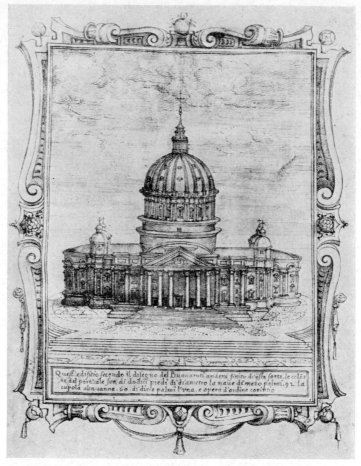

62a. St Peter's. East elevation, based on Michelangelo.

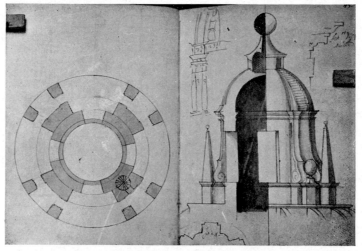

62b. St Peter's. Vignola's(?) project for lanterns of major dome.

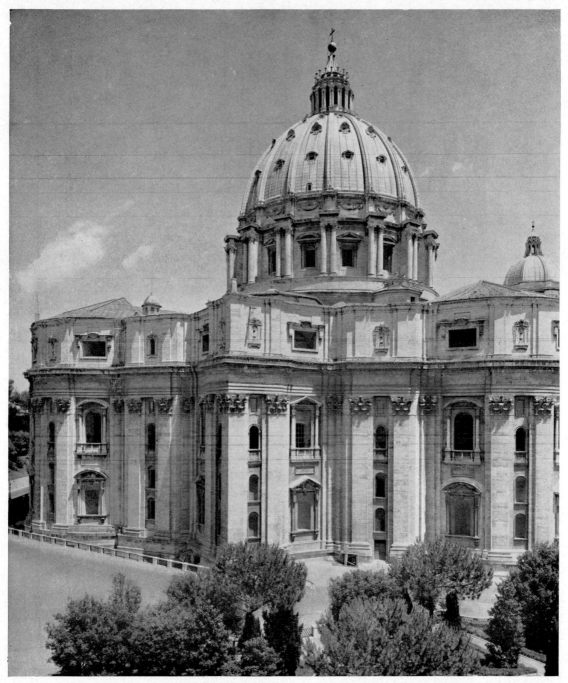

63. St Peter's. View from the Vatican gardens.

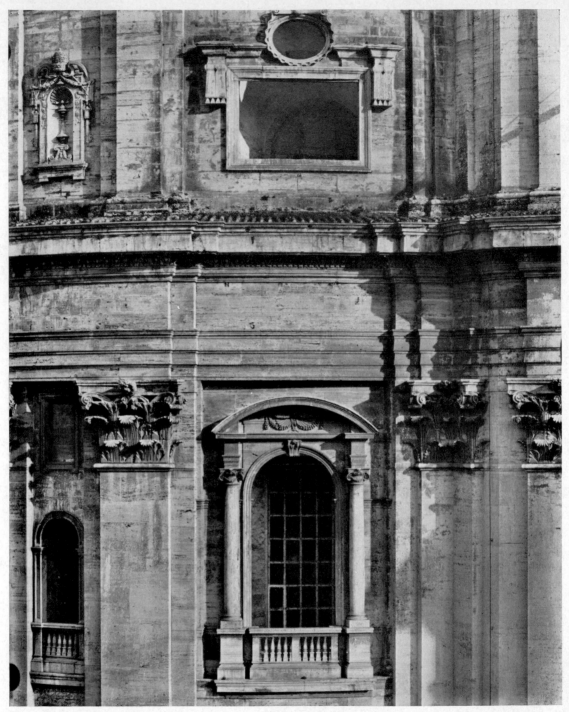

64. St Peter's. Apse. Detail.

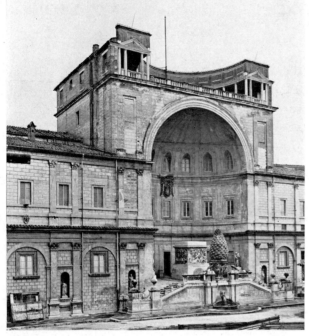

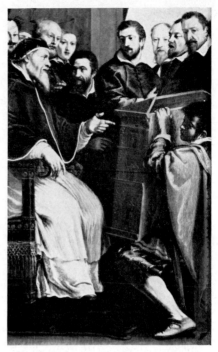

65a. Vatican. Belvedere. Michelangelo's stairway (1550–1551).

65b. F. Boschi. *Michelangelo presenting a model to Julius III.*

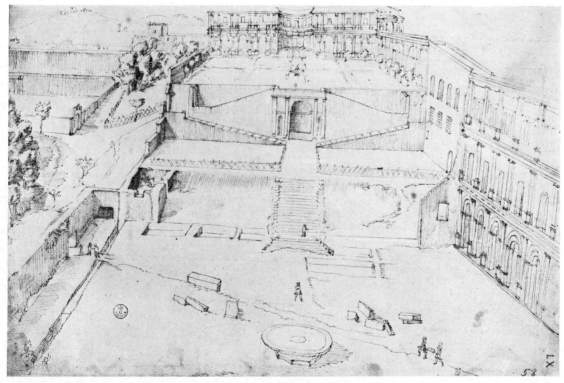

65c. G.-A. Dosio. The Cortile del Belvedere, *ca.* 1558–1561.

66b. San Giovanni de' Fiorentini. Plan project, 1559.

66a. A. Sangallo. San Giovanni de' Fiorentini. Plan project, *ca.* 1525.

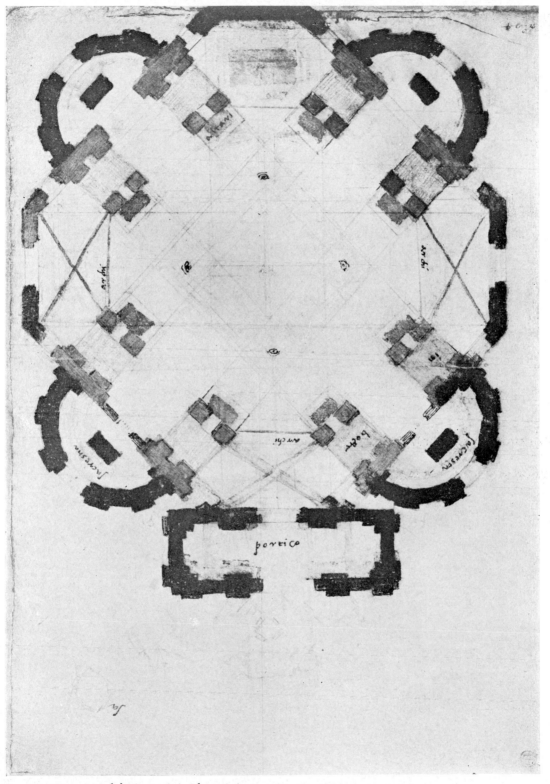

67. San Giovanni de' Fiorentini. Plan project, 1559.

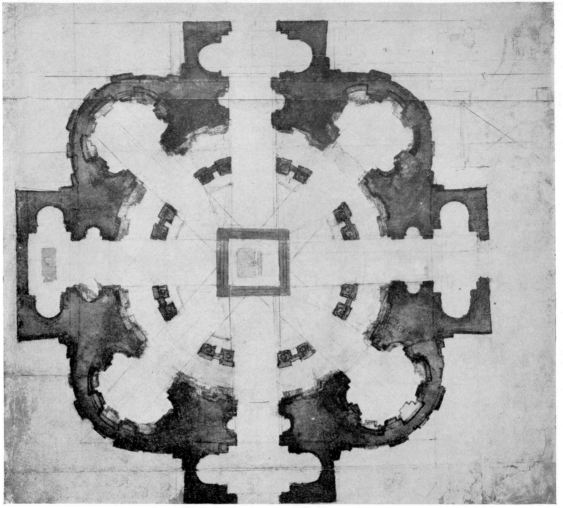

68. San Giovanni de' Fiorentini. Plan project, 1559.

69b. San Giovanni de' Fiorentini. Plan project, after Michelangelo.

69a. Calcagni. San Giovanni de' Fiorentini. Plan for the final model.

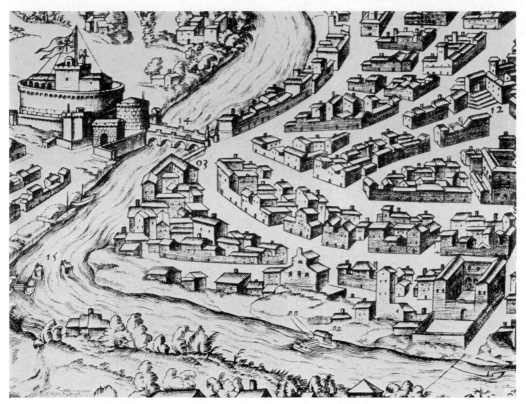

70a. San Giovanni de' Fiorentini. (lower centre, on river bank), 1555.

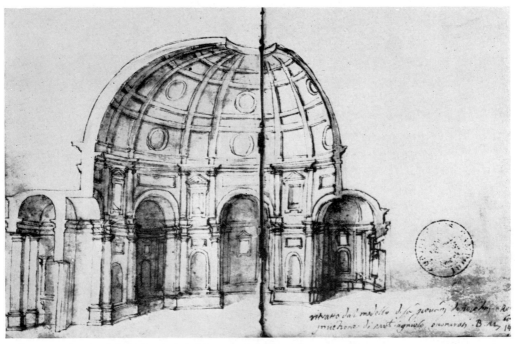

70b. San Giovanni de' Fiorentini. First model (Dosio).

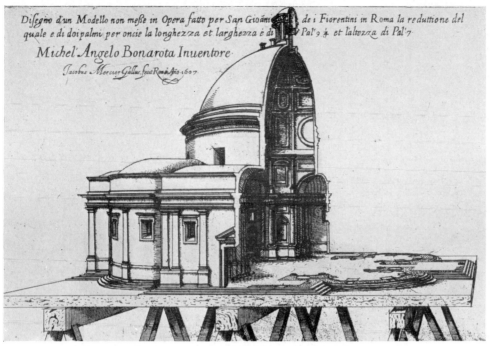

Disegno d'un Modello non messe in Opera fatto per San Gioan... de i Fiorentini in Roma la reduttione del quale e di doi palmi per oncie la longhezza et larghezza è di ... Pal 9 ¾ et laltezza di Pal 7

Michel Angelo Bonarota Inuentore

Jacobus Mercier Gallus fecit Romæ Aio 1607

71a. San Giovanni de' Fiorentini. Final model (Le Mercier).

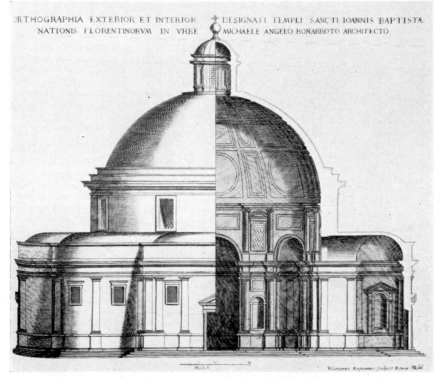

ORTHOGRAPHIA EXTERIOR ET INTERIOR ✠ DESIGNATI TEMPLI SANCTI IOANNIS BAPTISTÆ NATIONIS FLORENTINORVM IN VRBE MICHAELE ANGELO BONARROTO ARCHITECTO.

Valeranus Regnartus sculpsit Romæ Bild.

71b. San Giovanni de' Fiorentini. Final model (Régnard).

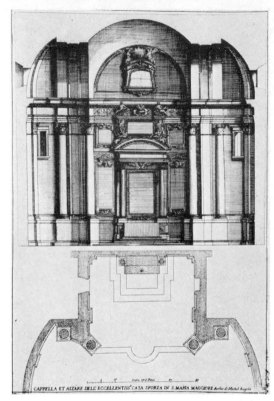

72a. Sforza Chapel. Plan and cross-section.

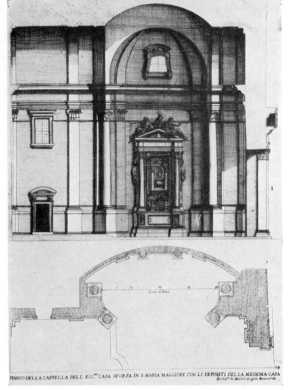

72b. Sforza Chapel. Plan and longitudindal section

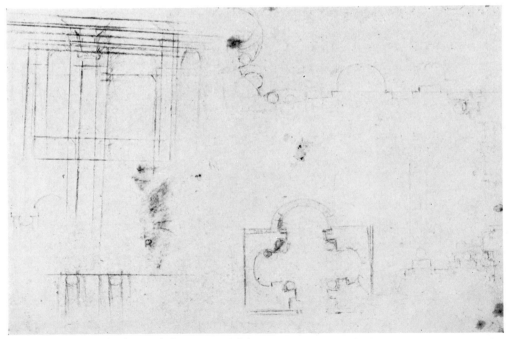

72c. Sforza Chapel. Plan and elevation studies.

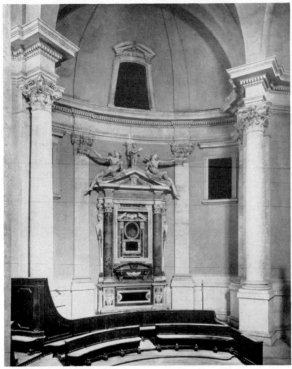

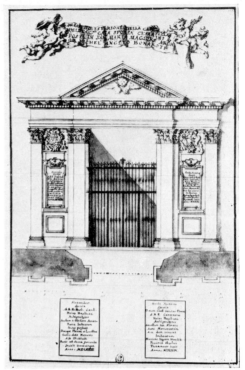

73a. Sforza Chapel. Right chapel.

73b. Sforza Chapel. Façade (destroyed).

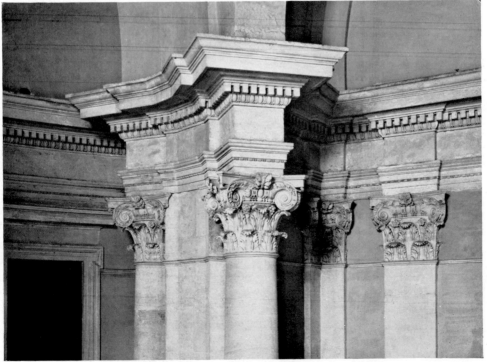

73c. Sforza Chapel. Detail of Order.

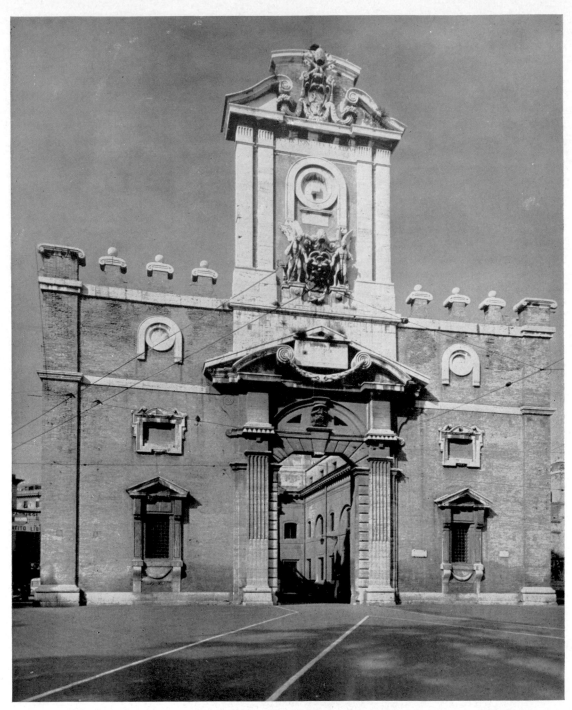

74. Porta Pia. City façade.

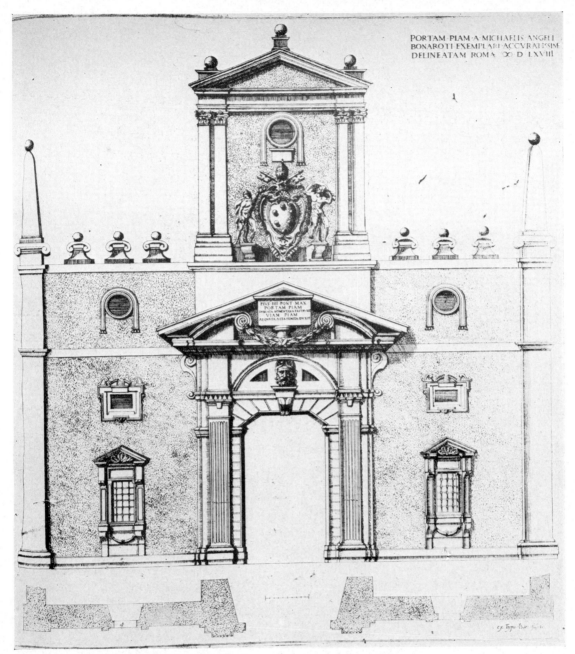

PORTAM·PIAM·A·MICHAELIS·ANGELI
BONAROTI·EXEMPLARI·ACCVRATISSIM
DELINEATAM·ROMA·M·D·LXVIII

75. Porta Pia. Façade project, 1568.

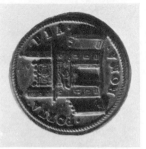

76b. Porta Pia. Initial façade project, 1561.

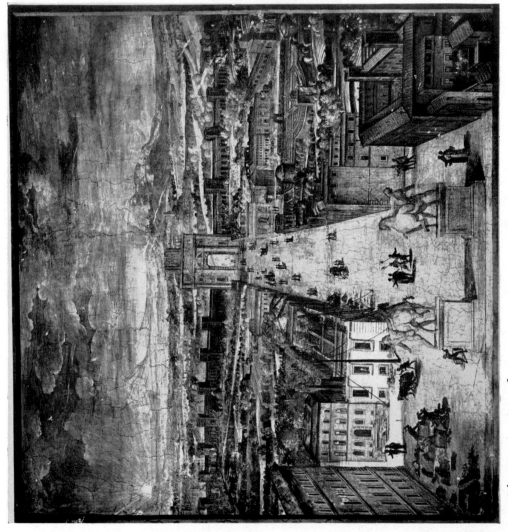

76a. The Via Pia, view of, *ca.* 1590.

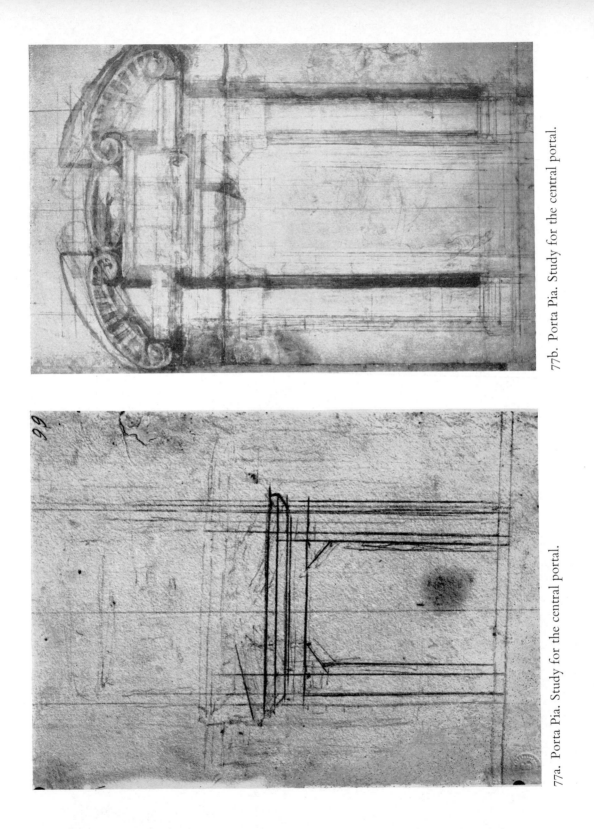

77b. Porta Pia. Study for the central portal.

77a. Porta Pia. Study for the central portal.

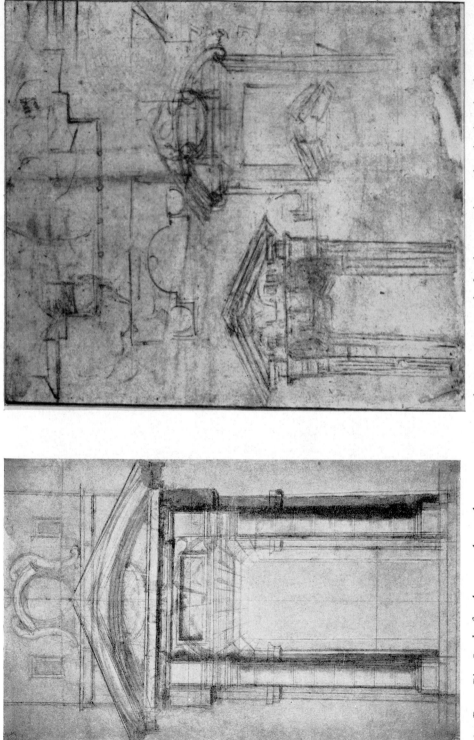

78b. Porta Pia. Study for the central portal and other details.

78a. Porta Pia. Study for the central portal.

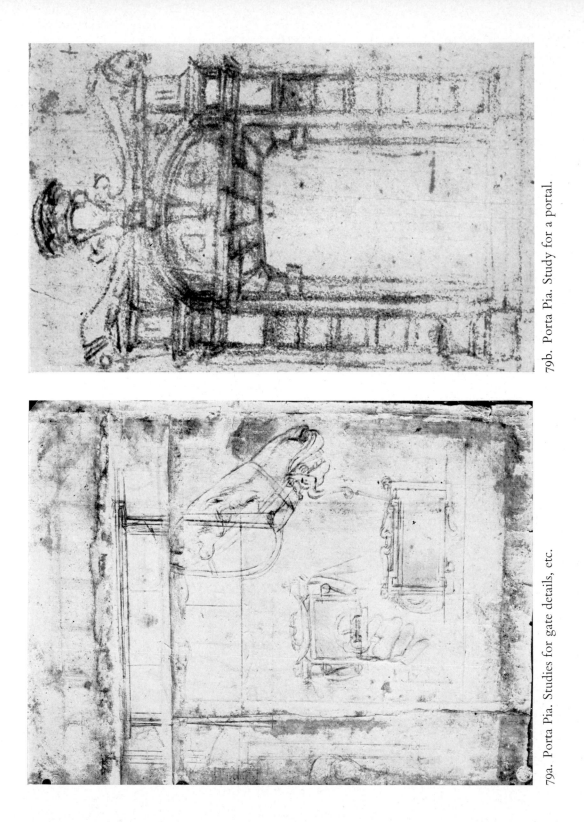

79b. Porta Pia. Study for a portal.

79a. Porta Pia. Studies for gate details, etc.

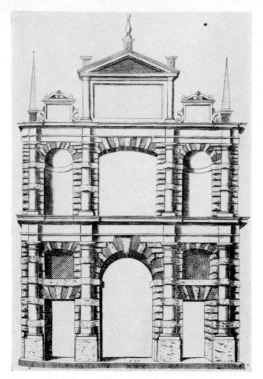

80a. S. Serlio. City-gate design, 1551.

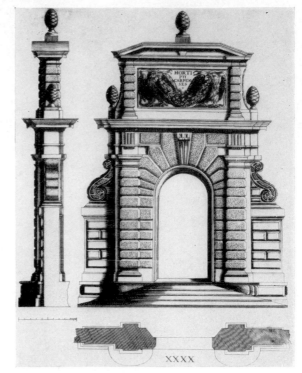

80b. Villa gate, Via Pia, *ca.* 1565.

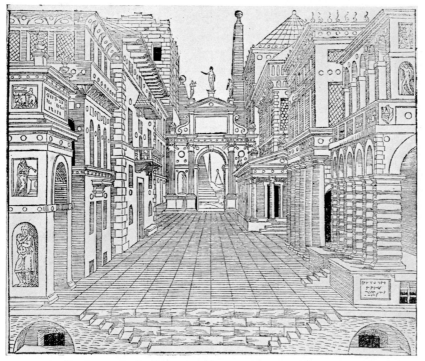

80c. S. Serlio. Stage design, 1545.

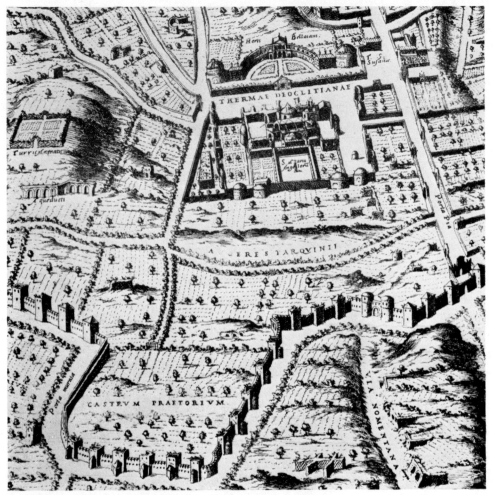

81a. Porta Pia and S. M. degli Angeli, 1577.

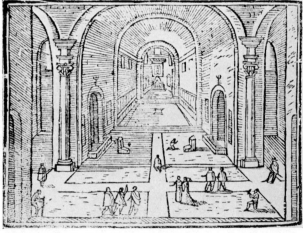

81b. S. M. degli Angeli. View into the chancel, 1644.

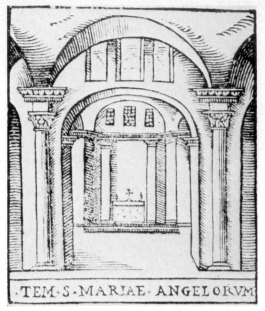

.TEM.S.MARIAE.ANGELORVM.

82a. S. M. degli Angeli. Altar in its original
     position, 1588.

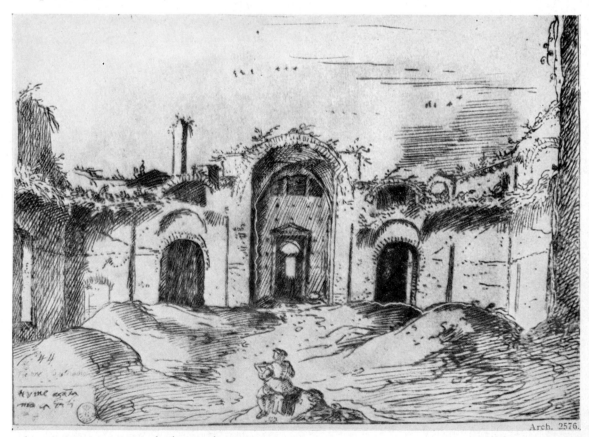

Arch. 2576.

82b. G.-A. Dosio. S. M. degli Angeli. View, *ca.* 1565.

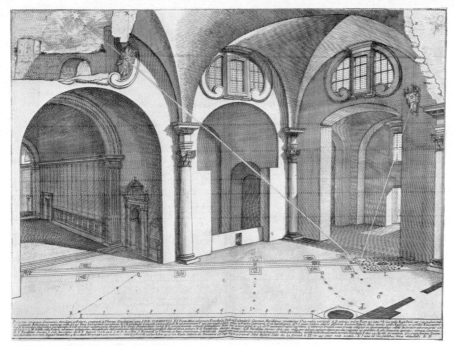

83a. S. M. degli Angeli. View of chancel and southeast vestibule, 1703.

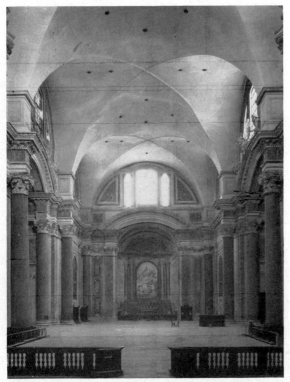

83b. S. M. degli Angeli. The great hall.

Bibliography*

Ackerman, James S. (1954), *The Cortile del Belvedere* (Studi e documenti per la storia del Palazzo Apostolico Vaticano, III), Vatican.

(1954 *bis*), "Architectural Practice in the Italian Renaissance", *Journal of the Society of Architectural Historians*, XIII, pp. 3–11.

(1956), Review of H. Siebenhüner's *Das Kapitol in Rom*, Art Bulletin, XXXVIII, pp. 53–57.

(1957), "*Marcus Aurelius* on the Capitoline Hill", *Renaissance News*, X, pp. 69–75.

Alker, H. R. (1920), *Die Portalfassade von St Peter nach dem Michelangelo-Entwurf*, dissertation (manuscript), Karlruhe.

(1921), "Das Michelangelo-Modell zur Kuppel von St Peter in Rom", *Repertorium für Kunstwissenschaft*, XLIII, pp. 98–99.

Ancel, D. René (1908), "Le Vatican sous Paul IV", *Revue Bénédictine*, XXV, pp. 48–71.

Apollonj Ghetti, Bruno M. (1934), *Opere architettoniche di Michelangelo a Firenze* (I monumenti italiani, II), Rome.

(*et al*) (1951), *Esplorazioni sotto la confessione di San Pietro in Vaticano*, Vatican, 2 vols.

Appolloni, A. (1912), "Vicende e restauri della statua equestre di Marco Aurelio", *Atti e Memorie della R. Accademia di San Luca*, II, pp. 1–24.

Arrigoni, Paolo and Bertarelli, A. (1939), *Piante a vedute di Roma e del Lazio conservate nella raccolta delle stampe e disegni*, Milan.

Arslan, W. (1926–1927), "Forme architettoniche civili di Giacomo della Porta", *Bollettino d'Arte*, VI, pp. 508–528.

Ashby, T. (1904), "Sixteenth Century Drawings of Roman Buildings Attributed to Andreas Coner", *Papers of the British School at Rome*, II, pp. 1–96.

(1916), *Topographical Study in Rome in 1581*, London.

(1927), "The Capitol in Rome: its History and Development", *Town Planning Review*, XII, pp. 159–173.

Baglione, Giovanni (1642), *Le vite de' pittori, scultori et architetti . . .*, Rome.

Bartoli, A. (1914–1922), *I monumenti antichi di Roma nei disegni degli Uffizi di Firenze*, Rome 6 vols.

Battisti, E. (1961), "Disegni cinquecenteschi per San Giovanni dei Fiorentini", *Quaderni dello Istituto di Storia dell'Architettura*, ser. vi-vii, fasc. 31-48, Rome, pp. 185-194.

Beltrami, Luca (1901), "Michelangelo e la facciata di San Lorenzo in Firenze: Disegno e note inediti", *Rassegna d'Arte*, I, pp. 67–72.

(1929) *La cupola vaticana*, Vatican.

Berenson, Bernard (1938), *The Drawings of the Florentine Painters*, 2nd ed., Chicago.

Bertolotti, A. (1875), "Documenti intorno a Michelangelo Buonarroti trovati ed esistenti in Roma", *Archivio storico-artistico, archaeologico e lettarario della città e provincia di Roma*, I, pp. 74–76.

* See also the List of Abbreviations, p. xix.

Bianchini, Francesco (1703), *De kalendario et cyclo Caesaris . . . dissertationes duae . . . his accessit enarratio . . . de nummo et gnomone Clementino*, Rome.

Boffito, Giuseppe and Mori, A. (1926), *Piante e vedute di Firenze*, Florence.

Bonanni, Philippo (1699), *Numismata Pontificum Romanorum*, Rome, 2 vols.

Bonelli, Renato (1960), *Da Bramante a Michelangelo*, Venice.

Borgatti, M. (1931), *Castel Sant'Angelo in Roma*, Rome.

Bourdon, Pierre (1907), "Un plafond du Palais Farnèse", *École française de Rome: Mélanges d'archéologie et d'histoire*, XXVII, pp. 3–22.

   and Laurent-Vibert, Robert (1909), "Le Palais Farnèse d'après l'inventaire de 1653", *École française de Rome: Mélanges d'archéologie et d'historie*, XXIX, pp. 145–198.

Brinckmann, A.E. (1921), "Das Kuppelmodell für San Pietro in Rom", *Repertorium für Kunstwissenschaft*, XLIII, pp. 92–97.

Brockhaus, Heinrich (1909), *Michelangelo und die Medici-Kapelle*, 1st ed., Leipzig.

Broglie, R. de (1953), *Le Palais Farnèse*, Paris.

Buonarroti, Michelangelo (1960), *Rime*, a cura di Enzo N. Girardi, Bari.

Burckhardt, Jacob (1912), *Geschichte der Renaissance in Italien*, 5th ed., Esslingen.

Burger, Fritz (1908), "Uber zwei Architekturzeichnungen Michelangelos in der Casa Buonarroti in Florenz", *Repertorium für Kunstwissenschaft*, XXXI, pp. 101–107.

Caflisch, N. (1934), *Carlo Maderno*, Munich.

Cecchelli, Carlo (1925), *Il Campidoglio*, Rome, Milan.

   (1944), "Il Campidoglio nel medio evo e nella rinascità", *Archivio della R. Dep. romana di storia patria*, LXVII, pp. 209–232.

Clausse, Gustave (1900–1902), *Les San Gallo: Architectes, peintres, sculpteurs, médailleurs, XVe et XVIe siècles*, 3 vols., Paris.

Clements, Robert J. (1961), *Michelangelo's Theory of Art*, New York.

Coolidge, John (1942), "Vignola, and the Little Domes of St Peter's", *Marsyas*, II, pp. 63–123.

   (1948), "The Arched Loggie on the Campidoglio", *Marsyas*, IV, pp. 69–79.

Corti, G. and Parronchi, A. (1964), "Michelangelo al tempo dei lavori di San Lorenzo in una 'ricordanza' del Figiovanni", *Paragone*, 175, pp. 9–31.

De Angelis d'Ossat, G., and Pietrangeli, C. (1965), *Il Campidoglio di Michelangelo*, Milan.

de' Rossi, G.G. (n.d.), *Disegni di vari altari e cappelle . . . di Roma*, Rome.

Di Stefano, (1963), *La cupola di San Pietro: storia della costruzione e dei restauri*, Naples.

D'Onofrio, Cesare (1957), *Le fontane di Roma*, Rome.

Dorez, Léon (1917; 1918), "Nouvelles recherches sur Michel-Ange et son entourage", *Bibliothèque de l'École de Chartres*, LXXVIII, pp. 448–470; LXXIX, pp. 179–220.

Dougill, W. (1927), "The Present Day Capitol", *Town Planning Review*, XII, pp. 174–180.

Egger, Herrmann (1911–1932), *Römische Veduten*, vol. I, Vienna, Leipzig, vol. II, Vienna. (In the second edition of volume I, published in 1932, the plate numbering differs from the first edition, which is cited here.)

   (1935), "Turris campanaria Sancti Petri", *Mededeelingen van het Nederlandsch historisch Instituut te Rome*, 2nd ser., V, pp. 59–82.

Ehrle, Francesco (1908), *Roma prima di Sisto V* (The Dupérac-Lafreri Rome plan of 1577), Rome.

(1911), *Roma al tempo di Giulio III* (The Bufalini Rome plan of 1551), Rome.

(1932), *Roma al tempo di Clemente VIII* (The A. Tempesta Rome plan of 1593), Vatican.

Fasolo, Vincenzo (1923–1924), "La Cappella Sforza di Michelangelo", *Architettura e arti decorative*, III, pp. 433–454.

(1926–1927), "Disegni architettonici di Michelangelo", *Architettura e arti decorative*, VI, pp. 385–401; 433–455.

Ferrerio, P. (1665?), *Palazzi di Roma de' più celebri architetti*, Rome.

Ferri, P.N. (1885), *Indici e cataloghi, III: Disegni di architettura esistenti nella R. Galleria degli Uffizi in Firenze*, Rome.

(1904), "Disegni e stampe del secolo XVI riguardanti la basilica di San Pietro a Roma", *Rassegna d'Arte*, IV, No. 6, pp. 91–94.

Ferri, P.N., and Jacobson, E. (1903), "Disegni sconosciuti di Michelangelo", *Miscellanea d'Arte* I, pp. 73–87.

(1904), "Nuovi disegni sconosciuti di Michelangelo", *Rivista d'Arte*, II, pp. 25–37.

(1905), *Neuentdekte Michelangelo-Zeichnungen in den Uffizien zu Florenz*, Leipzig.

Fichard, J. (1815), "Italia", *Frankfürtisches Archiv für ältere deutsche Literatur und Geschichte*, III, pp. 48 ff.

Fontana, Carlo (1694), *Templum Vaticanum . . .*, Rome.

Fontana, D. (1589), *Del modo tenuto nel trasportare l'obelisco vaticano e delle fabbriche fatte da N. S. Sisto V*, Libro primo, Rome.

Förster, Otto H. (1956), *Bramante*, Vienna – Munich.

Frankl, Paul (1914), *Die Entwicklungsphasen der neueren Baukunst*, Leipzig – Berlin.

Frey, Dagobert (1915), *Bramante-Studien, I: Bramantes St. Peter-Entwurf und seine Apokryphen*, Vienna.

(1920), *Michelangelo-Studien*, Vienna.

(1922), "Eine unbeachtete Zeichnung nach dem Modell Michelangelos für die Fassade von San Lorenzo", *Kunstchronik und Kunstmarkt*, N.F. XXXIV, pp. 221–228.

(1923), *Michelangelo Buonarroti architetto*, Rome.

Frey, Hermann-Walther (1951), "Zur Entstehungsgeschichte des Statuenschmuckes der Medici-Kapelle in Florenz", *Zeitschrift für Kunstgeschichte*, XIV, pp. 40–96.

Frey, Karl (1895), "Studien zu Michelagniolo I", *Jahrbuch der königlichen preuszischen Kunstsammlungen*, XVI, pp. 91–103.

(1896), "Studien zu Michelagniolo II", *Jahrbuch der königlichen preuszischen Kunstsammlungen*, XVII, pp. 5–18; 97–119.

(1907), *Michelagniolo Buonarroti; Quellen und Forschungen zu seiner Geschichte und Kunst*, Berlin.

(1909), "Studien zu Michelagniolo Buonarroti und zur Kunst seiner Zeit", *Jahrbuch der königlichen preuszischen Kunstsammlungen*, Beiheft zum XXX, pp. 103–180.

(1911), "Zur Baugeschichte des St. Peter", *Jahrbuch der königlichen preuszischen Kunstsammlungen*, Beiheft zum XXXI, 1910, pp. 1–95.

(1913), "Zur Baugeschichte des St. Peter", *Jahrbuch der königlichen preuszischen Kunstsammlungen*, Beiheft zum XXXIII, pp. 1–153.

(1914), *Die Briefe des Michelagniolo Buonarroti*, Berlin.

(1916), "Zur Baugeschichte des St. Peter", *Jahrbuch der königlichen preuszischen Kunstsammlungen*, Beiheft zum XXXVII, pp. 22–135.

Frutaz, Amato P. (1956), *Piante e vedute di Roma e del Vaticano dal 1300 al 1676* (Studi e documenti per la storia del Palazzo Apostolico Vaticano, I), Vatican.

Fulvio, A. (1588), *L'antichità di Roma di Andrea Fulvio con le aggiuntioni e annotationi di Girolamo Ferrucci*, Venice.

Gaye, Giovanni (1839–1840), *Carteggio inedito d'artisti dei secoli XIV–XVI*, Florence, 3 vols.

Geymüller, Heinrich von (1875), *Les projets primitifs pour la basilique de Saint-Pierre de Rome*, Paris – Vienna, 2 vols.

(1904), *Michelagnolo Buonarroti als Architekt nach neuen Quellen*, vol. VIII of *Die Architektur der Renaissance in Toscana*, Munich.

Gioseffi, Decio (1960), *La cupola vaticana; un ipotesi michelangiolesca* (Ist di storia dell'arte antica e moderna, 10), Università degli studi di Trieste.

Giovannoni, Gustavo (1921–1922), "Tra la cupola di Bramante e quella di Michelangelo", *Architettura e arti decorative*, I, pp. 418–438. (Republished in the author's *Saggi . . .*, pp. 145–176.)

(1935), *Saggi sull' architettura del Rinascimento*, 2nd ed., Milan.

(1941), "Spigolature nell'archivio di San Pietro in Vaticano", *Istituto di studi romani;* quaderno II (Storia dell'architettura).

(1959?) *Antonio da Sangallo il giovane*, Rome, 2 vols.

Gnoli, Umberto (1937), "Le palais Farnèse (notes et documents)", *École française de Rome: Mélanges d'archéologie et d'histoire*, LIV, Fasc. I–IV, pp. 200–210.

Goez, Werner (1963), "Annotationes zu Michelangelo's Mediceergräbern", *Festschrift für Harald Keller*, Darmstadt, pp. 235–254.

Gotti, Aurelio (1875), *Vita di Michelangelo Buonarroti . . .*, Florence, 2 vols.

Gramberg, Werner (1964), *Die düsseldorfer Skizzenbücher des Guglielmo della Porta*, 2 vols., Berlin.

Gronau, Georg (1911), "Dokumente zur Entstehungsgeschichte der neuen Sakristei und der Bibliothek von San Lorenzo in Florenz", *Jahrbuch der königlichen preuzischen Kunstsammlungen*, Beiheft zum XXXII, pp. 62–81.

(1918), "Uber zwei Skizzenbücher des Guglielmo della Porta in der Düsseldorfer Kunstakademie", *Jahrbuch der königlichen preuszischen Kunstsammlungen*, XXXIX, pp. 171–200.

Guasti, Cesare (1857), *La cupola di Santa Maria del Fiore illustrata con i documenti dell'archivio dell'opera secolare*, Florence.

Guglielmotti, Alberto (1887, 1893), "Storia delle fortificazioni nella spiaggia romana risarcite e accresciute dal 1560 al 1570" (vols. V, X of *Storia della marina pontificia*), Vatican.

Hagelberg, L. (1931), "Die Architektur Michelangelos in ihren Beziehungen zu Manierismus und Barock", *Münchner Jahrbuch, der bildenden Kunst*, N.F., VIII, pp. 264–280.

Hess, Jacob (1961), "Die päpstliche Villa bei Araceli", *Miscellanea Bibliothecae Hertzianae* (Röm. Forsch. der Bibl. Hertziana, xvi), Munich, pp. 239–254.

Hofmann, Theobald (1928), *Entstehungsgeschichte des St Peter in Rom*, Zittau.

Hubala, Erich (1964), "Michelangelo und die florentiner Baukunst", *Michelangelo Buonarroti*, Würzburg, pp. 157–180.

(1965), "Eine Anmerkung zu Michelangelo's Grundrissskizze für die Medici-Kapelle in Florenz", *Kunstchronik*, XVIII, pp. 37-42.

Huelsen, C. and Egger, H. (1913, 1916), *Die römischen Skizzenbücher von Marten van Heemskerk*, Berlin, I, 1913; II, 1916.

Jacobsen, Emil (1904), "Die Handzeichnungen der Uffizien in ihren Beziehungen zu Gemälden, Skulpturen und Gebäuden in Florenz", *Repertorium für Kunstwissenschaft*, XXVII, pp. 113-132; 251-260; 322-331; 401-429.

Körte, Werner (1932), "Zur Peterskuppel des Michelangelo", *Jahrbuch der preuszischen Kunstsammlungen*, LIII, pp. 90-112.

(1932 bis), Review of Luca Beltrami, *La cuploa vaticana*, *Zeitschrift für Kunstgeschichte*, I, pp. 161-162.

(1933), "Giacomo della Porta", *Allgemeines Lexikon der bildenden Künstler*, XXVII, Leipzig.

Kriegbaum, F. (1941), "Michelangelo e il Ponte a S. Trinita", *Rivista d'Arte*, XXIII, pp. 137-144.

Künzle, P. (1956), Review of H. Siebenhüner, *Das Kapitol in Rom*, *Mitteilungen des Institut für österreichische Geschichtsforschung*, LXIV, pp. 349-351.

(1961), "Die Aufstellung des Reiter vom Lateran durch Michelangelo", *Miscellanea Bibliothecae Hertzianae*, (Rom. Forsch. der Bibl. Hertziana, xvi), Munich, pp. 255-270.

Lanciani, R. (1902-1912), *Storia degli scavi di Roma e notizie intorno le collezioni romane di antichità*, Rome, 4 vols.

Letarouilly, P. (1849-1866), *Édifices de Rome moderne*, Liège, 3 vols.

Limburger, Walther (1910), *Die Gebäude von Florenz: Architekten, Strassen und Plätze in alphabetischen Verzeichnissen*, Leipzig.

Lotz, Wolfgang (1955), "Die ovalen Kirchenräume des Cinquecento", *Römisches Jahrbuch für Kunstgeschichte*, VII, pp. 7-99.

(1956), "Das Raumbild in der italienischen Architekturzeichnung der Renaissance", *Mitteilungen des kunsthistorischen Institutes in Florenz*, VII, pp. 193-226.

(1958), "Architecture in the Later 16th Century", *College Art Journal*, XVII, pp. 129-139.

Lowry, Bates (1958), "High Renaissance Architecture", *College Art Journal*, XVII, pp. 115-128.

Luporini, Eugenio (1957, 1958), "Un libro di disegni di Giovanni Antonio Dosio", *Critica d'Arte*, N.S., IV, pp. 442-467, N.S., V, pp. 43-72.

MacDougall, Elizabeth (1960), "Michelangelo and the Porta Pia", *Journal of the Society of Architectural Historians*, XIX, pp. 97-108.

Machiavelli, N. (1929), "Relazione di una visita fatta per fortificare Firenze", *L'Arte della guerra e scritti militari minori*, Florence, p. 207.

Mackowsky, Hans (1925), *Michelagniolo*, 4th ed., Berlin.

Marchini, Giuseppe (1956), "Quattro piante per il San Pietro di Roma", *Bollettino d'Arte*, XLI, pp. 313-317.

Marcuard, F. von (1901), *Die Zeichnungen Michelangelos im Museum Teyler zu Haarlem*, Munich.

Mariani, Valerio (1943), *Michelangelo e la facciata di San Pietro*, Rome.

Meliù, A. (1950), *Santa Maria degli Angeli alle Terme di Diocleziano*, Rome.

Meller, Simon (1909), "Zur Entstehungsgeschichte des Kranzgesimses am Palazzo Farnese in Rom", *Jahrbuch der königlichen preuszischen Kunstsammlungen*, XXX, pp. 1–8.

Metternich, Franz Graf Wolff, "Eine Vorstufe zu Michelangelo's Sankt-Peter Fassade", *Festschrift für H. von Einem*, Berlin, pp. 162–170.

Nava, Antonia (1936), "La storia della chiesa di San Giovanni dei Fiorentini nei documenti del suo archivio", *Archivio della R. deputazione romana di storia patria*, LIX, pp. 337–362.

   (1935–1936), "Sui disegni architettonici per San Giovanni dei Fiorentini in Roma", *Critica d'Arte*, I, pp. 102–108.

Navenne, F. de (1895), "Les origines du Palais Farnèse à Rome", *Revue des deux mondes*, 4e pér., CXXXI, pp. 382–406.

   (1914), *Rome. Le Palais Farnèse et les Farnèse*, Paris.

Orbaan, J.A.F. (1917), "Zur Baugeschichte des Peterskuppel", *Jahrbuch der königlichen preuszichen Kunstsammlungen*, Beiheft zum XXXVIII, pp. 189–207.

   (1919), "Der Abbruch Alt-Sankt-Peters 1605–1615", *Jahrbuch der königlichen preuszischen Kunstsammlungen*, Beiheft zum XXXIX.

Paatz, Walter and Elizabeth (1952–1955), *Die Kirchen von Florenz*, 2nd printing Frankfurt am Main, 6 vols.

Panofsky, Erwin (1920–1921), "Bemerkungen zu D. Frey's 'Michelangelostudien' ", *Archiv für Geschichte und Ästhetik der Architektur als Anhang zu Wasmuths Monatshefte für Baukunst*, V, pp. 35–45.

   (1921–1922), "Die Michelangelo-Literatur seit 1914", *Wiener Jahrbuch für Kunstgeschichte*, I (XV), (1923), Buchbesprechungen, Cols. 1–64.

   (1922), "Die Treppe der Libreria di San Lorenzo", *Monatshefte für Kunstwissenschaft*, XV, pp. 262–274.

   (1924), *Idea . . .*, Leipzig, Berlin.

   (1927), "Bemerkungen zu der Neuherausgabe der haarlemer Michelangelo-Zeichnungen durch Fr. Knapp", *Repertorium für Kunstwissenschaft*, XLVIII, pp. 25–58.

Papini, G. (1949), *Vita di Michelangelo*, Florence.

Parker, K. T. (1956), *Catalogue of the Collection of Drawings in the Ashmolean Museum*, vol. II, Italian Schools, Oxford.

Pasquinelli, Pio (1925), "Ricerche edilizie su Santa Maria degli Angeli", *Roma*, III, pp. 349–356; 395–407.

   (1932, 1935), "Santa Maria degli Angeli: la chiesa di Michelangiolo nelle Terme Diocleziane", *Roma*, pp. 152 ff., pp. 257 ff.

Pastor, Ludwig von (1885–1933), *Geschichte der Päpste seit dem Ausgang des Mittelalters*, Freiburg im Breisgau.

   (1922), *Sisto V, creatore della nuova Roma*, Rome.

Pecchiai, P. (1950), *Il Campidoglio nel Cinquecento sulla scorta dei documenti*, Rome.

   (1952), *Il Gesù di Roma*, Rome.

Pirri, Pietro (1941), "La topografia del Gesù di Roma e le vertenze tra Muzio Muti e S.

Ignazio", *Archivum historicum societatis Iesu*, X, pp. 177–217.

Podestà, B. (1875), "Documenti inediti relativi a Michelangelo Buonarroti", *Il Buonarroti*, X, pp. 128–137.

Pollak, Oskar (1915), "Ausgewählte Akten zur Geschichte der römischen Peterskirche (1535–1621)", *Jahrbuch der königlichen preuszischen Kunstsammlungen*, Beifeht zum XXXVI, pp. 21–117.

Pommer, R. (1957), "Drawings for the Façade of San Lorenzo by Giuliano da Sangallo", Unpublished thesis, New York University.

Popham, A. E. and Wilde, J. (1953), *Summary Catalogue of Exhibition of Drawings by Michelangelo*, London (Britisch Museum).

Popp, Anny E. (1922), *Die Medici-Kapelle Michelangelos, Munich*.

(1927), "Unbeachtete Projekte Michelangelos", *Münchner Jahrbuch der bildenden Kunst*, N.S., IV, pp. 389–477.

Portoghesi, P. and Zevi, B., editors, (1964) *Michelangiolo Architetto*, Turin.

Reymond, M. and C.-M. (1922), "Vanvitelli et Michel-Ange à Sainte Marie-des-Anges", *Gazette des Beaux-Arts*, 5e per., VI, pp. 195–217.

Ricci, Corrado (1900), *Michelangelo*, Florence.

(1906), *Cento vedute di Firenze*, Florence.

(1909), "Sta. Maria degli Angeli e le Terme Diocleziane", *Bollettino d'Arte*, III, pp. 361–372; 401–405.

Rocchi, Enrico (1902), *Le piante icnografiche prospettiche di Roma del secolo XVI*, Turin, Rome.

(1908), *Le fonti storiche dell'architettura militare*, Rome.

Rodocanachi, E. (1904), *Le capitole romain antique et moderne*, Paris.

Rose, Hans (1924), "Michelangelo als Architekt von St Peter", *Münchner Jahrbuch der bildenden Kunst*, N.F.,, I pp. 304–306.

(1925), Commentary to H. Wölfflin, *Renaissance und Barok*, 4th ed., Munich.

Rossi, Giuseppe Ignazio (1739), *La Libreria Mediceo-Laurenziana architettura di Michelagnolo Buonarruoti*, Florence.

Rufini, Mons. Emilio (1957), *S. Giovanni de' Fiorentini* (Le chiese di Roma illustrate No. 39), Rome.

Saxl, F. (1957), "The Capitol during the Renaissance: A Symbol of the Imperial Idea", *Lectures*, London, pp. 200–214.

Schiavo, Armando (1949), *Michelangelo architetto*, Rome.

(1952), "La cupola di S. Pietro", *Bollettino del centro studi di storia dell'architettura*, No. 6, pp. 14–26.

(1953), *La vita e le opere architettoniche di Michelangelo*, Rome.

(1954), *Santa Maria degli Angeli alle Terme*, Rome (reprinted from *Bollettino del centro studi di storia dell'architettura*, No. 8).

(1960), *San Pietro in Vaticano, forme e strutture*, (Quaderni di storia dell'arte, IX), Rome.

(1961), "Il modello della cupola di San Pietro nel suo quarto centenario", *Studi Romani*, IX, pp. 519–532.

Schmarsow, August (1888), "Aus dem Kunstmuseum der Schule zu Rugby", *Jahrbuch der königlichen preuszischen Kunstsammlungen*, IX, pp. 132–136.

Schottmüller, Frida (1927), "Michelangelo und das Ornament", *Jahrbuch der kunsthistorischen Sammlungen in Wien*, N.F., II, pp. 219–232.

Schüller-Piroli (1950), *2000 Jahre St Peter*, Olten.

Scully, Vincent, jun. (1952), "Michelangelo's Fortification Drawings, a Study in the Reflex Diagonal", *Perspecta*, I, pp. 38–45.

Sedelmayr, Hans (1931), "Die Area Capitolina des Michelangelo", *Jahrbuch der preuszischen Kunstsammlungen*, LII, pp. 176–181.

(1934), "Das Kapitol des Della Porta", *Zeitschrift für Kunstgeschichte*, III, pp. 264–274.

Serlio, Sebastiano (1584), *Tutte l'opere d'architettura*, Venice.

Siebenhüner, Herbert (1952), "Der Palazzo Farnese in Rom", *Wallraf-Richartz-Jahrbuch*, XIV, pp. 144–164.

(1954), *Das Kapitol in Rom; Idee und Gestalt* (Italienische Forschungen, 3rd ser., I), Munich.

(1955), "S. Maria degli Angeli in Rom", *Münchner Jahrbuch der bildenden Kunst*, 3rd ser., VI, pp. 179–206.

(1956), "S. Giovanni dei Fiorentini in Rom", *Kunstgeschichtliche Studien für Hans Kauffmann*, Berlin, pp. 172–191.

(1961), "Umrisse zur Geschichte der Ausstattung von St Peter in Rom . . . (1547–1606)", *Festschrift für Hans Sedelmayr*, pp. 229–230.

Steinmann, Ernest (1913), *Die Porträtdarstellungen des Michelangelo*, Leipzig.

(1930), *Michelangelo im Spiegel seiner Zeit*, Leipzig.

Steinmann, Ernest and Pogatscher, Heinrich (1906), "Dokumente und Forschungen zu Michelangelo", *Repertorium für Kunstwissenschaft*, XXIX, pp. 387–424; 485–417.

Steinmann, Ernest and Wittkower, Rudolf (1927), *Michelangelo Bibliographie 1510–1926*, Leipzig.

Supino, I. B. (1901), "La facciata della basilica di San Lorenzo in Firenze", *L'Arte*, IV, pp. 245–262.

Tacchi-Venturi, Pietro (1899), "Le case abitate in Roma da Ignazio di Loiola secondo un inedito documento del tempo", *Studi e documenti di storia e di diritto*, XX, pp. 287–356.

(1930–1951), *Storia della Compagnia di Gesù in Italia*, 2nd ed., Rome, 2 vols.

Thode, Henry (1908), *Michelangelo, kritische Untersuchungen über seine Werke* (Supplement), Berlin, 3 vols. (Although vol. III. was published in 1913, all three volumes are designated here by (1908).)

Thoenes, C., (1963), "Studien zur Geschichte des Petersplatzes", *Zeitschrift für Kunstgeschichte*, XXVI, pp. 97–145.

(1965), review of Wittkower 1963, in *Kunstchronik* XVIII, pp. 9–20.

Tolnay, Charles de (1927), "Die Handzeichnungen Michelangelos im Codex Vaticanus", *Repertorium für Kunstwissenschaft*, 48, pp. 157–205.

(1928), "Die Handzeichnungen Michelangelos im Archivio Buonarroti", *Münchner Jahrbuch der bildenden Kunst*, N.F., V, pp. 377–476.

(1930, 1932), "Zu den späten architektonischen Projekten Michelangelos", *Jahrbuch der preuszischen Kunstsammlungen*, Part I, LI, pp. 1–48; Part II, LIII, pp. 231–253.

(1934), "Michelange et la façade de St Lorenzo", *Gazette des Beaux-Arts*, 6e ser., XI, pp. 24–42.

(1934 *bis*), "Studi sulla Capella Medicia", L'Arte, N.S., V, pp. 5–44; 281–307.

(1935), "La Bibliothèque Laurentienne de Michel-Ange", *Gazette des Beaux-Arts*, 6e ser., XIV, pp. 95–105.

(1940), "Michelangelo Studies", *Art Bulletin*, XXII, pp. 127–137.

(1948), *The Medici Chapel*, Princeton.

(1949), *Werk und Weltbild des Michelangelo* (Albae Vigiliae, N.F., VIII), Zurich.

(1951), *Michelangiolo*, Florence.

(1954), *The Tomb of Julius II*, Princeton.

(1954 *bis*), "Un dessin inédit représentant la façade de Michel Ange de la Chapelle Sforza à Sainte Marie Majeure", *Urbanisme et architecture*, Études écrites et publiées en l'honneur de Pierre Lavedan, Paris.

(1955), "Michelangelo architetto", *Il Cinquecento*, Florence.

(1955 *bis*), "Un 'pensiero' nuovo di Michelangelo per il soffito della libreria Laurenziana", *Critica d'Arte*, N.S., II, pp. 237–240.

(1956), "Unknown sketches by Michelangelo", *The Burlington Magazine*, XCVIII, pp. 379–380.

(1960), *The Final Period*, Princeton.

(1964), *The Art and Thought of Michelangelo*, New York (Translation of Tolnay 1949).

(1965), "A Forgotten Architectural Project by Michelangelo: The Choir of the Cathedral of Padua", *Festschrift für H. von Einem*, Berlin, pp. 247–251.

Tormo, E. (1940), *Os disenhos das antigualhas que vio Francisco d'Ollanda*, Madrid.

Tosi, Luigia Maria (1927-1928), "Un modello di Baccio d'Agnolo attribuito a Michelangelo", *Dedalo*, VIII, pp. 320–328.

Valentini, Roberto and Zucchetti, Giuseppe (1940–1953), *Codice topografico della città di Roma*, Rome. (Fonti per la storia d'Italia, vols. LXXXI, LXXXVIII, XC, XCI.)

Varchi, Benedetto (1888), *Storia fiorentina di Benedetto Varchi con i primi quattro libri e col nono secondo il codice autografo; quale fu pubblicata la prima volta per cura di Gaetano Milanesi*, Florence, 3 vols.

Vasari, G. (1927), *Le vite d' più eccellenti pittori, scultori e architetti*, first edition of 1550, ed. C. Ricci, Milan, Rome.

(1962), *La vita di Michelangelo nelle redazioni del 1550 e del 1568*, curata e commentata da Paola Barocchi, 5 vols, Milan.

Vignola, G. Barozzio (1602), *Regola delli cinque ordini* with *Nuova ei ultima aggiunta delle porte d'architettura di Michel Angelo Buonaroti*, Rome, 1602, 1607, Amsterdan, 1617, Siena, 1635, *etc.*

Wachler, Ludwig (1940), "Giovannantonio Dosio, ein Architekt des späten Cinquecento", *Römisches Jahrbuch für Kunstgeschichte*, IV, pp. 143–251.

Wilde, Johannes (1953), *Italian Drawings in the British Museum; Michelangelo and his Studio*, London.

(1955), "Michelangelo's Designs for the Medici Tombs", *Journal of the Warburg and Courtauld Institutes*, XVIII, pp. 54–66.

Wittkower, Rudolf (1933), "Zur Peterskuppel Michelangelos", *Zeitschrift für Kunstgeschichte*, N.F., II, pp. 348–370.

(1934), "Michelangelo's Biblioteca Laurenziana", *Art Bulletin*, XVI, pp. 123–218.

(1949), *Architectural Principles in the Age of Humanism*, London.

(1962), "La cupola di San Pietro di Michelangelo", *Arte antica e moderna*, XX, pp. 390–437 (translation, with revisions, of Wittkower 1933).

(1963), editor, *Disegni de le ruine di Roma e come anticamente erono*, 2 vols, Milan

Zanghieri, Giovanni (1953), *Il Castello di Porta Pia d Michaelangiolo (1564) al Vespignani (1864) e ad oggi*, Rome.

Zevi, Bruno (1964), "Michelangiolo e Palladio", *Bollettino del Centro internazionale di studi di architettura Andrea Palladio*, VI, 2, pp. 13–28.

INDEX